Preface

The research reported here was sponsored by the U.S. Air Force, Director of Operational Planning and Strategy (A5X), Headquarters United States Air Force, and conducted within the Strategy and Doctrine Program of RAND Project AIR FORCE for a fiscal year 2008 study "Iraq Effects: Emerging Threats to U.S. Interests in the Greater Middle East." This monograph should be of interest to U.S. security policymakers, military planners, and analysts and observers of regional affairs in the Middle East and Central and South Asia.

The goal of this work is to advance understanding of the regional implications of the Iraq War by offering an assessment of trends, threats, and opportunities in the Middle East, drawing from extensive field-based research and primary sources. The monograph covers balance-of-power realignments, focusing on Iranian activism, Arab diplomatic disarray, and Turkey's new prominence; shifting local perceptions of U.S. credibility and the increased roles of such extraregional powers as China and Russia; the war's effects on sectarianism, ethnic activism, and political reform; and how the conflict has shaped future terrorist strategy, ideology, and tactics. By referring to an "Iraq effect," we do not suggest that the war is the sole driver behind these important regional dynamics. Rather, we use the expression as a framework or a lens to capture the ways in which key U.S. policy challenges—the stability of pro-U.S. regimes, terrorism, and Iranian power, to name a few—have been affected by the Iraq W

RAND Project AIR FORCE

RAND Project AIR FORCE (PAF), a division of the RAND Corporation, is the U.S. Air Force's federally funded research and development center for studies and analyses. PAF provides the Air Force with independent analyses of policy alternatives affecting the development, employment, combat readiness, and support of current and future aerospace forces. Research is conducted in four programs: Aerospace Force Development; Manpower, Personnel, and Training; Resource Management; and Strategy and Doctrine.

Additional information about PAF is available on our website:
http://www.rand.org/paf

Contents

Preface iii
Figures and Table ix
Summary xi
Acknowledgments xxv
Abbreviations xxvii

CHAPTER ONE

Introduction 1
The Effects of the Iraq Conflict Range Broadly 2
Previous Analyses Have Not Captured the Full Implications of
    These Shifts 4
The Future Trajectory of Iraq Will Not Significantly Alter Our
    Analyses of Current Regional Trends. 7
The U.S. Air Force and the Department of Defense Must Anticipate
    and Prepare for These New Realities. 10
This Monograph Surveys the Multiple Dimensions of the Iraq Effect 12
Organization of This Monograph 14
Our Research Methodology Is Grounded in Primary Sources and
    Fieldwork. 15

CHAPTER TWO

An Altered Strategic Landscape: The Shifting Regional Balance
    of Power 17
Traditional Balance-of-Power Dynamics Are Shifting to Non-Arab
    States. 18
The Rise of Iran: The Big Winner of the Iraq Conflict? 21

The Arab Response: More Hedging Than Balancing........................ 26
    The Two Faces of Iran in the Arab World 26
    Suspicion of Iran Does Not Necessarily Translate into Pro-American
        Positions... 30
    Regional Ambivalence Toward Both Iran and the United States
        Undermines U.S. Attempts to Create an Anti-Iranian Alliance 32
The Iraq War Has Reinforced and Created Strategic Challenges
    for Israel 38
    Iran Has Become Israel's Key Regional Concern 38
    Potential Instability in Jordan Is a Further Concern 40
    Israeli Views on an American Withdrawal Hinge on Perceptions
        About Whether a Withdrawal Will Strengthen or Weaken
        U.S. Regional Influence.. 41
The Iraq War Has Complicated Turkey's Strategic Relations with
    the United States and Iran 43
    The Conflict Exacerbated the Kurdish Challenge for Turkey............ 43
    The Conflict Has Led Turkey Toward Greater Regional Activism
        and More Cooperation with Iran 45
    Turkey's Economic Interests Provide Opportunities for Convergence
        with U.S. Interests 46
Conclusion... 47

CHAPTER THREE
New Challenges to American Influence: Chinese and Russian
    Roles in the Middle East.. 49
Perceptions of Eroding U.S. Credibility.................................... 50
Changing Extraregional Roles.. 55
    China... 55
    Russia... 62
Conclusion... 73

CHAPTER FOUR
Domestic Reverberations of the War: Internal Challenges to
    Regime Stability 75
The Iraq War Is Not the Main Driver of Increased Sectarian
    Tensions 77

Sectarianism Has Spread in the Gulf, but Regimes Are Mostly
to Blame... 77
Fears of Sunni-to-Shi'a Conversions Suggest Deeper Problems
in the Levant and Egypt 83
Local Dynamics, Not Iraq, Drive Most Sectarian Strife in Lebanon 85
Tribalism in Iraq May Animate Tribal Activism in Neighboring
States... 88
Developments in Iraq Have Inspired Kurdish Ambitions in Turkey,
Syria, and Iran... 92
Iraqi Refugees Present One of the Most Significant Long-Term
Challenge..95
Conclusion: The Iraq War May Ultimately Strengthen Neighboring
Regimes but Not the State 101

CHAPTER FIVE

**The Iraq War and the Future of Terrorism: Lessons Learned
and New Strategic Trends** 105
Existing Reports Present Contradictory Evidence on the Net Effects
of the Iraq War 106
The Iraq Conflict Has Boosted al-Qa'ida's Recruitment but Reduced
Its Long-Term Base of Popular Support............................. 109
Iraq Has Offered an Attractive Narrative of Resistance to Aggrieved
Muslims.. 109
But al-Qa'ida Has Failed to Translate Popular Support for
Resistance in Iraq into Broad Backing for Its Global Jihad Bid.... 111
Al-Qa'ida in Iraq's Violent Tactics Have Alienated Muslim Publics ... 113
Al-Qa'ida's Experience in Iraq Has Exposed Its Ideology and
Strategy... 115
Al-Qa'ida's Demonization of Iran and the Shi'a World Is
Backfiring.. 116
Al-Qa'ida Is Losing the Battle Between Nationalist and
Transnationalist Agendas 120
Palestine as al-Qa'ida's Misguided New Raison d'Être.................. 122
AQI's Franchise Model Has Arguably Sidelined the Role of
Ideology 125

Iraq Has Provided Sunni and Shi'a Militants with Tactics,
    Techniques, and Procedures for Asymmetric Warfare.............. 126
  Improvised Explosive Devices.. 128
  Indirect Fire 128
  Snipers.. 130
  Foreign Volunteerism and Suicide Bombing 130
  Recruiting Women and Children... 131
  Targeting Economic Assets.. 132
  Kidnapping, Torture, and Assassinations............................... 133
  Strategic Communications... 133
The Greatest Effects on Terrorism May Be Felt After the Conflict,
    and Outside of the Region.. 134
  The Impact of Volunteers from Iraq Is Lower Than Anticipated........ 134
  The Most Promising New Jihadi Fronts May Not Be Iraq's
    Neighbors.. 136
Conclusion.. 140

CHAPTER SIX
Conclusion: Managing the Aftershocks of Iraq and Seizing
    Opportunities 143
Key Findings.. 144
Policy Implications... 152

Bibliography 159

Figures and Table

Figures

2.1. Arab Popular Opinion Regarding U.S. and Iranian
     Roles in Iraq.. 31
3.1. 2008 Views of the United States: Six-Country Total........... 52
4.1. Regional Distribution of Iraqi Refugees as of March
     2008.. 97

Table

3.1. China's Oil Imports, January–June 2008........................ 59

Summary

Close to seven years after the invasion of Iraq, the Middle East is a region in flux. Regardless of the outcome in Iraq, the ongoing conflict has shaped the surrounding strategic landscape in ways that are likely to be felt for decades to come.

The Iraq War's reverberations in the region are broad ranging, affecting relations between states, political and societal dynamics inside states, the calculations of terrorists and paramilitaries, and shifts in public views of American credibility. The balance sheet of these changes does not bode well for long-term U.S. objectives in the Middle East. That said, a better understanding of how Middle Eastern states and nonstate actors are responding to the war's aftermath can help contribute to U.S. policies that may better contain and ameliorate the negative consequences of the conflict and perhaps even increase U.S. leverage.

Key Findings

The removal of Saddam Hussein upset a traditional balance of power in the region. While largely psychological, this was nonetheless significant for Sunni Arab regimes. Until the 2003 Iraq War, the regional balance of power has always involved Arab powers and Iran. Today, that balance has shifted toward Iran, although the internal unrest within Iran following its 2009 presidential election may significantly constrain Iran's maneuverability abroad. Still, the perceived removal of the Iraqi buffer to Iran following the Iraq War led to widespread concern among Arab states that Iran can more easily maneuver in the core of the Middle East, from Lebanon to Gaza. The ousting of the Iraqi leader created the perception of increased vulnerability on the Arab side, resulting in a tendency to exaggerate the specter of Iran and its associated nonstate allies. (See pp. 19–21.)

Iran is seizing opportunities the Iraq War has afforded but faces greater obstacles to expanding its influence in the region than is commonly assumed. There is no doubt that Iran skillfully exploited the strategic openings the aftermath of the Iraqi invasion and the resulting shake-up in regional order have provided. Buoyed by several years of windfall oil profits and imbued with the nationalistic outlook of Ahmadinejad's "new conservatives," Iran has endeavored since 2003 to safeguard not just its near abroad in Iraq but also to assert its primacy on the wider regional stage. This momentum was accelerated by the concurrent ascendancy of its Levantine allies—the electoral victory of HAMAS in Gaza and Hizballah's battlefield performance against the Israel Defense Forces in 2006. These events heightened the post-Saddam view in Arab capitals of Iran's inexorable rise and created the impression among Arab publics that Iran—and by extension, Shi'ism—was now the "winning" side. (See pp. 21–23.)

Yet Iran faces more constraints on its regional influence than is commonly acknowledged. The electoral losses for Hizballah in the 2009 Lebanese elections and the internal unrest in Iran following its own 2009 presidential election have further exposed Iranian vulnerabilities and limits to its regional reach. Another example of mixed regional views toward Iran became apparent when the groundswell of support it garnered among Arab publics from its role in the 2006 Lebanon war proved fleeting and was effectively reversed by widespread perceptions of Iran's misbehavior in Iraq. Tehran's policy in Iraq became even more of a liability for Iran's standing following revelations of its support to the fratricidal campaign of Muqtada al-Sadr's Jaysh al-Mahdi against opposing Shi'a factions and the resulting anti-Iranian backlash within the Maliki government and among the Iraqi public. Inside Iran, Ahmadinejad's bellicose posturing on Arab issues has provoked criticism from multiple Iranian factions along the ideological spectrum, particularly in light of the country's deteriorating economy. (See pp. 23–25.)

The perceived "rise" of Iran has not produced a consensus of opposition from Sunni Arab regimes; Arab states' responses to Iran have blended engagement, hedging, and balancing. Arab regimes and publics have responded to the rise of Iran in diverse and often contradictory ways. The Arab world holds two images of Iran. The "bad" Iran reflects Iran's influence in Iraq and its challenge to Arab regimes and Arab Sunni identity, while the "good" Iran defies the West, opposes Israel, and criticizes corrupt Arab regimes (although its ability to do so will be severely limited by the perception that its own government is not considered legitimate in the wake of the contested 2009 presidential election). (See pp. 26–28.)

In addition, Arab disagreements over how to respond to Iran are rooted in the different geostrategic imperatives of individual Arab states. Arab populations that either neighbor Iran (such as Gulf states) or have been exposed firsthand to Iranian involvement in local affairs (the Levantine states) are more wary of Iran than those that have the luxury of regarding Iran from a distance. Many Arab states have tended toward a policy of hedging and accommodation because of what they perceive as inconsistent and ambiguous U.S. policies toward the Islamic Republic and suspicions about the possibility of U.S.-Iranian collusion at their expense if rapprochement efforts move forward. (See pp. 28–32, 36–37.)

Even if consensus on confrontation existed among Arab states, there is currently no viable Arab state "balancer" to Iran. The result is that the most viable state powers in the region are now non-Arab: Israel, Turkey, Iran, and the United States. (See pp. 18–21.)

Uncertainty about U.S. intentions and capabilities in the region has increased local states' receptivity to assistance from China and Russia. Post-invasion disarray in the Arab world was accompanied by a corresponding erosion of confidence in the United States as a security guarantor, stemming from the perception of U.S. entanglement in Iraq, which some viewed as limiting both U.S. capabilities and willingness to intervene elsewhere. The net effect has been the increased willingness of traditional U.S. Arab allies to consider patronage from other extraregional powers—most notably Russia and China. (See pp. 50–55.)

The foreign policy of these two powers since 2003 has been marked by a new assertiveness and interest in the Middle East. Russia appears to be particularly active in challenging traditional domains of U.S. influence, claiming to be a more-balanced mediator on the Arab-Israeli front and through such symbolic gestures as its engagement with HAMAS. Yet the full potential of Russian influence is constrained by Moscow's historical "baggage" in the region and its frequent strategic blunders, such as its decision to brand the Muslim Brotherhood a terrorist organization. (See pp. 62–73.) For its part, China appears more narrowly focused on energy security, and it remains much more economically significant than politically or militarily influential in regional affairs. (See pp. 55–62.)

Our fieldwork suggests that while some Arab voices may welcome Moscow and Beijing's activism as a check against unrestrained U.S. hegemony, Arab regimes ultimately see Russian and Chinese assistance as a way to supplement, but not supplant, the traditional U.S.-led regional security order.

The war has heightened awareness of Shi'a and Sunni identity, yet in many cases, regimes have cynically exploited these loyalties to discredit oppositionists and blunt Iranian influence. Iraq's descent into sectarian strife in 2006 reverberated inside a number of states in the region, creating new pressures on regimes and stoking societal tensions. Although the threat of a direct spillover of the fighting has not materialized, Sunni-Shi'a and tribal divisions have sharpened as forms of substate identities. (See pp. 88–92.) The effects of the war in this area are felt most strongly in states marked by authoritarianism and/or a fractured body politic—Bahrain, Saudi Arabia, and Lebanon. Kuwait is an important case in which the negative effects of the war on Sunni-Shi'a relations were mitigated by a more liberal and participatory political culture. (See pp. 77–83, 85–88.)

Warnings of increased Shi'a activism, however, have emanated from regimes that have relatively little to fear from Shi'a agitation, such as Egypt and Jordan. This dynamic illustrates the political utility of fear-mongering on the sectarian issue. In many cases, authoritarian rulers have skillfully exploited the fear of Shi'a ascendancy to counter Iranian populist appeal at home, discredit and divide the political opposition along sectarian lines, and portray themselves as the only viable "buffers" against the chaos and uncertainty unleashed by the war. (See pp. 83–84.)

The war has stalled or reversed the momentum of Arab political reform; local regimes perceive that U.S. distraction in Iraq and the subsequent focus on Iran have given them a reprieve on domestic liberalization. In tandem with sectarian tensions, the war has produced a stalling or backtracking on post-9/11 progress on reform, however halting and incomplete. RAND discussions with activists and reformists in the Gulf and the Levant yielded a near consensus that 2003 was a turning point in reform, with authoritarian rulers sensing reduced U.S. interest in their domestic affairs and a subsequent return to Cold War–style balancing politics against Iran. Similarly, preemptive counterterrorism measures against returning jihadists provided a convenient pretext for the dragnet arrests of a broad spectrum of domestic opponents. (See pp. 80–83.)

In several instances, the war appears to have increased toleration and even the support of Arab publics for unpopular rulers who, whatever their faults, are still preferable to the unknown. Some of this may stem from the declining cachet of democratization, given its image as a "U.S. project" whose forcible implementation in Iraq was widely blamed for sowing the seeds of the country's descent into sectarian violence. (See pp. 102–103.)

Increased Kurdish agitation in Syria, Turkey, and Iran is the war's most pronounced and visible spillover effect. The 2003 invasion and the subsequent push by Iraqi Kurds for increased federalism has animated Kurdish activism in neighboring states, offering both inspiration and more-tangible support, such as a physical safe haven. Such events as the election of Kurdistan Workers' Party (PUK) leader Jalal Talabani as Iraq's president and the signing of the Transitional Administrative Law sparked celebratory rioting among Iranian Kurds and a serious uprising in Syria that left 40 dead. Violent Kurdish groups, such as the Kurdistan Workers' Party (PKK) in Turkey and the Free Life Party of Kurdistan (PJAK), have enjoyed increased sanctuary in postinvasion northern Iraq, posing new threats to domestic stability in Turkey and Iran. This challenge is spurring tripartite intelligence and operational coordination between Damascus, Ankara, and Tehran that will complicate U.S. diplomacy to pry Syria from Iran's orbit and solicit meaningful Turkish cooperation against Iran. In Turkey, the effects are particularly worrisome because intensified PKK activity threatens to undermine many of Turkey's recent gains in human rights, possibly even sabotaging its efforts to join the European Union. (See pp. 92–95.)

The influx of an estimated 2 million Iraqi refugees has created socioeconomic stresses in Syria and Jordan; the resulting public discontent and demographic changes could challenge stability in these states over the long term. The Iraq War created the largest refugee crisis in the Middle East since the 1948 Arab-Israeli War, potentially jeopardizing the long-term stability of Jordan, Syria, and—to a lesser extent—Lebanon. At least in the short term, the refugee challenge has not transformed into a security risk to the degree anticipated. Indeed, some studies have pointed to beneficial effects, such as the injection of capital by the mostly middle-class refugee population in Jordan following the war, which reportedly fueled Amman's housing boom during that period. That said, as resources run out for these refugees, their situation is becoming more dire, particularly because most are unable to find legal work and are reportedly charged inflated rates for housing. Prostitution and female trafficking have become significant problems, particularly in Syria. Still, the Iraqi refugees have not yet carried Iraq's political and sectarian violence to neighboring soil. Most Iraqi refugees in neighboring states appear more concerned with surviving than with fomenting instability in their host countries.

Yet a strong tendency exists to scapegoat the refugees. The refugees are increasingly blamed for the end of fuel subsidies, unemployment, inflation, and housing shortages. The effect over the long term may be pressure on regimes from key constituents to curtail and reduce services for Iraqis. The Jordanian and Syrian governments have already toughened their policies, and Jordan has largely closed its doors to new refugees. After significant international pressure, children have been allowed to go to school in some host countries (including Jordan and

Syria), but few do because parents fear that attendance may compromise their illegal or quasi-legal presence in the country and because many children work illegally to keep their families housed and fed. Another worrisome trend is the presence of unemployed college-age Iraqi males whose profile of displacement and anomie could make them vulnerable recruits to Salafi-jihadism. Previous refugee crises in the region and globally suggest that poverty and resentment can feed radicalization among the displaced and host populations.

Finally, the long-term urban demographics of refugee settlement bear watching; thus far, the Syrian and Jordanian governments have avoided constructing any parallel institutions—schools, clinics, and camps specifically for Iraqis—to prevent a repeat of the Palestinian camp experience. But certain urban areas are nevertheless becoming increasingly Iraqi in character, displacing indigenous populations and possibly sowing the seeds of future discord. Moreover, if future instability in Iraq led to renewed refugee flows, Jordan and Syria would be unlikely to accept them as they have done to date, and refugee camps could develop. A large Iraqi diaspora, combined with continuing conflict in Iraq, has the potential to spread conflict to neighbors as Iraqis living abroad funnel support to Iraqi groups, are recruited to fight, or lobby governments to provide aid to combatants. If camps are indeed set up, these risks increase, as camps have often been a primary source of militant recruiting for fighting and unrest in other cases (e.g., Lebanon). (See pp. 95–101.)

The war offered a universalizing narrative of resistance to occupation that has proven attractive to potential jihadist recruits, but al-Qaʻida in Iraq's abhorrent tactics have undermined this appeal. The invasion was an initial boon to al-Qaʻida, offering a compelling arena to conduct defensive jihad against an occupying force that had defiled Muslim honor, even if the original grievances of many of its recruits were more local and parochial.

While initially receiving applause from Arab publics and even tacit approval from the media, al-Qaʻida's battlefield emir in Iraq, Abu Musʻab al-Zarqawi, squandered this capital through the negative publicity generated by his abhorrent tactics, and in particular, the fallout in public opinion from the Amman hotel bombings. Populations that had previously cheered al-Qa'ida from afar now turned against it when afflicted with its violence firsthand, as in the cases of Saudi Arabia and Jordan, or when forced to live under its stifling social mores, as were the Anbar tribes. Although this downturn in public opinion may not significantly affect potential recruits, it has bolstered the ability of neighboring regimes to absorb and mitigate the threat from returning veterans of the Iraq jihad. (See pp. 106–126.)

Shi'a insurgents have proven the most proficient at using technological innovations against the United States because of the provisions and training Iran's Quds Force has provided, yet the potential for widespread migration is offset by Tehran's control. Much of the focus on terrorist spillover from Iraq has focused on Sunni jihadists, but Shi'a Iraqi insurgents have actually been the most adept at using technological innovations against U.S. and Iraqi forces. These groups have benefited from strong external links to Lebanese Hizballah and Iran's Islamic Revolutionary Guards Corps (IRGC)–Quds Force. U.S. forces accused the Lebanese Hizballah of training Iraqi insurgents in improvised explosive device ambush techniques and imparting technology it had honed during its campaign against the Israel Defense Forces during the 1990s. In tandem, the Quds Force has provided training and supplied explosively formed projectiles and rocket-assisted mortars that have penetrated U.S. armor and challenged the best defenses of coalition air bases and other facilities.

A cyclical sharing network has likely emerged, with Iraqi Shi'a groups honing techniques Hizballah has imparted, then briefing Hizballah and the Quds Force on the battlefield applications, and then transferring the lessons back to the Quds Force training camps inside Iran, from which they have migrated eastward to the Taliban. Yet the potential for truly widespread and unregulated dispersal of these tactics, techniques, and procedures is partially offset by Tehran's sensitivity to crossing certain "redlines," i.e., giving the United States an unequivocal pretext to attack Iran or provoking an intolerable anti-Iranian backlash among Arab audiences—as was the case in Iraq following the mid-2008 violence by Muqtada al-Sadr's Jaysh al-Mahdi and its splinter militias known as "special groups." (See pp. 126–134.)

Policy Recommendations

Taking these emerging trends and dynamics into account, we offer the following policy recommendations to mitigate evolving threats and to better position the United States to seize unexpected opportunities (see pp. 152–157):

Pursue a U.S. regional security strategy that recognizes local preferences for hedging and that seeks to encourage more-positive Iranian behavior. In terms of adapting to regional strategic shifts, particularly to Iran's growing influence in regional affairs, the United States faces the challenge of regional allies more interested in hedging and even accommodating Iran than in balancing it. Arab regional allies (particularly governments) no doubt worry about and dislike Iran, but they will not unequivocally antagonize and provoke it. Indeed, many of our closest allies, particularly Turkey, found new reasons to expand their ties to Tehran in the years following the Iraq War. U.S. policy should thus steer away from efforts to forge an anti-Iranian regional alliance of Arab "moderates" (e.g., the Gulf Cooperation Council states, Jordan, Egypt) to counter Iranian influence.

Such an alliance is not only unrealistic but may also backfire by bolstering Iranian hard-liners at a time of unprecedented internal factionalism and escalating regional tensions. And the focus on Arab states, particularly the Saudis, as bulwarks against Iran misreads regional capabilities and interests. While the United States should continue to demonstrate support for key regional allies through continued security cooperation activities and exercises, such cooperation should remain low-key and bilateral to avoid the impression that the United States is attempting to create a broad Cold War–style collective security organization arrayed against Iran.

Explore multilateral security and confidence-building measures between Iran and its neighbors. The United States can engage in efforts to create multilateral regional security structures that leave the door open to Iran and that focus on confidence-building measures and dialogues in areas of common interest, such as counterterrorism, narcotics trafficking, and maritime security. Regional security dialogues involving military personnel, including Air Force officials, can allow the airing of threat perceptions and avoid unintended conflict. They can also open up an indirect line of communication between Iran and Israel to avoid an unintended military confrontation, particularly if Iranian nuclear capabilities remain ambiguous. Although Iranian involvement in regional security discussions is unlikely in the aftermath of the contested 2009 election, such options should be developed and available for when political conditions in Iran improve. If such security dialogues eventually transpire and do not lead to a change in Iranian behavior, the United States will still gain important insights into Iranian decisionmaking and garner greater regional and international support for tougher actions against Iran should they become necessary. If they succeed, such dialogues can lead to enhanced security cooperation and a less threatening regional security environment where the potential for armed conflict is reduced.

Strengthen U.S. relations with Turkey, leveraging its unique role as a geopolitical bridge to mediate between Syria, Iran, and the Arab world. Another policy focus at the regional level that flows from our analysis is the need to strengthen U.S. relations with Turkey. Turkey can serve as a bridge for improving relations and modifying the behavior of current adversaries, such as Iran and Syria (as mentioned earlier, Turkey's relationship with both countries has strengthened because of common concerns over Kurdish separatism and terrorist acts within their nations in the aftermath of the Iraq War). Turkey has already demonstrated an interest in regional mediation by facilitating indirect dialogue between Israel and Syria, and the United States should encourage such efforts. Rather than force our allies into a bloclike containment approach, we should view regional allies' relationships with such countries as Iran and Syria as an opportunity and leverage their roles to the extent possible.

Turkey's interests in and extensive economic ties with northern Iraq also present an opportunity for assisting in U.S. efforts to rebuild Iraq. Indeed, unlike Iraq's Arab neighbors, Turkey has proven far more forthcoming in contributing to Iraqi stability and reconstruction, even though, like Iraq's other neighbors, it opposed the war. As a consequence, The U.S. Air Force should continue assisting the Turkish military with counterterrorism operations in Northern Iraq and increase security cooperation activities and training with the Turkish air force. In the current threat environment, U.S. security cooperation with Turkey may be as or more critical than security cooperation with America's Arab allies.

Continue the policy of encouraging responsible stakeholder involvement from China and, to the extent possible, Russia; harness these countries' respective niche interests to promote regional economic growth and stability. In the same vein, the U.S. should avoid alarmist reactions to Chinese or Russian influence in the region, particularly their economic activities, because many of these activities are more likely to complement, rather than supplant, U.S. regional interests. For example, China and the United States have a strong converging interest in creating a stable regional security order conducive to the flow of the region's oil and gas. U.S. policy should also distinguish among extraregional powers' pursuit of their economic interests and more-aggressive attempts to move the regional system toward multipolarity, which is a greater concern in the case of Russia than China.

Encourage Arab regimes to adopt incremental yet meaningful political reform as part of a long-term push to counter radicalization and ensure the viability of key U.S. partners. To mitigate the war's effects inside key regional states, U.S. policy should focus both on ensuring that governing regimes do not abuse their newly entrenched power to crack down on domestic opposition and should take measures to prevent weakening state conditions from evolving into failed states (with all the accompanying problems that involves: shelter for extremists, a magnified proliferation danger, greater potential for massive human rights abuses). This suggests that U.S. policy should recognize the long-term security implications of continued repression and should avoid putting regional reform on the back burner, even if the focus shifts from holding elections to strengthening democratic institutions and practices.

Provide U.S. assistance for Iraqi refugees and encourage more regional support to mitigate the potentially destabilizing consequences of the influx. The Iraqi refugee population is placing a strain on the domestic infrastructures of Jordan and Syria, particularly their education systems. The long-term political ramifications of the Iraqi refugee community are still unclear but could prove destabilizing to key allies, such as

Jordan. Rather than ignore the extent of this problem because of political sensitivities (the Jordanian government refuses to use the term refugee, for example, preferring guests because the latter assumes an eventual return to Iraq), the United States should be actively addressing this new regional challenge. The United States can continue to support efforts to relocate Iraqis to other countries (including the United States) and can provide and marshal significant financial assistance (particularly from Arab Gulf allies) to improve housing and education opportunities in both Syria and Jordan. Such policies could capitalize on this otherwise negative development and humanitarian crisis by improving long-term infrastructure and human development needs in key Arab states, reducing the possibility for future radicalization and challenges to friendly regimes.

In partnership with local allies, use strategic communications to broadcast al-Qa'ida's failures in Iraq across the region to further discredit the jihadist movement in the eyes of public audiences. The terrorist trends emerging over the last six years also suggest a number of U.S. policy actions that can enhance opportunities for U.S. influence. The United States should exploit al-Qa'ida's failure to appeal to some of its target audiences, in particular the Sunni tribes and nationalist Islamic groups. Forging better regional intelligence sharing, tracking Iraq War veterans, and identifying recruitment networks are also important policy initiatives that can capitalize on the declining cachet of al-Qa'ida following its brutal tactics in Iraq. Other policy actions include encouraging greater involvement of women in regional security services to conduct female searches in the light of the growing trend of female suicide bombers and refocusing efforts on the potential establishment of Shi'a militant networks outside of Iraq, such as the IRGC-Quds Force's transfers of tactics, techniques, and procedures to Hizballah in Lebanon.

Prepare the U.S. Air Force to shoulder new responsibilities in America's post-Iraq strategy. The threats and opportunities the aftermath of the Iraq War presents will likely demand a broad continuum of strategic options that airpower is uniquely positioned to provide. The Iranian challenge, for instance, will demand that U.S. policy adopt a new balance among deterrence, the reassurance of local allies, and even the possibility of limited and incremental military-to-military engagement with Iran down the road. Intelligence, surveillance, and reconnaissance assets will be in high demand to mitigate the potential "bleed-out" of terrorists from Iraq. Air Force regional engagement strategy should be used to encourage local militaries to respect civil society and support a liberalizing political culture as part of a more-comprehensive view of long-term regional security.

Acknowledgments

The authors wish to thank a number of people for their support of this research. Maj Gen William Rew, Director of Operational Planning, Policy and Strategy, HQ United States Air Force, was the sponsor of this study. Lt Col Guermantes Lailari, Deputy, Regional Plans and Issues (AF/A5XX), was instrumental in guiding this project throughout its various stages and provided helpful insights based on his own extensive experience in the region. We would also like to thank Andrew Hoehn, Vice President and Director, RAND Project AIR FORCE (PAF), and David Ochmanek, then Director of PAF's Strategy and Doctrine Program, for supporting the initial project concept and guiding the research to its conclusion. At RAND, we thank Jennifer Moroney, Paula Thornhill, Leslie Thornton, Richard Mesic, Eric Larson, David Thaler, Audra Grant, Nadia Oweidat, Olga Oliker, James Quinlivan, Jed Peters, Todd Helmus, Christopher Dirks, Roberta Shanman, and Isabel Sardou for their insights and assistance. 1st Lt Dave Shulker, a Pardee RAND Graduate School Fellow, provided helpful background on Air Force regional engagement strategy. Conversations with several U.S. scholars and analysts advanced our thinking on this topic: Michael O'Hanlon, Michael Eisenstadt, LTC Bill Wunderle, Larry Rubin, Jeremy Sharp, Tamara Coffman Wittes, Marc Lynch, and Michele Dunne. We also benefited from excellent reviews by Nora Bensahel and Dan Byman, which significantly improved this monograph. Finally, we are grateful to our interlocutors in the Middle East for sharing their unique perspectives with us.

Abbreviations

AMAL	Afwaj al-Muqawama al-Lubnaniya [Lebanese Resistance Detachments]
AQI	al-Qaʻida in Iraq
AQIM	al-Qaʻida in the Islamic Maghreb
DoD	U.S. Department of Defense
EIA	Energy Information Agency
FY	fiscal year
GCC	Gulf Cooperation Council
GECF	Gas Exporting Countries Forum
IED	improvised explosive device
IRAM	improvised rocket-assisted mortar
IRGC	Islamic Revolutionary Guard Corps
ISI	Islamic State of Iraq
MIPT	Memorial Institute for the Prevention of Terrorism
NIE	National Intelligence Estimate
PJAK	Kurdistan Free Life Party
PKK	Kurdistan Workers Party

PUK	Kurdistan Workers' Party
QAP	al-Qaʿida in the Arabian Peninsula
START	Study of Terrorism and Responses to Terror
TTPs	tactics, techniques, and procedures
UAE	United Arab Emirates
UN	United Nations
UNHCR	United Nations High Commissioner for Refugees
VBIED	vehicleborne improvised explosive device

CHAPTER ONE

Introduction

The 2003 U.S. invasion of Iraq and its aftermath have arguably been the most pivotal events in the Middle East region since the end of the Cold War.[1] For regional commentators, the war has elicited a range of comparisons to other historic and cataclysmic events resulting in foreign occupation, Arab defeat, and regional disarray: the creation of post–World War I colonial protectorates through the 1916 Sykes-Picot agreement, the 1967 Arab-Israeli War and the end of the pan-Arab project, and the 1979 Iranian revolution. Like such events, the ongoing conflict has had widespread effects on the regional security landscape. While the internal outcome in Iraq is indeterminate and is likely to be so for some time as the United States begins its drawdown from the country, the strategic implications of this war and its aftermath have already affected the broader region.

The implications of these changes are diverse, affecting relations among states, dynamics inside states, the calculations of nonstate actors, and shifts in public opinion. Taken in sum, the balance sheet of these changes does not bode well for long-term U.S. objectives in the region. That said, a better understanding of how Middle Eastern states and nonstate actors are responding to this war's aftermath can

---

[1] In assessing the strategic effects of the Iraq conflict, we define *the Middle East region* as consisting of the Arab League states plus Turkey, Iran, and Israel. While the states to the east of Iran have felt some of the aftershocks of the Iraq War—particularly in the realm of foreign fighters—the ongoing conflict in Afghanistan is a more proximate and significant strategic concern. When we use the terms *Iraq War* or *Iraq conflict*, we mean the full spectrum of conflict and coalition operations that defined the aftermath of the invasion from 2003 to 2009, when U.S. forces began withdrawing from the country.

help contribute to U.S. policies that may better contain and ameliorate the negative consequences of this conflict and perhaps increase U.S. leverage. Indeed, while the *diagnoses* of local observers about the war's consequences largely match U.S. analyses, a disparity emerges over *how to respond* to post-Iraq challenges. This disconnect is partially rooted in an inadequate U.S. appreciation for the Iraq War's full range of effects on the Middle East, including the complex and often contradictory way in which local players are adjusting to the new reality.

The goal of this monograph is to portray these new dynamics, which we collectively refer to as the *Iraq effect*, as accurately as possible. By referring to an Iraq effect, we do not suggest that the war is the sole driver behind the emergence of recent threats and opportunities. Rather, the expression is intended to capture the ways in which key policy challenges in the Middle East—the legitimacy and stability of pro-U.S. regimes, terrorism, and Iranian assertiveness—have been affected by the war, either directly or indirectly. In some cases, these pressures and threats predate the 2003 invasion but were exacerbated or strengthened by the ensuing internal conflict in Iraq. In other cases, the linkages to the Iraq War are not as explicit as is commonly assumed, yet *local actors themselves* may perceive a strong correlation. This in itself is an important observation with implications for U.S. efforts to solicit regional burden-sharing and cooperation.

The Effects of the Iraq Conflict Range Broadly

The most proximate and immediate effects of the conflict relate to the physical "spillover" across the country's porous and expansive borders. The war has created the largest external refugee movement in the region since 1948, and foreign militants have traversed Iraq's frontiers with alarming ease and regularity. Cross-border smuggling of weapons and contraband goods, always a feature of Iraq even under the authoritarian Ba'ath, assumed a new prominence with the weakness of the new regime and its inability to police large swaths of its peripheral territory. The war has also sparked fears that hardened jihadists would "bleed out" to fronts in the Middle East, Europe, and elsewhere, where lessons learned, tradecraft, and tactical know-how can be applied with increasing lethality.

More strategically, the war has affected new shifts in the regional balance-of-power equation that, in the minds of Arab regimes and their publics, have assumed almost seismic qualities. Much of this stems from the perceived disappearance of Iraq as the Arab world's "eastern flank" and, since 1979, as a military bulwark against a seemingly expansionist and predatory Iran. The rise of Iraqi Shi'a parties and their militias has amplified Iran's existing leverage in Iraq and imparted a jingoistic hue to its policy across the region.[2] Regional fears of this dynamic are well known and often shrill. King 'Abdullah of Jordan famously warned of a Shi'a crescent unfolding across the Middle East, while Saudi Foreign Minister Saud al-Faisal argued that the war and the U.S. administration of Iraq had effectively "handed Iraq to Iran" (Gibbons, 2005). These worries are not just limited to Iraq's western neighbors; even in Egypt, a prominent analyst told a RAND Corporation researcher that "the Iraq War brought Iran to the shores of the Mediterranean."[3]

Given the fallout over Iran's 2009 presidential elections and the regime's use of force to quell demonstrations, it remains to be seen whether Iran's rejectionist appeal will retain their luster among Arab publics. Indeed, a number of prominent Arab commentators have openly challenged Iran's allies in the region (Syria, Hizballah, and HAMAS) to justify their allegiance to the Islamic Republic in light of the regime's response to postelection dissent (al-'Utaybi, 2009; al-Rashid, 2009). That said, while the 2009 Iranian presidential election has exposed Iranian domestic vulnerabilities and may limit its maneuverability in the broader region, post-Iraq concerns over rising Iranian influence and, particularly, its nuclear ambitions are unlikely to subside.

---

[2] For an example of Arab media commentary on the Iranian threat, see al-Rashid, 2006. Valbjørn and Bank, 2007, p. 7, provides a nuanced analysis of Sunni Arab fears of the Iranian threat as stemming less from sectarian hegemony and more from a challenge to the stagnant political order. For an example of how Saudi Arabia has cultivated anti-Iranian sentiment using sectarianism, see Gause, 2007. For analysis of Iran's influence and calculations in the region post-Iraq, see Lowe and Spencer, 2006, and Ehteshami, 2004.

[3] Interview with Egyptian analyst, Cairo, Egypt, February 2008.

In addition to these regional dynamics, the war has created new societal tensions and political dynamics that have arisen inside the Middle Eastern states themselves. Historic and seemingly dormant affiliations—to sect, tribe, or ethnicity—have apparently reasserted themselves as local populations take increasingly partisan positions on Iraq's internecine war.[4] Some commentators have warned that centrifugal forces in Iraq could cause the eventual breakdown of states throughout the region, either through the spillover of sectarian conflict into fractured societies in the Gulf or a cascading drive for local autonomy by aggrieved ethnic minorities (Kurds, Baluch, Druze, and Iranian Arabs, to name a few), who feel inspired by the example of the Iraqi Kurds.[5]

Many of these dynamics stem from the fact that the war has exposed the artificiality of Iraq's post-colonial borders, which divided long-standing tribal, ethnic, and religious communities (Vissar, 2007). Some U.S. commentators have even argued that the United States should encourage, rather than resist, this momentum, seizing the war as an opportunity to "redraw" the Middle Eastern map along lines that reflect the sociocultural realities on the ground more accurately and that will make the region less prone to conflict (Peters, 2006).

Previous Analyses Have Not Captured the Full Implications of These Shifts

Surprisingly, few of these dire prognostications have been subjected to a rigorous analysis that is rooted in field-based research and primary sources. Similarly, many studies have focused solely on the twin narratives of regional "fragmentation" and the "rise" of Iran and failed to capture the war's second-order and corollary effects on societies and

---

[4]   Much has been made of the Shi'a "awakening" or "revival" and the Sunni counterreaction. For a pessimistic interpretation about the spread of this conflict, see Mansharof et al., 2007. Norton, 2007, offers a less-extreme view: "Reverberations from the 2003 invasion of Iraq may last for decades. But an inexorable spread of Sunni-Shi'a conflict is only the worse case, and frankly it is not very likely." See also Hiltermann, 2006, and Abdel-Latif, 2007.

[5]   For a recent example, see Goldberg, 2008.

interstate relations.[6] There are many such effects, each with important implications for U.S. policy.

First, and contrary to widely held assumptions, the specter of Iranian influence is not viewed with equal alarm across the Middle East and has not produced a firm Arab consensus on how to respond. Indeed, for some Arab states, the war's upheaval of the *inter-Arab* hierarchy may in some cases outweigh the threat from Iran. This is particularly visible in the new diplomatic assertiveness of Saudi Arabia, which arose in reaction to the Iranian challenge and which has provoked alarm from Egypt, the kingdom's traditional rival for Arab leadership, and from smaller peninsular states that have long-resented Saudi dominance in Gulf affairs.[7] These disagreements and insecurities have important implications for U.S. efforts to build a regional coalition against Iran.

Adding to this dynamic, the Iraq War is viewed in Arab capitals as "America's problem," resulting in an ambivalence that might best be characterized as "Iraq fatigue." This important dynamic has influenced the willingness of Iraq's neighbors to contribute financially to the country's reconstruction or to help legitimize the Iraqi government by opening embassies in Baghdad, although some progress began in the summer of 2008 as violence in Iraq began to go down. And the U.S. drawdown from Iraq could further encourage more regional involvement in Iraqi affairs. But the regional fieldwork documented in this monograph reveals a surprising degree of Arab defeatism on Iraq, including a self-admission that Arab hesitation and unpreparedness prior to the war had effectively paved the way for Iran to assert its dominance in Iraq. With this in mind, many regional officials and experts now see the most promising arenas for checking Iranian ambitions as Beirut and Gaza, rather than Baghdad.

---

[6] Prominent examples of the spillover thesis include Byman and Pollack, 2007, and Terrill, 2005. For more-comprehensive surveys, see Ottaway et al., 2008, and Russell, 2007.

[7] Interviews in Oman, Kuwait, and the United Arab Emirates (UAE) highlighted these intra-Arab tensions within the Gulf Cooperation Council (GCC). For more on this within the context of deliberations on the Iranian nuclear program, see Kaye and Wehrey, 2007, pp. 111–128. For Egyptian fears of a possible Saudi-Iranian rapprochement and the increased marginalization of Egypt's role in pan-Arab affairs, see Gaballah, 2007, p. 4.

The Iraq War has also strongly affected popular and official views of U.S. credibility, reliability, and maneuverability. The perception that the United States has been entangled and distracted by Iraq has potentially given new leeway to a range of actors in the neighboring countries, both hostile and supportive of U.S. goals, to "review" their previous assumptions about U.S. power.[8] Among traditional allies, this may be reflected in a drift toward "security diversification," in which long-standing security partnerships with the United States are being supplemented by support from other extraregional powers, most notably Russia and China.

In terms of its effects on internal politics within neighboring states, the Iraq conflict appears to have strengthened key U.S.-allied regimes, despite popular resistance to these governments.[9] Fearing the spread of chaos from Iraq, some segments of the citizenry have coalesced around unpopular governments, viewing them as the lesser of two evils. Regimes themselves have skillfully exploited this perception to entrench their legitimacy, portraying their states as indispensable buffers against the spread of civil and sectarian strife from Iraq. "Without the al-Khalifa," noted a Bahraini official referring to the kingdom's ruling family, "this country would go the way of Iraq."[10]

Closely related to this effect is the war's influence on the appeal and momentum of democratic reform in the Middle East. Regional commentators have frequently located the root of Iraq's internecine strife in the Iraqi elections, which had the effect of formalizing sectarian fissures that later manifested themselves in violent conflict. "The Iraqi elections were the birth certificate of sectarianism in the Middle East," noted a prominent Saudi reformist in 2007.[11] Similarly, authoritarian regimes have pointed to Iraq, and to the victory of HAMAS in the Palestinian elections, to defer moves toward reform or other

---

[8] Interview with Egyptian foreign ministry official, Cairo, February 2008.

[9] Ottaway, 2007, makes this argument.

[10] Interview with Bahraini government official, Manama, Bahrain, November 2006.

[11] Interview with Saudi Salafi reformist, Riyadh, March 2007.

"domestic experiments."[12] In Saudi Arabia, an oft-quoted phrase attributed to the late King Fahd has acquired a new resonance, "Why start fires on the inside when there are fires on the outside?"[13]

Finally, the war has certainly affected regional and even global terrorist dynamics, but these effects may be related less to tactical innovation and more to shifts in strategy and ideology.[14] The conflict has spawned an entire genre of jihadi "after-action reports" that analyze and critique the fratricidal career of Abu Mus'ab al-Zarqawi, the establishment of the Islamic State of Iraq (ISI), and other jihadi developments in Iraq.[15] Jihadi debates about lessons learned from Iraq center around the balance sheet of gains and losses from attacking Shi'a and civilians, the importance of co-opting rather than alienating tribes, and the advisability of declaring a liberated "emirate" prior to completely evicting an occupying force.[16] These deliberations have important implications for the future of al-Qa'ida, as well as for other forms of militancy across the globe.[17]

The Future Trajectory of Iraq Will Not Significantly Alter Our Analyses of Current Regional Trends

To be sure, whether Iraq "succeeds" (i.e., continues on its current trajectory of reduced violence and some degree of political reconciliation) or "fails" (i.e., returns to widespread sectarian or ethnic violence and

---

[12] RAND telephone interview with a European scholar on Syria, March 2008. Also, Daniel Brumberg (2006, pp. 97–116) wrote that Arab rulers are pointing to the Iraq War to "enforce a winter of authoritarianism."

[13] Interview with Saudi reformists, Eastern Province, March 2007. For more on the chilling effect of the war inside Saudi Arabia, see Jones, 2005.

[14] For a discussion of how the operational environment in Iraq differs from that in Afghanistan, see "Iraq Offers Training Opportunities . . . ," 2006.

[15] See, for example, al-Qa'ida in Iraq (AQI), undated.

[16] The most well-known debates occurred between al-Zarqawi and his clerical mentor, Abu Muhammad al-Maqdisi (Kazemi, 2005; Fishman, 2006; Fishman, 2009).

[17] For analyses on the future of jihadism after Iraq, see Bergen and Cruickshank, 2007; Hegghammer, 2006; and Paz, 2004a.

instability) will greatly affect the long-term position and prospects of the Iraqi state. But while regional actors are by no means insulated from such developments, regional trend lines are unlikely to shift significantly in response to internal Iraqi outcomes. For example, renewed violence in Iraq and massive repression and exclusion of the Sunni minority would no doubt anger Sunni Arab regimes and publics and would undermine Iran's outreach efforts to the broader region. But Iran's regional influence does not depend just on its leverage in Iraq, which, even under the best of circumstances, would still face resistance because of Iraqi nationalist sentiment. Even in the event of failure in Iraq, Iran is likely to continue its pursuit of other regional levers of influence that are of greater concern to its Arab neighbors, such as its ties to militant groups fighting Israel, as well as its pursuit of nuclear capabilities. Indeed, such levers would prove valuable to any type of Iranian leadership, but they are certainly valuable to hard-liners, who are attempting to consolidate power after the contested 2009 elections. Or, on the other hand, if the United States successfully withdraws from Iraq, leaving it with some level of stability, its improved regional credibility is not likely to deter regional states from continuing to pursue a hedging strategy with respect to Iran and to diversify extraregional security relationships by developing closer ties to such states as China and Russia.

Although the surge has been credited with restoring a measure of stability to Iraq, tensions had surfaced by mid-2009 regarding the integration of the *Majalis al-Sahwa* [Awakening Councils], intra-Shi'a power struggles, and the legitimacy of provincial governance.[18] Regional Arab states, particularly in the Gulf, remain fundamentally suspicious of the Maliki government, and promises to open embassies made in mid-2008 have not materialized.

This hesitation suggests deep ambivalence among Iraq's neighbors about Iraq's place in the regional order and, in particular, about the prospect of a return to sectarian internecine conflict. Should this happen, however, the trend lines identified in this monograph, particu-

---

[18] See Meyers, 2009; Rubin, 2009; al-Humayd, 2008; "U.S.-Allied Sunnis Alarmed . . . ," 2009.

larly in the domestic societal realm, would not significantly change—in many respects, the worst effects of "failure" in Iraq have already been felt in the 2006–2007 time frame, and neighboring states have proven largely resilient. Saudi interlocutors in particular had noted that the kingdom had nearly written off Iraq to Iranian influence and sectarian chaos by late 2006 and were pursuing a policy of containing the state's implosion up until mid-2008.[19]

If internal stability deteriorates, the impetus to intervene would certainly be stronger in the absence of a significant U.S. troop presence, although conventional military intervention is probably remote, with the exception of Turkey. Jordan, Saudi Arabia, Syria, and other Gulf states are likely to pursue a mix of subversion, strategic communication, and the funding of tribal allies and political partners while eschewing conventional military intervention. Much will depend on the trajectory of Iraq's weakening: The emergence of ungovernable areas outside the central government's control, viable political opposition movements, smuggling networks, or tribal or sectarian-based militias would be compelling magnets for outside intervention, both through official channels and from actors outside the government's control.

Failure in Iraq could have more-significant consequences for the refugee challenge. Syria and Jordan are not likely to accept additional refugees into their countries in the event of renewed violence in Iraq, and this could lead to the establishment of refugee camps. As we know from other cases, refugee camps can lead to increased poverty, desperation, and—ultimately—radicalization. On the other hand, if stability in Iraq continues to improve, some refugees may consider returning to Iraq, greatly reducing the long-term negative effects of this crisis. That said, even under the improving stability of the 2008–2009 period, very low numbers of refugees have been returning to Iraq. This suggests that, in the long term, the refugee challenge is likely to be problematic regardless of the outcome in Iraq, given the large numbers of Iraqis likely to remain in the diaspora under any scenario.

In terms of terrorism trends, the worsening of internecine strife and the collapse of government control in key areas could invite

---

[19] Interviews with Saudi analysts, Jeddah, Saudi Arabia, March 2007.

increased jihadist recruitment and training. In many respects, however, al-Qaʿidaʾs enterprise in Iraq may never again reach the level it attained in 2005–2006. The memory of its draconian rule in al-Anbar is still fresh, and tribal intolerance will deter al-Qaʿida from establishing a strong foothold. From the outside, such prospects would be a deterrent for jihadist volunteers seeking a new front. Other areas, such as Somalia or Yemen, are more promising from the jihadist perspective.

The U.S. Air Force and the Department of Defense Must Anticipate and Prepare for These New Realities

The broad-reaching changes under way in the region in the aftermath of the war argue a need for Department of Defense (DoD) and U.S. Air Force planners to reexamine recent and traditional strategic paradigms. The 2008 National Defense Strategy "emphasizes building the capacities of a broad spectrum of partners as the basis for long-term security" (DoD, 2008). Yet the societal and political pressures on states in recent years may affect their calculations about military-to-military cooperation and previous security partnerships.[20]

Similarly, the Iranian challenge will demand that U.S. planners adopt a new balance among deterrence, reassurance of local allies, and the possibility of limited and incremental military-to-military engagement with Iran, although significant engagement measures are unlikely in the aftermath of Iran's contested 2009 election. This approach would depart from previous U.S. efforts to form a coalition of "moderate" Arab states (the so-called "GCC plus two": Kuwait, Saudi Arabia, Bahrain, UAE, Oman, and Qatar plus Egypt and Jordan) arrayed against Iran, Syria, the Palestinian HAMAS, and the Lebanese Hizballah.[21]

---

[20] Russell, 2007, p. iii, has advanced this argument persuasively: "The war has dramatically altered internal political dynamics throughout the region, placing the regimes and their historically close relations with the United States under new pressures."

[21] Speaking en route to her 2006 tour of the region, Secretary of State Condoleezza Rice stated, "I do think that the GCC+2 effort is new and it gives us an opportunity in a new configuration to work with the moderate states and the moderate voices in the region." See Shelby, 2006.

For many regional analysts, this formula appears to be a retooled version of previous balancing attempts to create "blocs" to confront threats that were, in many cases, ideological and not easily "contained" through traditional diplomatic structures.[22] Given the changes that have occurred in the region since the Iraq War, the United States may find it more prudent to pursue an approach that acknowledges the diversity of regional views toward Iran and the nonconventional nature of the Iranian challenge. We discuss such an approach within this monograph.

Strategic communications and public diplomacy, of which deployed military forces are an integral part, will become increasingly important in light of shifting perceptions of U.S. credibility, intentions, and maneuverability, as well as the gap between official and public sentiment in the region.[23] An illustrative example is the March 2008 visit of the USS *Cole* off the coast of Beirut, ostensibly to show support for the embattled Siniora government and to spur resolution of the presidential crisis. For local commentators, however, the visit was interpreted through the lens of the Iraq invasion—political change and democracy promotion through a show of force. "We expected the *Cole* to bombard us with ballot boxes like you did in Iraq," noted one Lebanese observer.[24]

To be better able to confront and manage the dynamic forces affecting the region after the Iraq War, Air Force planners—as well as the larger U.S. policy community—need a more-nuanced understanding of the region's changed strategic landscape. This monograph aims to contribute to that understanding.

---

[22] Although the parallels are not precise, these other structures and paradigms include the Central Treaty Organization (1955–1979), which tried to organize Turkey, Iran, Pakistan, and—prior to 1958, Iraq—against Soviet encroachment; the Eisenhower Doctrine, which tried unsuccessfully to stanch the regional appeal of Nasserist pan-Arabism; and Nixon's "twin pillars" approach, which empowered the Shah's Iran and Saudi Arabia as America's surrogates in the Gulf.

[23] For the argument about a renewed U.S. emphasis on "soft power" post-Iraq, see Steinberg, 2008.

[24] Interview with Lebanese analyst, Beirut, Lebanon, March 2008.

This Monograph Surveys the Multiple Dimensions of the Iraq Effect

Our research on the multiple effects of the Iraq War is grounded in the following assumptions and caveats.

First, the role of Iraq as the central engine or catalyst for the region's strategic changes should not be overstated. The "domino" theory is tempting to apply in regional affairs, particularly in the Arab Middle East, where the artificiality of borders, the enduring appeal of pan-Arab and Islamist norms, and the presence of transnational linkages among ethnic groups, sects, and tribes would seem to increase the likelihood of instability spreading from one state to another.[25] Similarly, there is a tendency in the region to attribute a range of social and political ills to the "Pandora's box" of the Iraq conflict and U.S. policy in that country. Inevitably, these perceptions are inflated and, in some cases, patently false. Yet capturing these views is important because they offer important insights into the gaps between U.S. intentions in the region, its credibility, and the willingness of regional actors to share burdens with the United States on other U.S. initiatives.[26]

Additionally, the real and observable effects of the Iraq War have been offset by other events that have had similarly profound effects on state stability and the regional balance of power. For states in the Levant, the Arab-Israeli conflict, the ongoing strife in Gaza, and the aftershocks of the 2006 war in Lebanon dominate the official security agenda and the public's imagination. Indeed, our fieldwork in Egypt, Jordan, and Lebanon revealed a sort of "Iraq-fatigue." These states are certainly worried about instability in Iraq and the Iranian influence there, but they are more immediately concerned about curtailing Iranian influence and mitigating conflict in Gaza and Lebanon. A Jorda-

---

[25] For an analysis of this dynamic using post-1979 Gulf fears about the spread of revolutionary contagion from Iran as an example, see Gause, 1991.

[26] For example, recent polling suggests that Arab publics are more concerned about the direct effects of the Iraq conflict than a regional threat from Iran. When asked about their greatest regional worry, respondents were split, with U.S. permanence in the region, the fragmentation of Iraq, and the spillover of the Iraq War generally outweighing the direct threat of Iranian hegemony. See Zogby International/Arab American Institute, 2007.

nian official noted that confronting Iran in Iraq would simply "take too long" and "meanwhile, the house [Gaza] is burning down."[27] As one Lebanese scholar noted, the contours of an emerging Arab diplomatic strategy against Iran seem to suggest the "rollback of Iran in the Levant, containment in Iraq and engagement in the Gulf."[28]

Finally, we recognize that the Iraq War may be far from over and that the trajectory of the conflict, the state's political evolution, and the nature of its security relationship with the United States are not fixed in stone.[29] The reemergence of a strong Sunni regime in Baghdad that enforces complete control over its territory and borders, enjoys a modicum of stability, and has eliminated the militia scourge would almost certainly mitigate or reverse many of the concerns among Iraq's Arab neighbors that we have discussed. Yet existing trend lines do not appear to point in this direction, and it is therefore reasonable to expect that Iraq's future over the next five to ten years will resemble a variation of the present: a Shi'a-dominated Iraq marked by endemic instability, lawlessness, and violence in key portions of territory. We certainly cannot rule out the possibility that the worsening of internal strife, the emergence of ungoverned territories, and an increasing drift toward warlordism would exacerbate existing fears and possibly spur Iraq's neighbors to intervene. Yet as we have discussed, even such dire scenarios would not necessarily fundamentally alter broader regional trends and perceptions that have emerged since 2003.

With these caveats in mind, we approach the war as a useful lens for assessing the changing Middle East, rather than as the sole epicenter or catalyst for new strategic trends.

---

[27] Interview with Jordanian official, Amman, February 2008.

[28] Interview with Lebanese analyst, Beirut, Lebanon, March 2008.

[29] For assessment of alternative scenarios in Iraq and their effect on the region, see New York University Center for Global Affairs, 2007.

Organization of This Monograph

Chapter Two surveys the changing balance of power in the region, noting diverse reactions and responses to the perceived rise of Iran from Arab states, Israel, and Turkey. In particular, we assess the reach and limits of Iranian influence, as well as differing Arab threat perceptions of Iran across subregions and between regimes and their publics. Finally, we address the strategic effects of the war on Israel and Turkey, revealing mixed perceptions of the conflict's effects, as well as the appropriate policy responses to meet evolving regional challenges.

Chapter Three highlights how diminished perceptions of U.S. credibility and maneuverability following the war presented openings for increased involvement in the Middle East from other extraregional players, particularly China and Russia. We devote particular attention to local states' motives for soliciting extraregional patronage and the implications of this support for U.S. regional interests.

Chapter Four explores the war's effects on internal dynamics in a number of regional states, covering the new prominence of substate identities, such as sect, tribe, ethnicity, and locale. We also assess the potential for a "spillover" of sectarian strife in states marked by existing Sunni-Shiʻa fissures: Lebanon, Saudi Arabia, Kuwait, and Bahrain. Other challenges to regime stability resulting from the war include agitation by ethnic groups for increased autonomy and the Iraqi refugee crisis. At the same time, we highlight how the war may have entrenched some regimes and silenced their opponents. Finally, we address the war's consequences for the prospects for future political reform.

Chapter Five analyzes the Iraq War as a potential laboratory for future jihadist and insurgent strategy and tactics, highlighting the ongoing or potential migration of new tactics, techniques, and procedures (TTPs) outside the country. Importantly, we cover shifts in jihadist thinking about viable targets, allies, and fronts that have emerged as a result of the Salafi-jihadist experience in Iraq and how these doctrinal changes might affect the movement's fortunes elsewhere.

Chapter Six considers how the sum total of these effects and trends has altered U.S. security paradigms for the region and conceptions of military flexibility, deterrence, and power projection. We argue for a rethinking of traditional U.S. security policy in the region. More broadly, we consider the implications of the war for constructing a bloclike approach toward the Islamic Republic in light of more-nuanced Arab perceptions that appear to suggest a preference for elements of containment, rollback, and engagement.

Our Research Methodology Is Grounded in Primary Sources and Fieldwork

We have drawn from a range of primary and secondary sources and attempt to carefully distinguish between regional *perceptions* of the war's consequences and U.S. policy (both official and public) and the unfolding developments themselves.[30] Fieldwork throughout the region enabled us to build a foundation for discerning both categories of effects. We conducted over 50 interviews throughout 2007 and 2008 with a range of diplomatic, military, and security officials in Egypt, Jordan, Israel, Lebanon, Bahrain, Saudi Arabia, Kuwait, and the UAE. Yet we also see great value in unofficial views, from local think-tanks, scholars, and journalists and from Islamists, oppositionists, and other political actors. Several of the countries we studied also have a rich think-tank and analytical culture, even if the ultimate influence of their policy deliberations is open to debate. With this in mind, we drew from Arabic and Persian-language strategy pieces that offered interpretations of the war's effects that in most cases contrasted sharply with conventional U.S. and Western thinking. Finally, we drew from a number of opinion polls, indigenous news outlets, and Internet chat rooms.

As noted above, our intent is to provide an objective and field-based survey of the region's most important trends in the aftermath of the Iraq conflict, to better equip the Air Force and U.S. policymakers to plan against new threats and seize unexpected opportunities.

---

[30] For a good overview, see "The Widening Perception Gap . . . ," 2007.

CHAPTER TWO

An Altered Strategic Landscape: The Shifting Regional Balance of Power

This chapter considers how the Iraq conflict has affected regional diplomatic and military alignments, particularly local perceptions of rising Iranian power. How has the overall regional balance of power shifted, and to what extent has the Iraq War altered Iran's regional influence? How are regional states responding to the new strategic environment? Is there a viable regional "balancer" to Iranian power? Can balance-of-power paradigms adequately account for the complex nature of regional alignments and postures in this region?

Indeed, in the Middle East, internal state challenges and identity politics can weigh as heavily as external military threats in regional partnership calculations. Such calculations have contributed to Arab states responding to Iran's rise with a combination of alarm and accommodation. At the same time, these countries have not necessarily aligned themselves with the United States. In the following sections, we examine how these regional dynamics play out and their potential implications for U.S. policy toward the region.

The first section addresses the shift away from traditional balance-of-power dynamics involving Arab state powers toward a regional environment in which non-Arab powers dominate. The following section assesses the extent to which one of those non-Arab powers, Iran, has gained the most from the Iraq conflict, examining both the reach and limits of Iranian influence. We then turn to neighboring Arab states' reactions to Iran's apparent rise, noting differing threat perceptions across subregions and between regimes and their publics, including on the issue of Iran's nuclear capabilities. Finally, the chapter assesses the strategic effects of the war on Israel and Turkey, revealing mixed perceptions of the conflict's consequences and of the appropriate policy responses for addressing evolving regional challenges.

Traditional Balance-of-Power Dynamics Are Shifting to Non-Arab States

The traditional Middle East regional system since the Second World War has been dominated by competition among Iran and multiple Arab powers (most notably Iraq, Saudi Arabia, Egypt, and Syria) for regional primacy through shifting balances and alliances over the years.[1] These regional rivals have been backed by military assistance and political support from extraregional patrons (e.g., the United States and Soviet Union during the Cold War) to ensure that no one regional power or ideological bloc could dominate the region and, most critically, its oil supplies.

So, for example, to counter Egyptian President Gamal 'Abd al-Nasser's revolutionary pan-Arab ideology and Soviet military backing, the United States continued to strengthen its strategic partnership with Saudi Arabia. After the British withdrew from east of Suez in 1971, the United States added Iran as a regional balancer to Soviet-backed radical states, creating a twin-pillar approach to regional security, in which both Iran and Saudi Arabia received significant military assistance and advanced weapon systems. Indeed, before the overthrow of the Shah of Iran in 1979, the United States maintained strong military and political relations with Tehran, which also served as a balance to Soviet-supported Ba'athist Iraq. But after the Iranian revolution, the United States began supporting Saddam Hussein's Iraq to counter Iranian influence, tilting toward Iraq in the Iran-Iraq War of the 1980s. After the end of the Cold War and in the aftermath of the 1991 Gulf War, the United States changed its traditional offshore balancing

---

[1]   For an overview of traditional balance-of-power and threat dynamics among regional states, see Walt, 1990.

stance to a direct, regional balancing role with its growing military presence in Saudi Arabia and the GCC states, this time to contain *both* Iran and Iraq (the so-called dual-containment policy).

Until the 2003 Iraq War, the regional balance-of-power has always involved Arab powers, as well as Iran.[2] After the Iraq War, the fundamental balance shifted to non-Arab states, at least perceptually, creating a new strategic operating environment. The war reinforced the already steady relative decline of Arab state power and the concurrent rise of Iran. With the Iraq buffer removed, Iran can more easily maneuver in the core of the Middle East, from Lebanon to Gaza, even if the notion that Iraq ever served as a serious bulwark to Iran is debatable. Indeed, analysts have questioned the extent to which Iraq actually served as a buffer against Iran, given the international sanctions that severely limited Iraqi power and capabilities to effectively "balance" Iran after the 1991 Gulf War.[3] Some military analysts similarly argue that Iraq was never a serious counter to Iran's largely naval and ideological sources of power, concluding that the idea that Iraq balanced Iran before the 2003 war is flawed.[4]

Yet the psychological effect of the demise of a stable Iraqi state and the rise of a Shi'a-dominated government with long-standing ties to Iran is significant, and has shifted the regional perception of Iranian power. Today, it is difficult to imagine that the current Iraqi government would desire to balance Iran even if it had the capability to do so. Although the internal unrest and contestation of the 2009 presidential election results has somewhat diminished Iran's reputation in the Arab world, concerns over its post-Iraq regional reach and its nuclear ambitions remain.

The conflict and the significant American military presence in an Arab country have also turned the United States into a de facto regional power to a much greater extent than its forward posture of the 1990s did. Indeed, as one former Jordanian official noted, two non-

---

[2] For an overview of regional balance-of-power dynamics prior to the Iraq War, see Russell, 2007.

[3] On this point, see Eisenstadt, 1996.

[4] Interview with U.S. military official, Washington, D.C., December 11, 2007.

Arab actors—the United States and Iran—are now the most influential regional players.[5] An analyst of regional affairs has similarly noted the fundamental shift in the regional balance of power to a bilateral system, in which, "[s]trangely enough, the external or at least non-Arab powers, i.e., the U.S. and Iran, are now the most powerful actors in the otherwise Arab Gulf region" (Furtig, 2007, p. 640). An Arab analyst similarly notes "that the non-Arab role in Iraq has become the hegemonic role. And here I mean the United States, Iran, and Turkey in that order" (Fandy, 2008).

The third non-Arab power, Turkey, is also playing an increasingly active role in regional affairs, militarily and diplomatically, because this conflict directly affects its own security and territorial integrity through the Kurdish prism. Turkey's relations with Iran have strengthened in recent years because of their common concerns about Kurdish separatism and Kurdish terrorism within their own borders, which has also led Turkey to launch military incursions into northern Iraq against Kurdish militants. Turkey's interest in playing a larger role in regional affairs is also evident in its mediation in back-channel talks between Israelis and Syrians.

The trend toward non-Arab dominance is strengthened by the lack of an effective Arab balancer to Iran. As a U.S. official observed, Iraq is gone, and other potential bulwarks, such as Egypt and Saudi Arabia, face significant internal challenges, so "who are counter-weights to Iran now in the Sunni world?"[6] With even the Iraqis now "on Iran's side," this official suggested that, for Sunni elites, the natural regional order has been overturned. Arab analysts have taken note of the weakening status of Arab regimes, particularly apparent in the aftermath of the Arab summit in Damascus in March 2008 (see Atwan, 2008).[7] In his address to the Arab summit, 'Amr Moussa, the Secretary General of the Arab League, noted: "We suffer from a crisis of confidence in us and

---

[5] Interview with former Jordanian official, Amman, February 18, 2008.

[6] Interview with U.S. official, Amman, February 19, 2008. For a particularly downbeat assessment of Egypt's waning influence in the region, see al-Dakhil, 2006.

[7] The Arab summit meeting sparked unusually visible division among Arab states. See also Worth, 2008a.

those around us. Yes, the status of Arab relations has reached an unacceptable level of disarray" (Moussa, 2008). Subsequent Arab summits have displayed similar divisions and inaction.[8] And despite indications of renewed inter-Arab cooperation and activism (e.g., Saudi-Jordanian cooperation on such issues as Iraq and the peace process), some analysts view the Saudis as a regional mediator lacking military or nationalist credentials and thus not as a serious regional power broker (see Kostiner, 2005).

In sum, the regional balance of power has shifted from Arab to non-Arab states. U.S. policies in the region will need to better understand the complexity of the new security environment to be effective. And no shift is more significant than changing perceptions over the role of Iran in the region.

The Rise of Iran: The Big Winner of the Iraq Conflict?

In the aftermath of the Iraq War, the growing aggressiveness of Iran—from its nuclear posturing to a seemingly expanded reach from the Gulf to the Levant—has become a defining feature of the new Middle East landscape, raising alarms in Washington and the region.

Numerous studies since the war have examined Iran's enhanced role in Iraq, where most of the Shi'a political factions that are emerging as the key power brokers in the evolving Iraqi political system have had long-standing ties and asylum in Iran before the war, even if Iraqi nationalism may at times trump the sectarian dimension.[9] On the military front, Iran's training of militants in Iraq through the Islamic Revolutionary Guard Corps (IRGC) and its supply of lethal impro-

---

[8]   For an overview, see Lynch, 2009.

[9]   On Iran's rising influence, see Nasr, 2006. For an assessment of Iran's influence and involvement in Iraq since the 2003 war, see International Crisis Group, 2005; Takeyh, 2008; and Ehteshami, 2003. For an Arab assessment of Iraqi pushback on Iranian influence, in which the author asserts that *uruqua* [Iraqiness] is stronger than Shi'ism, see Taheri, 2007.

vised explosive device (IED) technology to Iraqi insurgents is well documented.[10]

But Iran's influence and activism have expanded beyond what is arguably its natural sphere of influence in Iraq to the core of the Levant.[11] Jordanian King 'Abdullah voiced his fear over Iranian penetration into the Arab-Israeli conflict in sectarian terms by referring to a growing "Shi'a Crescent" in the region.[12] Indeed, there is widespread concern in Jordan regarding the growing Iranian reach into the Levant, with one former official calling this development a "fiasco," noting "Iran is winning everywhere and the U.S. is losing."[13] Iranian activism is most visible in its sponsorship of militant groups, such as Palestinian HAMAS and the Lebanese Hizballah, and through its development of short- and medium-range ballistic missiles (many of which Hizballah tested during the 2006 Lebanon war). While Iranian links to terrorist organizations are not new, regional analysts believe Iran has become bolder and more open in its support of such activity since the Iraq War.

In terms of its conventional military, some of Iran's capabilities are threatening to Western and allied Gulf interests, particularly on the naval front. Iran's mining capability, antiship cruise missiles, and innovative "swarming" tactics could impede maritime access in the Strait of Hormuz. The IRGC also possesses a significant arsenal of short- and medium-range ballistic missiles that can reach the small Persian Gulf states, Afghanistan, Israel, eastern Turkey, and most of Saudi Arabia. Although these missiles are currently inaccurate and thus have limited military utility, improvements in their range, ability to carry unconventional warheads, and accuracy would significantly enhance Iran's

---

[10] See, for example, Katzman, 2007, and Kagen, 2006–2007.

[11] For an example of an alarmist view toward Iran and its regional ambitions, which are common in the Arabic press, see Alhomayed, 2007.

[12] What is most revealing on this issue is that the strongest warnings of a Shi'a menace have come from two Arab states (Egypt and Jordan) with very little to fear from a Shi'a fifth column in their midst.

[13] Interview with former Jordanian official, February 18, 2008. Interviews with current Jordanian officials (Amman, February 2008) only reinforced such messages.

ability to threaten large population centers, economic infrastructure, and military bases. Overall, however, Iran's conventional capability remains mired in conventional doctrine due to bureaucratic inertia in procurement and frequent infighting between the IRGC and conventional forces. Most of its equipment is out of date and poorly maintained, and its ground forces suffer from both personnel and equipment shortages. The Iranian Air Force, in particular, has outdated aircraft and is no match for its neighbors and certainly not for U.S. airpower.[14]

This conventional inferiority contributes to Tehran's nuclear ambitions. Although questions remain about the pace and nature of the Iranian program, there is little doubt that Tehran is actively seeking an indigenous uranium enrichment capability that will, at the very least, allow a nuclear breakout capacity.[15] Finally, Iran also exerts significant regional influence through "soft" power projection, such as reconstruction aid, infrastructure development, media, and financial investments.[16]

Despite these strategic gains, it is important to understand how the Iraq War may have affected Iranian threat perceptions. For example, the invasion of Iraq brought the threatening presence of U.S. ground forces to Iran's doorstep, and despite the scheduled drawdown, Iran remains concerned about the potential reintroduction of U.S. forces into Iraq under the terms of the U.S.-Iraq Status of Forces Agreement. And while Iran benefits from some degree of instability in Iraq to keep residual U.S. forces distracted and to dilute the ability of the central government in Baghdad to exert control over the southern provinces, it is also worried about uncontained Iraqi instability spilling over its borders (see, for example, Dehghani, 2003).[17] Indeed, the Iraq War has exacerbated transnational threats that affect Iran's internal stabil-

---

[14] For more on Iran's conventional threat, see Wehrey et al., 2009.

[15] See, for example, Guldimann, 2007. For a similar assessment on Iranian capabilities and intentions on the nuclear front, see Fitzpatrick, 2008.

[16] For further details on Iranian influence in these areas, see Slavin, 2008.

[17] The Iranian Center for Strategic Research, which is affiliated with former president and current Expediency Council chairman 'Ali Akbar Hashemi Rafsanjani, has issued similar warnings. Also see Ahadi, 2008.

ity, such as ethnic separatism and Sunni radicalism (Ehteshami, 2004, p. 187). Iran is particularly concerned over its increasing Kurdish challenge since the Iraq War (there are 4 million Kurds in Iran), particularly the internal threat from the resurgent Kurdistan Free Life Party (PJAK), which maintains close links to the Kurdistan Workers' Party (PKK).

Aside from these effects, some observers have argued that Iraq's democratic experience and the reemergence of Shi'a clerical power in Najaf and Karbala have emboldened regime opposition in Iran—particularly the demand for greater electoral transparency and clerical criticism of the theological basis for the Supreme Leader's expansive authority.[18] In the wake of the June 2009 presidential elections, the Islamic Republic faced its worst internal unrest since the 1979 Revolution, with a broad-based opposition coalition (the so-called "Green Revolution," centered on defeated presidential contender Mir-Hossein Mousavi), challenging the results that handed victory to the incumbent, Ahmadinejad. The protest movement and the resulting crackdown spearheaded by the IRGC intensified existing fissures among the clerical elite, with former president and Expediency Council chairman 'Ali Akbar Hashemi Rafsanjani mounting the most vociferous critique of the Ahmadinejad administration.

Although it is tempting to read a "Sistani effect" into Iran's opposition and demands for greater pluralism, particularly given Rafsanjani's recent consultations with Grand Ayatollah 'Ali al-Sistani and his Qom-based representatives, such linkages should not be overstated. In press accounts and statements, Iraqi officials appeared lukewarm and ambivalent about events in Iran, while Najaf-based Iraqi clerics refrained from vocal partisanship (Shadid, 2009). What is certain, however, is that the Iranian regime is facing an unprecedented test of its political and ideological legitimacy that will undoubtedly constrain its maneuverability abroad, thus undermining the notion that the post-Iraq era will be one of unbridled Iranian supremacy.

Thus, it should come as no surprise that Tehran has strong incentives to assert a critical role for itself in the region's affairs—often in

---

[18] For a representative example, see Hitchens, 2009.

ways that are inimical to U.S. objectives. One regional analyst argues that the fluidity of the strategic environment reinforces both the fears and ambitions of the Islamic Republic to the extent that Iran is best understood as both "frightened" and "frightening":

> What does the frightened Iran want: A guarantee for [the continuity] of the regime or acknowledgement of Iran's role in the region or the two together? And what does the frightening Iran want: leadership of the region or laying claim to the position of senior partner to the "Great Satan" in [regional] oil affairs and security arrangements? (Charbel, 2008)

Indeed, what many view as an Iranian drive for hegemony may in fact be intended as a form of deterrence or a bid for increased stature and "indispensability." The "new assertiveness" in Iranian external behavior can be characterized as an attempt to *consolidate* and *preserve* the strategic gains that were in some sense handed to the Islamic Republic by the U.S. invasions of Iraq and Afghanistan. Analysts of Iran suggest largely defensive Iranian ambitions with respect to such key issues as Iraq, where "The overarching priority for Tehran is to prevent Iraq from once more emerging as a military and ideological threat" and where Iran is more interested in stabilizing Iraq to facilitate an American withdrawal than in seeking a preeminent position in the Gulf (Takeyh, 2008, pp. 23, 28).

Tehran's motives for pursuing a nuclear capability for both security (deterrent) and status (reinforcing its regional leadership) reasons are also not new, explaining why Iranian interest in such a capability dates back to the Shah.[19] Although there are tactical differences among Iranian domestic factions with respect to the acceptable costs for pursuing a nuclear option, there is broad support for the strategic decision and perceived right of Iran to acquire an indigenous enrichment capability. The Iraq War and the momentous 2009 Iranian presidential election have not fundamentally altered such calculations. This trend likely reflects Iran's interest in consolidating its regional stature, as well as its

---

[19] On Iranian nuclear motivations, see Sokolski and Clawson, 2005; Takeyh, 2003; Takeyh, 2004; Eisenstadt, 1999; Kemp et al., 2004; and Kemp, 2004.

interest in bolstering its deterrent capabilities to avoid a military attack from the United States. If Iran's recent regional activity in part reflects such deterrent and defensive interests, this may open up the possibility of cooperation or rapprochement with Iran for U.S. policymakers, a point the final chapter of this monograph explores further.

The Arab Response: More Hedging Than Balancing

The Two Faces of Iran in the Arab World

Arab regimes and publics have responded to the rise of Iran in diverse and often contradictory ways. The Arab world holds two images of Iran. The "bad" Iran reflects Iran's influence in Iraq and its challenge to Arab regimes and Arab Sunni identity, while the "good" Iran defies the West, opposes Israel, and criticizes corrupt Arab regimes.[20]

That said, Arab regimes and populations often have different views about the good and bad Irans.[21] While official Arab postures toward Iran are more hostile than among Arab publics, RAND interviews with government officials and political elites suggest a complex understanding of the Iranian challenge, and even some appreciation for the defensive motivations that may be partly driving Iranian regional behavior.

The bad Iran image is fostered by Iranian influence in Iraq and particularly its meddling with Shi'a groups in both Iraq and the broader region, challenging not only Arab regimes but also Arab Sunni identity. This image is most prevalent at official levels but at times also appears in popular Arab opinion. Saudi Foreign Minister Saud al-Faisal has argued, for example, that the Iraq War had effectively "handed Iraq to Iran" (Gibbons, 2005).[22] A former Jordanian official similarly sug-

---

[20] This characterization of the "two Irans" was made during an interview with a Jordanian journalist, Amman, February 18, 2008.

[21] For a sample overview of Arab threat perceptions, see al-Rashid, 2006.

[22] *Asharq Al-Awsat* columnist Zain al-'Abidin al-Rukabi used similar language, writing on the fifth anniversary of the Iraq invasion that "the naked truth is that the American neoconservative administration has handed Iraq to Iran" (al-Rukabi, 2008).

gested to RAND that "Arab Iraq has been lost to Iran."[23] Some analysts attribute Iran's gains in Iraq not only to American missteps but also to Arab states' neglect. A Bahraini commentator has noted that the "Arabs decided on their own accord to turn away from Iraq and remain at distance from its arena, and the result is that Iran has become, on the basis of influence, the northern neighbor of the Gulf" (al-Marhun, 2007). Because neighboring Arab states did not want to be associated with the war, they did not attempt to counter Iran in Iraq, and viewed Iraq as America's problem.[24] Indeed, dozens of RAND interviews with regional officials and analysts suggested that Iraq's neighbors are far more concerned with "local" problems, such as Gaza and Lebanon, than with Iraq.

The good Iran image of defiant postures toward the West and anti-Israeli rhetoric and actions resonates more with Arab publics. But these positive images also place constraints on Arab regimes because overly hostile official anti-Iranian stances feed into Iran's critique that these regimes are subservient to U.S. interests. Indeed, Iran has drawn applause from Arab populations in recent years based on its defiant nuclear posture; the escalatory, anti-Israeli rhetoric of Iranian President Ahmadinejad; its support for militant groups fighting Israel in Lebanon and Gaza; and its persistent critique of ruling Arab regimes as corrupt and illegitimate (see Valbjørn and Bank, 2007, and England, 2007). This last critique may no longer resonate among Arab publics in the wake of the regime's brutal repression of opposition forces following the 2009 election, but Iran's focus on double standards on the nuclear question and its anti-Israel rhetoric is still likely to generate broad appeal.

These two images of Iran can fluctuate rapidly among Arab publics. For example, the collateral acclaim for Iran after the 2006 Lebanon war rapidly dissipated in the wake of the December 2006 execution of Saddam Hussein, which was widely viewed as an Iranian and U.S.-engineered attempt to diminish Arab identity. By 2007, available polling and media surveys revealed a noticeable drop in Arab public

---

[23] Interview with former Jordanian military official, Amman, February 18, 2008.

[24] Interview with Jordanian researcher, Amman, February 19, 2008.

support for Iran. Zogby's February–March 2007 survey showed that a majority of Arab respondents believed Iran's role in Iraq was unhelpful (Zogby International/Arab American Institute, 2007).[25] The effect of this rising suspicion was a closer alignment with U.S. opposition to Iranian policies in Iraq; when the United States considered branding Iran's IRGC a terrorist organization, Arab press commentary was largely supportive.[26] Even though the GCC received Ahmadinejad at its December 2007 summit, Arab press commentary continued to express suspicion and concern over Iran's regional ambitions (Lynch, 2007). Indeed, Iranian analysts recognize that Arab fears of Iran have escalated in recent years because of Iran's activist regional policies.

Even on the nuclear question, reactions among Iran's Arab neighbors are diverse, reflecting both the good and the bad Iran images. Arab publics remain more supportive of Iran's ambitions for nuclear power than their regimes, largely as an indirect critique of what they perceive to be Western interference and double standards.[27] In discussions with RAND, a Jordanian researcher argued, for example, that the Jordanian government was exaggerating the threat, suggesting most Jordanians do not have an issue with an Iranian nuclear capacity and even see some advantage to it in terms of its potential to balance Israel.[28] An Egyptian reform activist similarly suggested that, while the Egyptian Muslim Brotherhood does not feel an affinity to Iran (the concept of clerical rule is alien to Egypt's Sunni Islamists), it supports Iran's right to nuclear power as a critique of the double standard with Israel.[29]

On the other hand, Iran finds a less-sympathetic audience among Sunni Arabs of the Gulf, who are more likely than their Levantine or

[25] A separate Al Arabiya poll in February 2007 revealed similar unease, extending to Iran's ambitions throughout the Arab world.

[26] For example, al-Dhiyabi, 2007.

[27] Osama al-Ghazali Harb writes, "The [Iranian nuclear] issue in the mind of an average Arab appears simple: by what logic is the Israeli nuclear weapon accepted—indeed disregarded—at the same time that Iran is deprived of a nuclear weapon?" (Harb, 2008).

[28] Interview with Jordanian researcher, Amman, February 19, 2008.

[29] Interview with Egyptian reform activist, Cairo, February 24, 2008.

North African counterparts to view Iranian ambitions as a threat to regional security. As countries that are firmly aligned with the United States, host significant U.S. military installations, and have been targets of Iranian force (both overt and covert), Gulf populations are generally more wary of Iran's growing influence, particularly in conjunction with the continued nuclear crisis. Joint polling undertaken by Al Arabiya and YouGov Siraj in 2007 found, for example, that 63 percent of respondents from the GCC states were anxious over Iran's position in the Arab World, nearly 10 percent higher than respondents from non-Gulf countries.[30] A similar regional split emerged in response to the question of whether the Iranian relationship with Hizballah strengthens the latter as a deterrent force in the conflict with Israel; 34 percent of North Africans supported this statement, in comparison to only 23 percent of those polled from the Levant and the GCC states. Thus, Arab populations that either neighbor Iran (the GCC states) or have been exposed firsthand to Iranian involvement in local affairs (the Levantine states) are more wary of Iran than those that have the luxury of regarding Iran from a distance.

Yet even in the Levant, there is significant concern about Iran in official circles.[31] As an Egyptian security analyst noted, one indication of official concern over Iran is the shift of the Iran portfolio from the Foreign Ministry to the president and the intelligence services: "this means it [Iran] is a threat. Period."[32] More-forceful language is also

---

[30] The Al Arabiya/YouGov Siraj poll surveyed 1,221 individuals between February 7 and 13, 2007. Thirty-six percent of respondents were from the Levant, 21 percent from the Gulf, 29 percent from Egypt, and 14 percent from the North African states minus Egypt. Ninety-six percent of respondents were Muslim and 80 percent male. The majority of those polled were under 30 (71 percent), with 19 percent between 30 and 39, and 10 percent 40 or over. A summary of the poll is available from Al Arabiya (February 2, 2007).

[31] That said, in interviews with RAND in Amman in 2007, senior Jordanian officials suggested there could be some benefits to an Iranian nuclear balance with Israel, perhaps creating an incentive for Arab-Israeli peacemaking, similar to what occurred in the Indian-Pakistani case (of course, they failed to note that these two South Asian countries nearly went to war before their most recent peacemaking efforts).

[32] Interview with Egyptian security analyst, Cairo, February 25, 2008.

evident in recent public statements from Egyptian officials, such as the August 2008 comments from Foreign Minister Abu al-Gheit:

> It is necessary for Iran to be mindful that the Gulf is not an Iranian lake. But that Iran is located on one side and the Arabs on the other side. And the Arabs have reserves and strategic depth—that being Egypt—and that Egypt is part of this equation. (al-Gheit, 2008)

Fears over Iran do not necessarily stem from concerns that Iran will launch a direct nuclear attack but rather from the ripple effects the advent of a nuclear-capable Iran would send through the region: the potential for an escalating regional arms race, a nuclear accident at one of Iran's reactors, and the prospect that a nuclear Iran will become more aggressive in its support for terrorism and Shi'a activism or more unyielding in its diplomacy.[33] An Arab analyst writes,

> Today, a non-nuclear Iran uses Iraq as a platform for its influence and dominance in Lebanon, Gaza, Yemen, Bahrain, Kuwait, and other Gulf countries. If Iran has this influence in the region without a nuclear weapon, what will be its weight [in regional affairs] when it acquires a nuclear weapon and joins the international nuclear club? (Fandy, 2008)

Suspicion of Iran Does Not Necessarily Translate into Pro-American Positions

Even when the "bad Iran" image prevails among Arab publics, such sentiments do not necessarily translate into support for U.S. policies in the region. Indeed, suspicion of Iran is often marked by equal distrust of U.S. regional policies. As Figure 2.1 shows, available polling suggests that Arab publics see U.S. influence *as equally or more harmful* than that of Iran's in the case of Iraq.

---

[33] This analysis is based on interviews with scholars, officials, and diplomats throughout the GCC and in Egypt and Jordan, February and March 2006 and July 2007. See also Kaye and Wehrey, 2007; Sadjapour, 2007; Russell, 2005; Yaphe and Lutes, 2005; Henderson, 2005; and el-Hokayem and Legrenzi, 2006.

Such distrust should caution U.S. policymakers against assuming that Arab allies will fall naturally in line behind U.S. containment measures against Iran. For example, the same regional commentators who endorsed Washington's criticism of the IRGC showed ambivalence about its policy prescription—economic sanctions—that they interpreted as a prelude to war, rather than as is more commonly accepted in the West, a measure short of war. Similarly, a $20 billion proposed U.S. arms package to Saudi Arabia and other regional allies, with its tacit goal of deterring and containing Iran, provoked reflection on the lost opportunities and the detrimental side effects of this policy. Other analysts view heightened concerns about the Iranian threat as a "card" that regimes like Egypt's play to strengthen their bona fides with the United States, but the reality is that neither the Egyptian regime nor Egyptian people are "truly afraid of Iran."[34]

In tandem with fears of excessive U.S. hostility toward Iran, there is parallel concern, especially among GCC states, about U.S.-Iranian engagement. These states, particularly Saudi Arabia, have benefited tre-

Figure 2.1
Arab Popular Opinion Regarding U.S. and Iranian Roles in Iraq

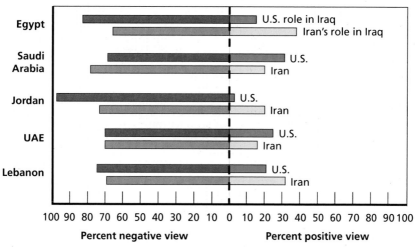

SOURCE: Zogby International/Arab American Institute Poll, conducted between February 26 and March 20, 2007. Sample included 3,400 Arabs in the above countries.
RAND MG892-2.1

---

[34] Interview with Egyptian reform activist, Cairo, February 24, 2008.

mendously from Washington's decades-long estrangement from both Iran and Iraq, and they fear a loss of status in the event of American-Iranian rapprochement. Unsurprisingly, there was widespread condemnation in the Arab press of the U.S.-Iraqi-Iranian talks in Baghdad in May 2007. For example, the pan-Arab daily *al-Arab al-Alamiya* noted, "The most important message that the meeting sends is that the role of the Arabs in Iraq has come to an end and that they have no value in the eyes of the masters in Washington."[35] Arab criticism over the 2007 U.S. National Intelligence Estimate (NIE) (National Intelligence Council, 2007), which claimed Iran was not seeking a nuclear weapon design (although it did acknowledge its continued nuclear enrichment capabilities) further bolstered Arab fears over weakening U.S. resolve toward Iran (Fleishman, 2007; al-Humayd, 2007b). And recent U.S. overtures toward Iran under the Obama administration are also making some Arab states nervous. As early as the U.S. Democratic primary, there was already concern with then-Senator Barack Obama's declared intention to negotiate with Iran, with one Saudi editorial arguing that this implied a dangerous naïveté about Iran's motives (al-Humayd, 2007a).

Regional Ambivalence Toward Both Iran and the United States Undermines U.S. Attempts to Create an Anti-Iranian Alliance

This regionwide ambivalence toward both Iran and the United States becomes even clearer when surveying particular state stances toward the notion of balancing or containing Iranian influence. While Iraqi nationalism and other sources of competition (e.g., among clerics and religious institutions) will likely provide natural buffers against Iranian overreach even in Shi'a-dominated Iraq, suffice it to say that there is no clear dividing line along which to draw a "green curtain" around Iran.[36] Even an independent-minded Iraqi government is unlikely to return to the hostile anti-Iranian positions and actions of Saddam Hussein's Iraq absent a radical shift in the political trajectory of that country.

Similarly, Turkey's common interest and even military cooperation with Iran in stemming PKK and PJAK activity in northern Iraq

---

[35] Quoted in U.S. Department of State, 2007.

[36] Wright, 2007, used the expression, *green curtain*.

and opposing Kurdish independence more broadly (along with extensive trade ties with Tehran totaling over $4 billion annually) will make it nearly impossible for Ankara to sign up to a broad-based containment strategy against Tehran.[37] Stephen Larrabee argues that Turkey's shared interest with Iran (and Syria) in preventing an independent Kurdish state and its growing energy ties with Iran suggest that Turkey "is unlikely to support U.S. policies aimed at isolating Iran . . ." (Larrabee, 2008, p. viii).

Another frequently discussed strategic goal in both American and Arab policy circles is the creation of conditions that could end up severing the Syrian-Iranian alliance. The logic behind such goals is that

> Iranian regional influence stretches into Lebanon and Palestine via Syria. [Thus] Returning Syria to the Arab fold is essential to the stability of Iraq and the region. It is also essential in any strategy that aspires to place a limit on Iranian influence. (Fandy, 2008)

Given that Syria maintains even closer political and military ties with Iran and shares similar common interests with respect to the Kurds, efforts to peel Syria entirely away from Iran may prove difficult, even in the context of a Syrian agreement with Israel.[38] A Syrian analyst has suggested that Syria is particularly inclined to turn toward Iran when facing threats and that, although Syria disagrees with Iran on many regional issues, it would not be in Damascus's interest to completely break its links to Tehran.[39]

Even in states, such as Jordan, that are more explicitly aligned in the moderate, "anti-Iranian" camp, ambivalent attitudes and positions show up. One Jordanian analyst expressed more concern over Salafi extremists than Iranian aggression because, in his view, the

---

[37] On Turkey's complex regional predicament and relationships with both the United States and Iran, see Cagapty, 2007.

[38] See, for example, Saab, 2007. For a lengthy survey of Syrian relations with Iran that illustrates the depth of the relationship, see Lawson, 2007.

[39] Views of a Syrian analyst expressed during a roundtable discussion, Santa Monica, Calif., July 30, 2008.

Salafi extremists are out to destroy the system itself, while Iran is "just maximizing its share and playing the cards it was dealt."[40] A former Jordanian official argued that, while less-educated Jordanians may respond to the official position that paints Iran as a dangerous threat, the middle class does not have a problem with Iran, believing that the United States is seeking to replace Israel with Iran as the new regional enemy. In his view, the Palestine problem needs to be resolved before the Arabs "can afford to antagonize Iran."[41] As a Jordanian official put it, containing Iran in Iraq would prove impossible while the "house was burning down" [in Palestine].[42] Another former Jordanian official acknowledged Iran's aggressive posture but called the idea of an Arab alliance to confront Iran "nonsense."[43] Even Jordanian King 'Abdullah has toned down the emphasis on the Iranian threat compared to the crisis in Arab-Israeli diplomacy (see Weymouth, 2008).[44]

What about the linchpin of regional containment, the Saudis? Indeed, some U.S. policymakers view Saudi Arabia as the most viable "Arab balancer" against Iran, as various arms sale proposals and other security initiatives suggest.[45] But the presumption of a bloc of "moderate Arab states" led by Saudi Arabia to counter Iranian influence is questionable.[46] It is true that Sunni Arab fears about Iran have strengthened regional support for Saudi Arabia's activism in the region.[47] Yet the

---

[40] Interview with Jordanian analyst, Amman, February 17, 2008.

[41] Interview with former Jordanian official, Amman, February 17, 2008.

[42] Interview with Jordanian official, Amman, February 20, 2008.

[43] Interview with former Jordanian official, Amman, February 17, 2008.

[44] However, many regional analysts, particularly Israelis, view the Iranian threat and the crisis in Gaza as linked.

[45] See, for example, Shadid, 2007; Slackman and Fattah, 2007; Solomon, 2007; Wright, 2007; La Franchi, 2007; and Bernard interview with Gary Sick in Gwertzman, 2007.

[46] For Gulf Arab wariness of both the U.S. and Iran, see Partrick, 2008. For a discussion of recent Saudi and Gulf engagement of Iran, see Kupchan and Takeyh, 2008.

[47] When asked about Saudi Arabia's relations with Iran in light of the Iraq conflict, the managing director of Al Arabiya, Abdelrahman Rashid, stated that "the possibility of having conflict is very high . . . who will face the Iranians tomorrow? Just the Israelis alone? I don't think that is possible" (Fattah, 2006b).

specter of Iranian influence and Saudi Arabia's resulting assertiveness have also intensified long-standing inter-Arab debates over regional primacy between the Gulf and the Levant and within the GCC.

For smaller Gulf states and for Egypt—Saudi Arabia's long-standing rival for Arab leadership—Riyadh's centrality in an Iranian containment strategy may be as alarming as the threat from Iran itself.[48] The role of the United States is particularly salient here; in some quarters, there is a sense that U.S. empowerment of Riyadh as its regional proxy against Iran could prove destabilizing in the long term, particularly concerning the growth of radical Islamism. Illustrating this during a discussion on the Iranian nuclear program, an Omani diplomat suggested that Saudi Arabia's radical Salafi ideology was "the Peninsula's real nuclear bomb."[49] One Israeli analyst claims that it was the Saudi threat to U.S. Vice President Richard Cheney that contributed to the U.S. troop surge in Iraq because the Saudis had suggested that, if the U.S. starting pulling out of Iraq, the Saudis would arm Iraqi Sunnis.[50] Some Egyptians share similar concerns over heightened Saudi activism, with one Egyptian reform activist suggesting that the "Saudis are a cancer in this region and the U.S. is feeding this cancer."[51] A former Egyptian foreign ministry official also noted increased Saudi activism with their "initiatives everywhere," which makes Egypt "edgy," even if, in his view, the Saudis do not have the capability to follow up and the Jordanians are often the "brains" behind most Saudi proposals.[52]

---

[48] For Egyptian fears about a possible Saudi-Iranian rapprochement and Egypt's general loss of stature on pan-Arab affairs, see Gaballah, 2007. For Arab and especially Saudi reactions to a possible Iranian nuclear capability, see Kaye and Wehrey, 2007.

[49] Interview with Omani diplomat, Muscat, Oman, February 2006. Commenting on the 'Abdullah-Ahmadinejad summit in March 2007, Egyptian analysts questioned whether the tentative Iranian-Saudi coordination on Lebanon, Palestine, and Iraq was "pulling the political rug from underneath Cairo's feet" and lamented Egypt's deepening retreat from Arab affairs.

[50] Interview with Israeli analyst, Tel Aviv, February 26, 2008.

[51] Interview with Egyptian reform activist, Cairo, February 24, 2008.

[52] Interview with former Egyptian foreign ministry official, Cairo, February 25, 2008. In another author interview in Jordan, a researcher similarly noted that the Jordanians often provide the content to Saudi initiatives, including the Arab peace initiative and the idea of

The result is that Iran's Arab neighbors, particularly the smaller GCC states, have pursued a mixed approach toward Tehran that incorporates some elements of accommodation and engagement, regardless of warnings from Riyadh and Washington. And indeed, even the Saudis themselves have adopted such an approach; the regional shakeup in the aftermath of the Iraq War has not fundamentally altered the Saudis' rapprochement with Tehran, which dates to the mid-1990s. When necessary, the two states have shown the propensity for pragmatic cooperation in specific geographic areas and on issues where their interests intersect—even if, in other areas, there is concurrently open rivalry. As one analyst of Saudi Arabia argues, the United States may want the Saudis to head an anti-Iranian alliance, but they will not do this, preferring to act as mediators instead.[53] Ahmadinejad's invitation and attendance at the December 2007 GCC summit was a particularly public expression of the mixed approach toward Iran among the Arab Gulf states and underscores the obstacles U.S. attempts to solidify an anti-Iranian stance among Iran's neighbors face.

That said, Arab hedging toward Iran is nuanced, and Iran's reach into the region does face some significant redlines, even if its neighbors are at times accommodating. Author interviews with a variety of regional experts and officials suggest an emerging Arab diplomatic strategy toward Iran that can be summed up as engagement in the Gulf, containment in Iraq, and rollback in the Levant. According to a Jordanian official, Iran is most vulnerable in Gaza: Egypt, Jordan, Saudi Arabia, and others view Iranian penetration into the Arab-Israeli conflict as unacceptable. This official argued that, if Arabs focus on resolving the Palestinian-Israeli conflict, Iran could no longer use this card as a means to destabilize moderate Arab regimes. In this official's view, the Arab strategy to confront Iran should start in Gaza, not Iraq.[54]

Arab security guarantees for peace with Israel. Interview with Jordanian researcher, Amman, February 20, 2008.

[53] Interview with Israeli analyst, Tel Aviv, February 26, 2008.

[54] Interview with Jordanian official, Amman, February 20, 2008.

An Israeli analyst told a similar story, suggesting that Saudi King 'Abdullah met with Ahmadinejad in March 2007 and made it clear that, while the nuclear issue was not good for the Saudis, the Saudis would not fight Iran on it. That said, 'Abdullah reportedly told the Iranians that the Saudis would not tolerate Iranian dominance in other areas, particularly in Lebanon or Gaza.[55] An Egyptian analyst similarly observed the Saudis' nuanced approach toward Iran, inviting Ahmadinejad to the Hajj but, at the same time, working against Iran in Lebanon, focusing on "clipping Iran's wings" (e.g., protecting investments, mitigating Shi'a-Sunni clashes, pushing for the Hariri tribunal).[56] Similarly, Egypt accepts Iranian visits but, at the same time, wants to stop Iran's influence in Gaza, fearing the increased growth of Islamism or a completely failed state.[57] The Rafah border breach in January 2008 and the Gaza war of 2008–2009 brought Egypt back to a focus on external affairs and opened its eyes to the dangers of the Iran-HAMAS connection in Gaza.[58]

Understanding this nuanced Arab approach to Iran will help U.S. policymakers better leverage their influence in efforts to undermine malign Iranian actions and help capitalize on opportunities to facilitate more-constructive Iranian actions based on interests it shares with both the U.S. and its regional allies. The same may be said for understanding the views of Israel and Turkey, to which we now turn.

---

[55] Interview with Israeli analyst, Tel Aviv, February 26, 2008.

[56] Interview with Egyptian security analyst, Cairo, February 25, 2008; interview with Lebanese analyst, Beirut, March 6, 2008.

[57] Interview with Egyptian security analyst, Cairo, February 25, 2008.

[58] The border breach occurred when Palestinians in HAMAS-controlled Gaza tore down the separation barrier between Gaza and Egypt, allowing thousands of Palestinians to cross over into Egypt, including HAMAS activists whom Egypt views as a security threat because of their association with Egypt's own Muslim Brotherhood Islamist opposition. Details on Egypt's perspective on the Rafah border incident from interview with former Egyptian Foreign Ministry official, February 25, 2008.

The Iraq War Has Reinforced and Created Strategic Challenges for Israel

Although there is some concern in Israel about the Iraq War's effect on the export of terrorism, the two central concerns for Israel resulting from this war relate to rising Iranian power and the potential threat to Jordanian stability.

Iran Has Become Israel's Key Regional Concern

Israel has long been concerned about Iranian regional ambitions and hostility. It was no secret, for example, that a central motivation for Yitzhak Rabin in pursuing peace with the Palestinians in the early 1990s related to his desire to deal with Israel's immediate neighbors so that it could better manage its more significant "far enemies," such as Iran. Subsequent Israeli leaders have similarly viewed Iran as the most serious, even existential, threat their state faces. Perceptions of rising Iranian influence after the Iraq War, the continued Iranian nuclear crisis, and the inflammatory rhetoric of Iranian President Ahmadinejad (denying the Holocaust, suggesting Israel be "wiped off the map"), has led to especially heightened Israeli alarm in recent years. As one Israeli analyst told RAND, Israel takes Iranian threats to destroy Israel seriously, arguing that, even if Iran would never use a nuclear bomb against Israel, the specter of an Iranian bomb could lead Israelis to leave the country and question the future of Zionism. In his view, Israel has never faced as serious a threat as the one a nuclear Iran poses.[59]

Indeed, from many Israelis' perspective, the United States fought the wrong war in 2003.[60] According to Israeli analysts and officials, the Iraq War is nearly off the Israeli radar screen, while Israeli policymakers now view every issue through the prism of Iran.[61] Concern over Iran

---

[59] Interview with Israeli analyst, Tel Aviv, February 26, 2008. Israeli officials, such as Deputy Defense Minister Ephraim Sneh, have also expressed fears publicly that an Iranian bomb could lead to a massive exodus of Jews from Israel ("Israel's Deputy DefMin Interviewed . . . ," 2006).

[60] Interview with Israeli journalist, Tel Aviv, February 24, 2008.

[61] Interviews in Jerusalem and Tel Aviv, February 2008.

expands beyond the direct threat a nuclear Iran could pose to Israel. Many Israeli analysts believe Iran is seeking hegemony over the broader region, not just the Gulf, and that if Iran acquires a nuclear option, it will become even more aggressive in seeking regional dominance.[62] According to analysts knowledgeable about current Israeli decisionmaking, key personalities in the Israeli government may be moderate on issues relating to the Palestinians but are hawkish when it comes to Iran.[63] An Israeli defense official suggested to RAND that Iranian rhetoric and actions are reaching new heights, as Iran's political and material links to Hizballah are growing.[64] Such concerns have only increased with the perception among many Israeli analysts that the wars against Hizballah in 2006 and HAMAS in 2008 were as much about deterring Iranian aggression as deterring these nonstate actors.

Although such sentiments dominate both official and public discourse, less-conventional views toward Iran exist. Some Israeli analysts are beginning to question just how much of a threat Iran poses to Israel and whether a hard-line policy toward Tehran is effective. For example, although one Israeli analyst calls Iran "an expansionist aspiring hegemon," he also suggests that "Iranian aspirations should nonetheless be viewed in proper proportion. Iran is not the Soviet Union . . . . Tehran has its own serious vulnerabilities, domestic, economic, and military" (Susser, 2007b). Other Israeli analysts also do not believe that Israel would be the central target if Iran were to acquire a nuclear weapon capability and that deterrence could work in avoiding an Iranian attack, particularly if Israel acquires adequate second-strike capabilities.[65]

---

[62] Such sentiments were voiced in several interviews in Jerusalem and Tel Aviv in February 2008 and January 2009.

[63] Interview with former Israeli military official, Tel Aviv, February 27, 2008.

[64] Interview with Israeli defense official, Tel Aviv, February 25, 2008.

[65] Author discussion with Israeli analysts, Tel Aviv, December 4, 2005. For a discussion countering the suggestion that Iran is not deterrable (while acknowledging that regime factionalism can make a stable deterrent relationship difficult), see Eisenstadt, 1999, especially pp. 134–137. For further discussion regarding the complexities of deterring Iran, see Evron, 2008.

Former Israeli military officials also suggest neutralizing Iran by reaching a bargain with it and support American negotiations with Iran as long as engagement is not open ended.[66] Former Israeli intelligence officials similarly believe that Israel should support the Americans in opening channels to Iran to avoid a confrontation.[67] One of these former officials suggested that, if Iran were able to signal to Israel (through the United States) that "it's [Iran's nuclear capability] not about you," Israel could back off as it did in the Pakistan case.[68] Still, such assessments are in the minority. The prevailing view in Israel is that Iran is among Israel's gravest strategic threats and that the Iraq War and its aftermath exacerbated this threat.

Potential Instability in Jordan Is a Further Concern

The second major fallout of the Iraq War from Israel's perspective is the growing potential for instability in Jordan emanating from this conflict. As discussed in Chapter Four, the Iraq War sent over half a million refugees to Jordan, straining already limited domestic resources in education and health care and creating new political uncertainties about the future role of this community in Jordanian society. Jordan's loss of subsidized oil from Iraq after the war contributed to rising prices for food, heating oil, and other basic goods, creating a serious economic crisis and widespread discontent with the regime, even among the monarchy's traditional bases of support.

In addition to economic pressures, Jordanians also face the prospect of extremist violence spilling over from Iraq. The hotel bombings in Amman in 2005—the worst terrorist incident on Jordanian soil to date—were carried out by Iraqis, although the Jordanian security services have proven effective in preventing similar types of incidents. Still, with violence and political uncertainty surrounding Jordan, Israelis worry about the future stability of the friendly Hashemite-led Jordanian state. As one Israeli analyst suggested, Jordan is the "weakest link

---

[66] Interview with former Israeli military official, Tel Aviv, February 27, 2008.

[67] Interviews with former Israeli intelligence officials, Jerusalem, February 25, 2008, and Tel Aviv, February 27, 2008.

[68] Interview with former Israeli intelligence official, Tel Aviv, February 27, 2008.

in the aftermath of the war" and could be "in serious trouble" if waves of refugees attempt to enter Jordan in the future because Jordan risks being "squashed" between the absence of a solution on the Palestinian front to the west and the deterioration of Iraq to the east.[69] Before the Iraq War, Israel took Jordan's ability to serve as a buffer between Israel and Iraq as a given; now, Israelis worry about the loss of such a buffer shielding them from aggression from the east.[70]

Israeli Views on an American Withdrawal Hinge on Perceptions About Whether a Withdrawal Will Strengthen or Weaken U.S. Regional Influence

From the perspective of many Israelis, the erosion of and limitations on American power are serious strategic consequences of the Iraq War. Because Israel's key interest is a strong America that can credibly intervene elsewhere if necessary, many Israeli analysts worry that a prolonged U.S. presence in Iraq reduces the "U.S. appetite or ability to go to war" anywhere else and feel that the utility of the U.S. presence in Iraq has exhausted its use.[71] Israelis are primarily focused on Iraq to the extent that it affects broader U.S. power projection in the region, particularly vis-à-vis Iran.[72] Thus, it should not be surprising that opinions on an American drawdown from Iraq hinge largely on beliefs about whether withdrawal will weaken or strengthen U.S. capabilities and regional influence.

---

[69] Interview with former Israeli intelligence official, Jerusalem, February 25, 2008.

[70] Interview with Israeli analyst and former government official, Tel Aviv, February 22, 2008.

[71] Interview with Israeli analysts, Tel Aviv, February 2008.

[72] One possible exception is Israel's interest in building relations with Iraq's Kurdish north, and some reports claim that Israel is training the Iraqi Kurdish militia and establishing economic ties with Kurdish Iraq (although Kurdish and Israeli leaders deny such reports). See Hersh, 2004, and Judson, 2007, both also cited in Blanchard et al., 2008, p. 31. Moreover, according to a former Israeli intelligence official, although Israel has an interest in seeing a Kurdish entity emerge as an independent state in northern Iraq (in contrast to American interests), if Israel had to choose, it would still choose to maintain its relationship with Turkey over support for a Kurdish state. Interview with former Israeli intelligence official, Tel Aviv, February 27, 2008.

The conventional Israeli view is that an American withdrawal could be dangerous, further eroding U.S. influence. What one Israeli analyst calls the "Israeli neo-con school" thinks a U.S. withdrawal will be a disaster for U.S. image, prestige, and influence in the region. And since what is good for the United States is good for Israel in their view, a U.S. withdrawal can be very damaging. In March 2007, Israeli Prime Minister Ehud Olmert spoke publicly about concerns over the instability that would result if the U.S. withdrew from Iraq, and how the Americans would lose their authority in the Middle East (Rosner, Benn, and Barkat, 2007. Former Foreign Minister Tzipi Livni also warned of similar consequences if "we appease the extremists . . ." (Rosner, 2007). Echoing such sentiments, an Israeli defense official and other Israeli analysts expressed several central concerns regarding a "premature" American withdrawal from Iraq, including some of the concerns outlined above: a stronger Iran; the potential for renewed civil war that will challenge Jordanian stability as Iraqi refugees flee; a psychological victory for violent extremists leading to the export of terrorism to Jordan, Saudi Arabia, and even Israel; and the solidification of a "loser image" for the United States and, by extension, Israel.[73]

However, improved security conditions in Iraq in 2008–2009 reduced such Israeli concerns about the negative effects of a drawdown, particularly with respect to U.S. credibility. Some analysts also question whether a U.S. drawdown will significantly damage American credibility because the U.S. presence in Iraq has already eroded it. As one analyst put it, "what has happened in the last six years has created the perception of U.S. failure; withdrawal itself is not the test of the pudding, as the pudding is already sour."[74]

Some Israelis also see potential opportunities emerging from a U.S. drawdown from Iraq. For example, an Israeli official suggested that the Saudis could play a more-constructive role in regional security in the context of a U.S. drawdown, including supporting stabilizing steps for Iraq. Because Israel increasingly views itself as tacitly

---

[73] Interview with Israeli defense official, Tel Aviv, February 25, 2008, and interviews with Israeli analysts, Tel Aviv and Jerusalem, February 2008 and January 2009.

[74] Interview with former Israeli defense official, Tel Aviv, January 2009.

aligned with "moderate" Arab states, such as Saudi Arabia and Egypt, in a common concern about growing Iranian influence, Israelis view an expanded regional role for U.S. allies in the wake of a U.S. drawdown as potentially beneficial.[75] Israelis also view a U.S. drawdown as providing opportunities to enhance dialogue with Syria. For example, some Israeli officials believe that a U.S. withdrawal may help lead Syria away from Iran, at least in the context of a different U.S.–Syrian relationship, because Syria's concerns over Iranian dominance in Iraq could increase once the Americans leave.[76]

Most Israelis expected some sort of U.S. engagement and dialogue with Iran in the Obama administration. An Israeli official believes that the U.S. drawdown will allow a serious U.S. attempt at engagement with Iran, or at least improve U.S. leverage in such a dialogue.[77] But Israelis, regardless of their political perspective, do not want to see talks with Iran drag out in a way that would allow the nuclear issue to remain unresolved.

The Iraq War Has Complicated Turkey's Strategic Relations with the United States and Iran

The Conflict Exacerbated the Kurdish Challenge for Turkey

The most significant strategic repercussion for Turkey from the 2003 Iraq conflict relates to fears that a weak and destabilized Iraq will lead to the emergence of an independent Kurdish state on Turkey's southern border, threatening the secession of Turkey's own Kurdish population and providing a springboard for terrorist activities by Kurdish groups within Turkey's borders. As Stephen Larrabee explains,

> From the outset Turkish leaders had strong reservations about the U.S. invasion of Iraq. . . . Turkish leaders feared that [Saddam Hussein's] removal would lead to the fragmentation of Iraq, the

---

[75] Interview with Israeli official, Jerusalem, January 2009.

[76] Interviews with Israeli officials, Jerusalem, February 2008 and January 2009.

[77] Interview with Israeli official, Jerusalem, January 2009.

growth of Kurdish nationalism, and an overall decline in Turkish security. The aftermath of the invasion has seen Turkey's worst fears come true. (Larrabee, 2008, p. 8)

Turkey remains extremely concerned about the continuing threat from the PKK, which the United States, NATO, and the European Union list as a terrorist organization.[78] Violent PKK attacks have escalated significantly since 2003, killing more than 600 Turks (many from the Turkish security forces) in 2006 alone (Larrabee, 2008, p. 8). Such attacks have sparked a public outcry in Turkey and calls for military action against the PKK in Iraq. Turkish leaders and the Turkish public view the United States as responsible for the resurgence in Kurdish violence and have been frustrated by what they perceive as U.S. reluctance to deal with the PKK challenge because of Washington's strong ties with Iraqi Kurds, who have proven to be reliable allies.[79] Consequently, Turkey turned to unilateral military action against the PKK, beginning with military buildups on the Iraqi border in 2006 and, ultimately, incursions into northern Iraq in 2007–2008.[80]

Recognizing that the alignment of U.S. and Turkish interests in maintaining a unified and stable Iraqi state was at stake (not to mention the broader U.S.–Turkish relationship), the United States began expressing more high-level support for Turkish actions against the PKK by the end of 2007. When Turkish Prime Minister Recep Tayyip Erdogan visited the White House in November 2007, President George W. Bush referred to the PKK as "our common enemy" and offered "real time" and "actionable" intelligence (Blanchard et al., 2008, p. 14). The United States fulfilled its promise when it offered intelligence support for Turkish forces as they launched an incursion into northern Iraq to

---

[78] From 1984 to 1999, Turkey fought a costly war with the PKK in Southeast Turkey, losing 30,000 lives. An estimated 3,000 to 3,500 PKK fighters have also escaped to the mountainous region of Northern Iraq. For further details, see Blanchard et al., 2008, pp. 12–16.

[79] See, for example, Enginsoy, 2008.

[80] For further details, see Blanchard et al., 2008, p. 14. Also see Rubin and Tavernise, 2008. In late July 2008, Turkey bombed Kurdish rebel targets in northern Iraq after land mines killed three Turkish civilians. See "Kurdish Landmine Kills Three," 2008.

degrade PKK communications, supply depots, and training facilities in February 2008 (Blanchard et al., 2008, p. 14).

The Conflict Has Led Turkey Toward Greater Regional Activism and More Cooperation with Iran

The resurgent Kurdish challenge, along with Turkey's other significant interests in Iraq (particularly its related concern over the fate of Iraqi Turkmen who feel they are being outnumbered by Iraqi Kurds in the north and worry about Kurdish claims to oil-rich Kirkuk),[81] has led to increasing Turkish activism in regional affairs. Turkey's disappointment with the European Union and NATO and the ascendance of the Islamist Justice and Development Party, has also contributed to Turkey's turn toward the Middle East.[82] Yet Turkey's distancing from Europe has not warmed its relationship with the United States. Turkey's unhappiness with the initial lack of U.S. assistance in stamping out the Kurdish terrorist threat stemming from Northern Iraq has particularly soured U.S.–Turkish relations and popular Turkish perceptions of the United States.[83]

Although recent U.S. support for Turkish actions against the PKK in northern Iraq is certainly welcome in Ankara, the Kurdish challenge is likely to continue to be a source of friction in U.S.–Turkish relations in years to come. The Kurdish issue also aligns Turkish interests with those of key American adversaries, particularly Iran. As discussed earlier, Turkey shares fundamental security and extensive economic interests with Iran (as well as Syria) that will make it difficult, if not impossible, to bring Turkey into a firmly pro-Western camp.[84] As

---

[81] For further details, see Blanchard et al., 2008, p. 14.

[82] NATO's decision in 2003 not to give Turkey the air defense it requested contributed to Turkey's strategic shift away from the United States and Europe. On these points, see Susser, 2007a, p. 179.

[83] According to Pew, 2007, 83 percent of Turks have unfavorable views of the United States, with only 9 percent holding favorable views. Pew, 2008, shows views of the United States improving only slightly, up by only 3 points in Turkey (with 12 percent expressing favorable views of the United States).

[84] For example, in July 2004, Turkey and Iran signed a security agreement calling the PKK a terrorist organization and have increased security cooperation to protect their borders

Turkey asserts greater interest and activism in the Middle East arena, U.S. policymakers will need to contend with what some analysts view as a more independent-minded and nationalist Turkish orientation (see Larrabee, 2008).

Turkey's Economic Interests Provide Opportunities for Convergence with U.S. Interests

Turkey's role in Iraq is not merely about Kurdish secessionist tendencies. Turkey has also developed lucrative trade relations with Iraq that could help to stabilize and rebuild Iraq, contributing to U.S. efforts to build regional support for the Iraqi government. Turkish Prime Minister Erdogan visited Iraq in July 2008, making him only the second leader of a neighboring state to visit Iraq since the 2003 war (Tavernise and Robertson, 2008). Turkey also maintains a strong diplomatic presence in Iraq (in contrast to Iraq's Arab neighbors), with an ambassador in Baghdad, an ambassadorial-level Special Representative to Iraq, an ambassador in Ankara responsible for reconstruction in Iraq and Afghanistan, and consulates in Mosul and Basra (see Blanchard et al., 2008, p. 15).

On the economic front, Turkey's bilateral trade with Iraq reached $2.8 billion in 2007, and Turkey has expressed an interest in developing a free trade agreement with Iraq (see Blanchard et al., 2008, p. 15). Turkey and Iraq are also working to establish a pipeline to ship Iraqi natural gas through Turkey to Europe (see Blanchard et al., 2008, p. 15). And despite the cross-border tension and even conflict in Iraq's Kurdish north, Turkey is a critical trading partner for Iraq's Kurdish region. One study argues that, despite Turkish attacks and incursions into northern Iraq, Turkey appreciates its important geographic role as an "energy transportation corridor" and does not want to interfere with the supply line through northern Iraq (Brannen, 2007). For example, the Iraqi Kurdish leadership has awarded the Turkish business community several reconstruction contracts, including a $40-million air-

---

against PKK attacks (Larrabee, 2008, p. 11). Energy ties are especially strong. Iran is Turkey's second-largest supplier of natural gas, and the two countries have signed recent agreements to significantly expand the export of Iranian gas to Europe through Turkey (Larrabee, 2008, p. 12).

port construction project in Suleymaniyah (see Barkey, 2005, p. 16). Several Turkish firms have also signed production-sharing agreements with the Kurds in Northern Iraq to explore new oil and gas fields (see Beehner, 2006). The first high-level meetings between Turkish and Kurdish regional leaders occurred in May 2008, with the leaders expressing a desire to improve economic (as well as security and political) relations.[85] Such economic relations will not only bolster Iraq's struggling economy but could help erode Turkish mistrust of Iraq's Kurdish population.

Conclusion

This overview of the regional landscape in the years following the Iraq War suggests a fluid strategic environment with complex regional threat perceptions and behavior. Despite concerns over eroding American influence, the United States and Iran have emerged from this conflict as the major regional powers. That non-Arab states (the United States, Iran, and to some extent Turkey) now dominate regional security dynamics underscores the continuing weakness of the Arab state system and the lack of a viable Arab balancer to counter Iran, despite some renewed inter-Arab cooperation and activism.

Iranian motivations for its growing regional assertiveness, often grounded on perceptions of vulnerability, and ambivalent Arab responses to Iran's rise raise questions about balance-of-power strategies and the extent to which the region operates in bloclike terms. Alarm and dislike of Iran and its regional postures does not necessarily lead regional actors to embrace the United States or its regional security agenda. Even regional U.S. allies, such as Turkey, are not finding themselves aligned in all cases with U.S. regional interests and are facing new challenges in the aftermath of this conflict that may at times require accommodation with American adversaries.

---

[85] Kurdish Regional Government statement on first high-level talks with Turkey, May 2008.

A simplistic paradigm, such as a new Cold War between Iran and America's Arab allies, is thus not an accurate portrayal of the new Middle East, even if the old regional strategic balance has been fundamentally overturned. U.S. policymakers need to understand the complex nature of regional shifts and postures to develop policies that can best minimize regional threats and capitalize on opportunities to address them, policies that we consider in the concluding chapter.

New Challenges to American Influence: Chinese and Russian Roles in the Middle East

The decline in U.S. standing in the Middle East following the Iraq War created opportunities for other extraregional actors to expand their influence in regional affairs, notably China and Russia. Although the source of this decline cannot be reduced to a single event, the Iraq conflict contributed to doubts that the United States is no longer the guarantor of regional security it once was, to say nothing of its effect on perceptions of U.S. moral authority. This effect can be observed in Arab public opinion, in which U.S. favorability ratings sharply declined in the years following 2003. Although views of the United States have somewhat improved after the election of President Obama, polls in key countries, such as Egypt and Jordan, show continued negative views of the United States and its policies in the region.[1]

However, of even greater concern to U.S. strategic planners, America's declining authority is also reflected in the hedging strategies regional actors are using to diversify their security alliances. A combination of lowered confidence in the U.S. capacity to ensure regional security and a desire by some to return the region to a system of multipolarity have expanded opportunities for China and Russia to enhance their positions in regional affairs. To date, the Russian and Chinese advances have largely taken the form of strengthened economic ties. However, should the U.S. "brand" continue to suffer, Chinese and Russian engagement could spread into the security portfolio.

---

[1] See Pew, 2009, for example.

Perceptions of Eroding U.S. Credibility

Regional concerns related to growing Iranian influence after the war were compounded by a perception that the heavy U.S. commitment in Iraq constrained its ability to project power and enforce regional security. Specifically, the difficulties of prosecuting the war in Iraq have fed the view that the American "moment" in the Middle East may be waning, or at a minimum, that the war has clipped the Americans' wings. However, despite diminished standing in the region, the United States remains the balancer of choice, and the U.S. drawdown from Iraq may enable the United States to regain regional confidence if it proceeds smoothly.

The draining effect of the war in Iraq on U.S. resources and military readiness is advanced as the principal reason behind the United States' declining influence in the region (al-Rukabi, 2008). Despite recent improvement in the security situation in Iraq, many regional observers believe that the war in Iraq has revealed the limits of U.S. power. Similarly, the rise of Iranian influence inside Iraq and the continued development of its missile technology and nuclear program are cited as harbingers of a new regional security order, in which Iran will play an increasingly assertive role at the expense of U.S. interests (Harb, 2008). In an article in the *Arab Journal of Political Science*, 'Abdullah al-Shaiji observes,

> Iraq has become a theatre for Iran to settle scores with the United States and [for Iran] to increase the periphery of its power and its presence in the region, to play the role of the principal authority in the region, and to take hold of the trump cards, from Western Afghanistan to southern Iraq and from Yemen to the Persian Gulf. (al-Shaiji, 2008, p. 152)

Events in Lebanon are also advanced as evidence of Iran's growing influence in regional affairs. Specifically, Hizballah's staying power in the 2006 war with Israel, its ability to dictate the terms of the 2008 prisoner exchange, and its political gains vis-à-vis the March 14 majority coalition are all cited as further evidence of Iranian gains and the erosion of U.S. power. For example, in reference to Hizballah's May 2008 show of force in Beirut, one Arab commentator observed,

> Since the outbreak of the Lebanese internal crisis, the Lebanese political forces have been divided between two camps. One did not hide its alliance with the United States while the other aligned with Iran and Syria. . . . In the moment the crisis exploded, the United States was unable to protect its friends and left them completely exposed in the face of the sudden attack launched by Hezbollah and its allies. (Nafi'a, 2008)

Given deep skepticism in the region over both the strategic logic and prosecution of the war in Iraq, the recent improvements in the security environment that have followed the troop surge and the empowerment of the Awakening Councils have had little effect on restoring U.S. standing in the region. In a commentary appearing in *Dar al-Hayat*, Mahmoud 'Awad wrote,

> When we recall that the Green Zone in the Iraqi capital Baghdad is bombarded continuously every day despite being the area with the greatest protection from U.S. forces, and we recall the walls that were erected in order to divide [Baghdad's] neighborhoods from one another, and in addition to that the doubling of security check-points . . . then this does not mean progress in security but in fact means a deterioration in security. ('Awad, 2008)

That is to say, given that many in the region see the war in Iraq as a strategic error on par with the U.S. "gouging out its eyes with its own hand" (al-Rukabi, 2008), it should not be surprising that regional observers are slow to acknowledge progress on the ground.

The same skepticism is reflected in public opinion polls. For example, in Shibley Telhami's 2008 survey of regional attitudes, only 6 percent of the more than 4,000 Arabs polled were convinced that the American troop surge in Iraq is working (Telhami, 2008, p. 13). While there is a logical time-lag for public opinion to catch up with developments on the ground, this result underscores the importance of perceptions that may or may not reflect reality and the difficult task of reversing such views. Moreover, doubts over the efficacy of U.S. policy are not limited to the surge but extend more broadly to U.S. involvement in Iraq. In fact, 81 percent of those polled believed most Iraqis are worse off, given the net effect of the war in Iraq (Telhami, 2008, p. 6). These negative views on the Iraq War are also consistent with general attitudes toward the United States in that 83 percent of respondents identified their attitude toward the U.S. as very or somewhat unfavorable, and 70 percent reported having "no confidence" in the United States; see Figure 3.1 (Telhami, 2008, pp. 62, 65).

The official positions of regional actors also reflect doubts, in that states that were responsive to U.S. leverage in the past are now less willing to subjugate national interests or their own regime's stability to the U.S. regional agenda. For example, in countries in which the United States has shown a willingness to press a reform agenda, there is an attitude of "if you twist my arm to do issue X, maybe I won't want to do it because you can't do anything."[2] This dynamic is particularly evident

Figure 3.1
2008 Views of the United States: Six-Country Total

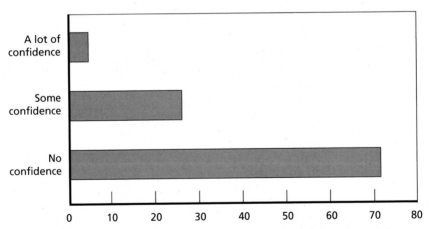

SOURCE: Shibley Telhami/Zogby International, "2008 Arab Public Opinion Poll," March 2008, p. 65.
NOTE: The six countries polled were Egypt, Jordan, Lebanon, Morocco, Saudi Arabia, and the United Arab Emirates.
RAND MG892-3.1

---

2   Interview with former Egyptian foreign ministry official, Cairo, February 25, 2008.

in Egypt, where observers widely credit U.S. pressure on the regime as a major impetus behind the political openings of 2003–2005 (al-'Anani, 2007, p. 195), a trend that was later reversed when the precariousness of the U.S. position in Iraq undermined U.S. credibility and leverage vis-à-vis its reform agenda. Some analysts believe that U.S. allies are "happy to see the U.S. with egg on its face," if this relieves pressure on regimes to move forward on internal reforms.[3]

Added to concerns over U.S. policies in Iraq is the perception that the United States "is simply not present" on the Arab-Israeli scene, either by design or again because of the constraints of Iraq.[4] Greater regional efforts to resolve local conflicts (e.g., Egypt's role in brokering an Israeli-HAMAS cease-fire in Gaza; Yemen's efforts to promote reconciliation between Fatah and HAMAS, Qatar's role in reaching a power-sharing agreement in Lebanon, and Turkey's role in mediating Israeli-Syrian peace overtures) have also underscored declining U.S. influence in the region.[5] President Obama's appointment of George Mitchell as a special envoy to the Arab-Israeli peace process early in his administration may help shift this regional perception, but widespread skepticism of the U.S. ability to alter its policies in the region remains strong.

The Iraq War also raised questions in the region about whether the United States is a power that can deliver. As a former Egyptian foreign ministry official put it, local actors are "watching the U.S. sink."[6] Similar views are prevalent in the Arab media. For example, a guest on the television program, *al-Ittijah al-Mu'akis* [The Opposite Direction], argued that "America is in a state of crisis, a predicament, the countries that America attempted to isolate and overthrow are now in a better situation [than prior to the war in Iraq]" ('Aloush, 2007).

That said, despite the view that U.S. preeminence in regional security is fading, author interviews found a recognition that the United

[3] Interview with Lebanese analyst, Beirut, March 6, 2008.

[4] Interview with former Egyptian foreign ministry official, Cairo, February 25, 2008.

[5] Such sentiments were expressed in multiple interviews, including by a Syrian analyst at a roundtable discussion, Santa Monica, Calif., July 30, 2008.

[6] Interview with former Egyptian foreign ministry official, Cairo, February 25, 2008.

States remains indispensable to finding a way out of current crises.[7] Indeed, despite some hedging and tentative moves toward "security diversification" from traditional U.S. allies in the region,[8] the United States remains the clear balancer of choice. For example, a Jordanian researcher noted that, because Iraq now exerts a much smaller pull in the regional balance of power, the United States has become that much more important to regional security. Because Jordan is less able to maneuver between regional alliances, it has come to view such options as secondary, instead choosing to focus on consolidating its strategic alliance with the United States.[9]

Thus, while the war in Iraq has deepened antipathy toward the United States, the hornet's nest it uncovered has also served to underscore the extent to which the regional security order depends on the United States. The duality of the Arab view of the U.S. regional role—characterized by a mix of animosity and dependence—was wryly captured by 'Abd al-Rauf Maqdimi:

> Despite the Arabs' dire need for the United States, and it is a need that manifests itself particularly through bilateral cooperation with the U.S. and via the logic of the nation state . . . the Arabs' common feature is that wish and continual search for the worst news that could reflect out from America or on America. But the issue is also not that simple. For if the [Arab] soul hopes for the defeat of the Americans in Iraq, it also fears its consequences, fearing a regression of the situation in favor of Iran, fearing the empowerment of those not in tune with an Arab in power [in Iraq], and fearing for Iraq itself [from the prospect of] its division. (Maqdimi, 2007)

---

[7] Interview with Lebanese analyst, Beirut, March 6, 2008.

[8] A former Egyptian ambassador used the term *security diversification* in an author interview, Cairo, February 25, 2008. Other interviews also referred to the trend toward diversification of security ties among regional actors, including interview with former United Nations (UN) official stationed in South Lebanon, Beirut, March 4, 2008.

[9] Interview with Jordanian researcher, Amman, February 20, 2008.

Thus, while the war in Iraq contributed to a decline in U.S. standing among regional actors, a trend that is even more pronounced at the level of public opinion (Zogby, 2007), a broad recognition of the United States' crucial role in regional security remains. Experienced observers, while at times incredulous of U.S. policy in the region, understand that the United States remains the heavyweight in regional security. However, over the long term, the emergence of greater parity in the regional system via the ascendancy of Iran and the surfacing of doubts about the capability and resolve of the United States to play the role of regional balancer have opened the door for greater influence by both regional and extraregional actors in shaping the future of regional security.

Changing Extraregional Roles

Despite the fact that the United States retains its status as the balancer of choice in the Middle East, the erosion of U.S. credibility and influence has created an opportunity for growing extraregional activism, even if such activism has to date largely complemented rather than supplanted the U.S. regional role. The following sections further assess the extent and nature of extraregional involvement in the Middle East in the years following the Iraq War.

China

Chinese Prospects in the Gulf. China's recent engagement in the Gulf has largely been driven by its status as a "stakeholder state" favoring regime stability.[10] That is to say, given the importance of China's economic growth as the source of its emerging power, China is heavily invested in promoting the stability conducive to the flow of Chinese exports to the region, as well as to the import of Middle Eastern oil and gas to China. However, the precariousness of regional security in light of the repercussions of the war in Iraq creates both challenges

---

[10] The term *stakeholder* was used in September 2005 by then–Deputy Secretary of State Robert Zoellick in remarks to the Committee on U.S.–China Relations.

and opportunities for China that are changing its posture vis-à-vis the region. Specifically, the disruption of Iraqi oil supplies is leading China to strengthen its relationships with other producers, notably Saudi Arabia and Iran. Moreover, the U.S. entanglement in Iraq and the move of some Gulf States to hedge against an erosion of American power by diversifying their security alliances creates opportunities for China to expand its influence in the Gulf. However, while China has sought to expand its footprint in the region and become more proactive in ensuring its access to Middle East markets and share of the region's oil and gas, this expansion of China's role in regional affairs is likely to proceed gradually and remain focused on the economic dimension.

The Chinese-Saudi Dimension. Violence in Iraq has thwarted Chinese ambitions to maximize oil potential there, and while it is pushing for major oil deals with the new Iraqi government, its biggest focus on the Arab side of the Gulf is Saudi Arabia. From China's vantage point, the calculus is simple: As the world's largest oil producer, Saudi Arabia is a natural provider of China's energy needs. The benefit is equally clear for Saudi Arabia: The Iraq War underscores the risk of reliance on a single power for maintaining regional security. Saudi Arabia is therefore keen to strengthen its relationships with other powers that can be employed to reinforce the kingdom's security in a dangerous neighborhood. Ambassador Chas Freeman describes the underlying logic this way:

> What do the Arabs and Chinese see in each other? Quite a bit. The Arabs see a partner who will buy their oil without demanding that they accept a foreign ideology, abandon their way of life, or make other choices they'd rather avoid. They see a country that is far away and has no imperial agenda in their region, but which is internationally influential and likely in time to be militarily powerful. (Freeman, 2006)

In short, Saudi Arabia and other Gulf states view China as a stable market for their oil and gas resources and a potential check on the use of force in the region but not an alternative to the U.S.-led regional security order. Alterman and Garver, 2008, p. 57, have observed that

China cannot supplant the United States in the Middle East as a military power, lacking anything close to the requisite military might. Yet, Middle Eastern countries can use a relationship to China to supplement the bilateral relations with the United States and perhaps give those countries the freedom of greater distance from Washington.

Put another way, China provides the Gulf states with an opportunity to reduce their dependence on the United States as the sole heavyweight in the region.

By any measure, China's ties in the Middle East are growing. In 2006, King 'Abdullah of Saudi Arabia and President Hu Jintao of China exchanged visits. 'Abdullah's visit was the first by a Saudi head of state since China and Saudi Arabia established formal diplomatic relations in 1990. This historic step culminated in an offer from Saudi Arabia to build and operate a strategic oil reserve in China that would hold 100 million barrels of oil, roughly 10 days' worth of Saudi oil output (Georgi, 2006). While there is nothing suspicious about China's pursuit of Saudi oil, there is concern that China's demand for Gulf oil may lead to an intensification of American-Chinese energy competition.

China is already the world's second-largest consumer of energy, and its demand for oil is forecast to rise faster than that of any other country over the next several decades (Energy Information Agency [EIA], 2006, p. 87). Over the 1998–2007 period, Chinese oil consumption grew nearly 85 percent.[11] By 2030, it is estimated that China will need to import roughly 14 million barrels of oil per day to close the gap between its consumption and domestic production (Alterman and Garver, 2008, p. 21). While a prolonged global recession could certainly change these forecasts, China is still likely to be a strong source of demand relative to other energy consumers even if global demand fails to keep pace with forecasts.

As for the regional breakout of the country's energy supply, the People's Republic of China currently imports a significant share of its

---

[11] From 4,105,835 barrels a day to 7,578,319 barrels a day (EIA, 2008).

oil from non–Middle Eastern producers, notably Angola. However, it is forecast that, by 2020, the Middle East and North Africa will be the source of more than 70 percent of China's oil imports (Lei, 2006). This has raised concerns about Chinese-American competition for Saudi oil, although an important countervailing factor is that, while China has shown an interest in purchasing discounted *heavy* crude from Saudi Arabia—and is further investing in its capacity to refine it—the United States is focused on importing lighter crude that is both easier to refine and less environmentally damaging (Alterman and Garver, 2008, pp. 58–59). Thus, although the United States and China are competing for limited resources, it is important to recognize the distinctions in the specific sources each state seeks to meet its energy needs.

In contrast to the global nature of energy markets, oil in particular because of the ability to transport it by sea, China's energy strategy places greater emphasis on developing strong partnerships with individual producers. Historically, this has taken the form of direct investment in countries that boast significant energy recourses but have been second choices to fulfill Western demand, such as Angola and Sudan, because of their chronic political instability. More recently, China appears to be applying a similar logic to Middle Eastern producers. Thus, with regard to Saudi supply, China has shown some deference to the long-standing U.S. relationship with the kingdom in its choice to pursue Saudi output that is less suited for the American market. Similarly, China is making a major push to cultivate Iran as a supplier of its energy needs. This is driven not only by geographic considerations but also by the fact that Iran's nuclear program puts it into a position (much like Angola and Sudan) in which political considerations trump market forces in linking specific energy producers and suppliers.

The Chinese-Iranian Dimension. Despite the radically different ideologies underpinning their respective regimes, the People's Republic of China and the Islamic Republic of Iran share considerable strategic interests. From the vantage point of China, Iran is an important energy source that is strategically located for the delivery of oil and gas to the Chinese market. Moreover, since Iran is outside the American orbit, China's interest in Iranian resources need not take a back seat to American demand. From the Iranian perspective, China represents a growing market for its oil and gas output and, given China's ambivalence about imposing sanctions on Iran for its nuclear ambitions, a potential conduit for Iranian oil should the West move to freeze Iranian energy exports. Moreover, Iran can reasonably assume that cultivating closer ties with China helps to deter any aggression against it and would provide a window to the outside world should the West choose to ratchet up its isolation of the Islamic Republic.

The economic ties between China and Iran are already considerable and are likely to grow. Iran, along with Saudi Arabia and Angola, provides the largest share of Chinese oil imports; see Table 3.1 (see also EIA, 2006, p. 5). China is also the second-largest importer of Iranian oil (EIA, 2007, p. 5), and by extension, an important source of foreign currency for the regime in Tehran. Moreover, economic cooperation has increased considerably in the aftermath of the Iraq War, in that China has looked to Iran to pick up the slack in Iraqi production that has gone off-line. In March 2004, China's state-owned oil trading company, Zhuhai Zhenrong Corporation, signed a 25-year deal to

Table 3.1
China's Oil Imports, January–June 2008

Sources of Oil	Barrels per Day	Share of Total Imports (%)
Angola	675,000	18.51
Saudi Arabia	656,000	17.99
Iran	433,000	11.88
Oman	285,000	7.82
Russia	252,000	6.91
Sudan	216,000	5.92
Venezuela	200,000	5.49
Kazakhstan	109,000	2.99
Libya	97,000	2.66
Congo-Brazzaville	95,000	2.61
Other	628,000	17.22
Total	3,646,000	100.00

SOURCE: Khadduri, 2008.

import 110 million tons of liquefied natural gas from Iran (Gundzik, 2005). In December 2007, China and Iran finalized a $2-billion deal awarding Sinopec the right to develop the Yadavaran field in Iran. In addition, China National Offshore Oil Corp recently signed a preliminary gas deal to develop Iran's North Pars Gas Field.[12]

With respect to Chinese direct investment in Iran's energy sector, Iran actually enjoys some advantage over Saudi Arabia in terms of its more-permissive regulatory environment. Specifically, Saudi Arabia still restricts foreign investment in its *upstream* oil sector (exploration and production), but Iran has a mechanism that allows China to develop Iranian fields in return for a share of that field's future production (Leverett and Bader, 2005–2006, p. 191). The existence of this mechanism helps explain why Chinese investment in Iran's energy sector is projected to exceed $100 billion U.S. over the next 25 years (Leverett and Bader, 2005–2006, p. 191).

On the political front, China has shown some willingness to support Western efforts to impose sanctions on Iran for refusing to suspend uranium enrichment. However, in 2006, China and Russia blocked a U.S.-led attempt to introduce a UN resolution against Iran, and China has consistently advocated a negotiated solution to the stand-off. This position is not only a reflection of China's preference for nonintervention but also speaks to China's economic interests in the region. Thus, China has been adamant that "actions to address this problem [nuclear proliferation] should not undermine normal trade and economic cooperation with Iran."[13] China's weaker resolve on the Iranian nuclear portfolio reinforces the view in Tehran that China and Russia are the weak links in the efforts of the international community to stop Iranian proliferation and thus constitute the best opening for Iran to play the great powers off against each other. However, while China is noticeably more averse to confronting Iran than the other permanent members of the UN Security Council, China's vested interest in a stable regional security order means that it is unlikely to use its position on the Security Council to shield Iran from future punitive measures.

---

[12] "CNOOC Confirms Preliminary Gas . . . ," 2007.

[13] Chinese Foreign Ministry spokesman Liu Jianchao, as reported in Bhadrakumar, 2008.

Regional Views of China. Within the region, China's noninterventionism is seen, on the one hand, as an attractive alternative to the more-muscular U.S. approach to regional affairs. It also exposes the limits of Chinese power. When Arabs are asked to identify what two countries pose the biggest threat to them, only 2 percent of respondents identify China as a threat, as opposed to 88 percent who feel threatened by the United States (Telhami, 2008, p. 89). Similarly, when asked hypothetically: In a world where there is only one superpower, which country would you prefer to be that superpower? China was tied for second with Germany and trailed only France (Telhami, 2008, p. 82). As Alterman and Garver (2008, p. 4) have noted:

> On the popular level, China carries little of the baggage that the United States does in the Middle East. Local publics (and their governments) conveniently elide China's rigorous atheism and its ongoing battle with Muslim Uighur separatists in the Western provinces, and they see a country that manufactures affordable goods and communicates respect.

As in much of the developing world, Arab publics see China as a model, not only in terms of China's impressive economic development but also its ability to transform itself from a position of dependence to a regional power capable of charting an independent course (al-Tariqi, 2008). On the other hand, among informed observers, China's inward-looking posture is recognized as a limitation in its ability to offset U.S. regional hegemony. For example, according to an Egyptian analyst (Talib, 2008),

> There is not much that is controversial in [China's Middle East] vision, but there remains the question: What is the actual role that China plays in order to achieve this vision? This is a question that reflects the chasm or the great distance between a positive vision in terms of its content, and the presumed role China would play by virtue of its international responsibility and as a permanent member of the Security Council. But China turns away from [this role] for one reason or another or often takes it up only in a symbolic manner.

China as an Extraregional Power in the Gulf. While the war in Iraq has created opportunities for the expansion of Chinese influence in the Gulf, it should not be assumed that China's advance will necessarily come at the expense of American interests in the region. In fact, American and Chinese interests intersect on many issues, most notably in terms of fostering the regional stability necessary for the free flow of the region's oil and gas production. The interruption of energy supplies is not in the interest of either state, and on this front there is considerable room for Sino-American cooperation.

Moreover, although China has shown greater initiative since the onset of the Iraq War in cultivating ties with Middle East energy producers, its role in the regional balance of power remains peripheral. That is to say, while China's status as a permanent member of the UN Security Council necessarily involves China in regional disputes, China has not made a significant effort to enhance its political role in the Middle East or offer itself as an alternative balancer to the United States in regional security. Indeed, its growing but still limited ability to project military power outside its neighborhood leaves China as more economically significant than militarily significant in regional affairs.

Given this backdrop, the extent of China's influence in the Middle East is likely to turn in large part on the degree to which the United States is able to improve its strategic position through the stabilization of Iraq. Thus, should the regional security environment improve—freeing up American forces and enhancing the U.S. ability to project its influence—this would certainly help keep China within the framework of a complimentary role in which it works to strengthen the U.S.-led regional security order. On the other hand, perceptions of U.S. weakness or a future push by China to move the international system toward multipolarity could lead China to play a spoiler role in regional affairs.

Russia

Russia in the Middle East. Unlike China, which does not currently boast the military capability to seriously challenge U.S. preeminence in the Middle East regional system, Russia has the wherewithal to be a more-immediate competitor. However, while Russia is more militarily capable, there is little to suggest that it has the intention to challenge the current regional order. Moreover, given that Russia has indirectly benefited from the U.S. intervention in Iraq—through its debilitating effect on U.S. standing, resources, and military readiness, to say nothing of the war's effect on the (temporary) surge in energy prices that helped to fuel Russia's economic resurgence—Russia has little incentive to follow the United States down a path of regional entanglement. Finally, unlike China, whose engagement is generally welcomed by actors in the region, Russia carries its own "imperial baggage" insofar as it continues to be viewed within the region with wariness and through the historical lens of the former Soviet Union's territorial expansionism.

In the run-up to the U.S. invasion of Iraq, Russia made no secret of its opposition to the war. Russia's leadership interpreted the war as a threat to its own economic and security interests. Of specific import, Russia feared a devaluation of its investments in Iraq and a loss of the estimated $8-billion Iraqi state debt to Russia (Verlin, 2003). Even more significantly, many in Russia viewed the war as a play by the United States to consolidate its hegemony in the region and further marginalize Russia. In a speech before parliament in March 2003, Vladimir Putin stated that

> As we predicted, the consequences of the war in Iraq are going outside the framework of a regional conflict. . . . [This is] perhaps, . . . the first time since the end of the Cold War [that] the international community has come up against such a difficult crisis. In essence, this threatens to shake the very basis of global stability and international rights. (Zaks, 2003)

In fact, in sharp contrast to Putin's warning, Russia has emerged as an indirect beneficiary of the war in Iraq. Although Russia and the United States continue to share important interests that transcend the zero-sum logic of the Cold War, U.S. entanglement in Iraq has emboldened Russia in that it has both demonstrated the limits of U.S. power and eroded international norms regarding the inviolability of national sovereignty. Similarly, while it is difficult to isolate the effect of the Iraq

War on the calculus underlying Russia's 2008 use of force in Georgia, it is apparent that Russia views the United States as operating from a position of relative strategic weakness.[14] Finally, because Russia is an important energy producer, the initial effect of the Iraq War on the cost of oil and gas (the so-called "security premium") served to bolster the nation's economic fundamentals.

Energy Interests. Like China, Russia has a significant interest in Middle East energy resources. However, unlike China, which has been a net oil importer since 1993 (Alterman and Garver, 2008, p. 5), Russia has more than adequate energy resources of its own. Russia's energy holdings include the largest natural gas reserves in the world, the second-largest coal reserves, and the eighth-largest oil reserves (EIA, 2008, p. 1). The Russian Federation's importance as an energy producer is further amplified by its strong capacity to develop its resources and bring them to market. In 2006, Russia's share in world oil production was 12.3 percent. As a point of comparison, Saudi Arabia, with by far the world's largest proven oil reserves, produced 13.1 percent (Sfakianakis, 2007). Russia's natural resource endowments mean that it has a vested interest in keeping prices high. Moreover, given that Russia and Iran control over 40 percent of the world's known gas reserves and that Russia and Iran both have a track record of using energy as a lever of foreign policy, the potential emergence of a Russian-led gas cartel looms as a long-term challenge to energy security.

Like China, Russia has invested heavily in Gulf energy, with particular emphasis on gas infrastructure. In January 2004, LUKOIL won a 40-year contract to develop the 30,000-km^2 Block A natural gas field in Saudi Arabia's Rub al-Khali desert.[15] Russia is also making strong inroads in the Syrian energy sector, having recently signed a $370-million contract to construct a gas pipeline leading to al-Rayyan and a gas processing plant near Palmyra, as well as a multibillion dollar preliminary contract to build an oil refining and petrochemical complex in Syria.[16] Similarly, LUKOIL negotiated swap deals with Iran in

---

[14] For Arab views of Russia's resurgence, see Malik, 2008, and al-Sayyid, 2008.

[15] "Russian-Saudi JV Finds . . . ," 2007.

[16] "Intelligence Brief: Russia's Moves in Syria," 2006; Smith, 2007, p. 5.

2003 whereby Russian crude oil is used in Iran's northern refineries for domestic consumption in return for the same amount of Iranian oil being delivered to Russian buyers at Iran's Persian Gulf oil terminals (Peimani, 2003).

In a potentially serious, although longer term, challenge to energy security, Russia has taken the initiative to push forward the establishment of a gas cartel loosely based on the model of the Organization of Petroleum Exporting Countries. Specifically, Russia has been a leader in bringing together the major gas producers under a single umbrella, the Gas Exporting Countries Forum (GECF), considered the initial step toward the establishment of a formal cartel. While the organization is still in its infancy, it has met with favorable reactions from representatives of Russia, Iran, Qatar, Algeria, Venezuela, and other important exporters.

The goals of the proposed gas cartel are to harmonize pricing between producer countries, coordinate pipeline development to limit competition between producer countries for specific markets, conduct joint exploration and development to leverage economies of scale, and develop member countries' liquefied natural gas capacity (Socor, 2007, pp. 114–115). Such an organization could wield significant power over gas pricing, given that GECF membership accounts for 73 percent of the world's gas reserves and 42 percent of its production. More threatening to energy security, its largest members—Russia and Iran—have shown a propensity for using energy as a coercive lever of foreign policy, for example, in Russia's withholding of gas from the Caucasus and Iran's behavior during the so-called "tanker war" episode (1984 to 1988) of the Iran-Iraq War. Given this background and the recent volatility of the oil market, the initiative has raised concerns that GECF could become an instrument of a political agenda in tandem with its primary objective—maximizing gas revenues.

That said, it is believed that the establishment of a functioning gas cartel is still 10 to 15 years away (Qadura, 2008), and important characteristics of gas production and export would constrain the effectiveness of such a cartel. The most important among these is that gas is still largely delivered through single-destination pipelines. While these tie consumers to specific producers, they also limit the leverage of producers because expanding a market requires substantial investment in new pipelines or alternative delivery mechanisms (Socor, 2007, p. 115). Moreover, in contrast to oil, gas contracts are typically negotiated on a long-term basis to provide a stable source of income for exporters and a predictable supply for importers. However, this is little comfort for European countries, which rely on Russia as a major supplier of their natural gas needs and saw Russia's willingness to use energy as a type of political blackmail when it suspended gas deliveries to the Ukraine in 2006 and again in January 2009.

Despite the challenges of establishing a gas cartel, to say nothing of enforcing subsequent cooperation among its membership, the initiative represents a long-term challenge to energy security and a potentially powerful instrument of Russian leverage in the region. According to Vladimir Socor (2007, pp. 115, 116),

> Russia would be strongly placed to set cartel rules for allocating gas markets by capitalizing on Russia's far superior export potential, its entrenched dominance in some European countries, and its control of some major transit systems and routes to Europe.

So, as the logical leader of any future gas cartel, Russia could use GECF as a vehicle for influence in the region. More immediately, discussion of the proposed cartel provides a useful point of leverage for Moscow in its negotiation of gas contracts with Europe, as well as an issue around which Russia can strengthen ties to other Gulf energy producers.

Regional Views of Russia. The erosion of U.S. standing in the Middle East has provided an opening for Moscow to present itself as a more-palatable alternative to the United States as a security partner. To this end, Russia has taken pains to portray itself as a more-balanced mediator for the Arab-Israeli conflict, more flexible than the Americans in engaging with such "resistance" groups as HAMAS and Hizballah, and less inclined to intervene in the domestic affairs of Middle East states. Although the charm offensive has succeeded to some degree,[17]

---

[17] For a supportive view of Russia's attempt to join the Organization of the Islamic Conference, see al-'Abidi, 2004.

particularly among those who are all too happy to see a check on U.S. influence and a measure of comeuppance for the power that has long dominated the regional security order, more-measured observers view Russia's rise cautiously. On the one hand, Russia's resurgence is seen as an opportunity to diversify the regional security framework. However, Russia's past, in terms of its direct involvement in the region during the Cold War, its invasion of Afghanistan, and its present approach to stamping out the Chechen rebellion, leaves many uneasy with its ascent.

Since the onset of the war in Iraq, Russia has taken a number of largely symbolic actions designed to improve its standing among Arab and Muslim publics. Most prominent among these were Russia's 2003 bid to join the Organization of the Islamic Conference (it was granted observer status), its 2006 decision to receive a delegation from HAMAS, its support for the Saudi-led initiative popularly known as the Arab peace proposal, its critique of Israel's prosecution of the 2006 war in Lebanon, and its March 2008 proposal to hold an Arab-Israeli peace conference in Moscow (Freedman, 2007a, 2007b, p. 20; Stepanova, 2006, p. 3; "Rusiya Tadraj . . . ," 2006). Taken together, these positions represent Russia's effort to rebrand itself within the Arab World.

That said, Russia's attempts to court Arab and Muslim sympathies have often been clumsy, eliciting an uneven reception inside the region. For example, in 2006, Russia broke with the United States in excluding both Hizballah and HAMAS from its list of terrorist organizations. (This is also consistent with Russia's calls for engagement with such groups in their capacity as representatives of significant constituencies within Lebanon and the Palestinian Territories.) However, instead of eliciting support from Arab publics, Russia's announcement of its list of terrorist organizations was greeted with bewilderment given its inclusion of the Muslim Brotherhood on the same list. This led to a segment on Al Jazeera's program *Ma Wara' al-Khabr* [Behind the News] in which the host repeatedly questioned Russia's representative as to what standards could have possibly been used to classify the Muslim Brotherhood as a terrorist organization while exempting HAMAS and Hizballah from that label.[18]

Just as Russia's occasional clumsiness in its outreach to the Muslim world reduces the extent to which it constitutes a challenge to U.S. influence, American strategic planners should also keep in mind that Russia's objectives in this realm have as much to do with domestic considerations as competing with the United States to win influence in the region. Russia's recent engagement with Saudi Arabia and its more-accommodative positions with such groups as HAMAS are aimed (in part) at convincing outside actors to abstain from supporting or expressing solidarity with Chechen rebels (Ghali, 2007). To this end, Russia has leaned heavily on Saudi Arabia, both in its invitation of then–Crown Prince 'Abdullah to Moscow in May 2003 and in Putin's February 2007 visit to the kingdom, to provide cover for Moscow's handling of the Chechen issue (Freedman, 2007a). Similarly, a predictable outcome of Khalid Mish'al's 2006 visit to Moscow was a statement distancing HAMAS from the Chechen cause (Freedman, 2007b, p. 21).[19]

More recently, Russia's show of force in Georgia, and the cautious response to it on the part of the United States and its European allies, was celebrated by some Arab commentators as further evidence of the decline of U.S. power. For example, commentary in the newspaper *al-Quds al-Arabi* trumpeted the development as "another sign of American retreat" ('Othman, 2008). However, other commentators were quick to throw cold water on the notion that Russia's ascendancy would necessarily be a boon to the Arabs.[20] Writing in *Dar al-Hayat*, 'Irfan Nizam al-Din (2008) warned,

> What is certain is that the Arabs will pay the price of what is happening on the international scene, and that the region will

---

[18] "Rusiya Tadraj . . . ," 2006.

[19] Khalid Mish'al has also defended Russia's recent military intervention in Georgia (see al-'Alam, 2008).

[20] See the arguments advanced by Qasim Muhammad Ja'afar on *al-Ittijah al-Mu'akis* (Ja'afar, 2008).

see changes in terms of conditions, positions, [and boundaries] of maps. And it is [also] certain that the Arab world is inattentive to these dangers that threaten it . . . while the international powers struggle and compete against one another to win new regions of influence in preparation for a new Yalta.

This sharp contrast in reactions to Russia's resurgence closely mirrors the ideological splits within the Arab World. So, while media associated with an Arab nationalist platform, such as *al-Quds al-Arabi*, have tended to cover Moscow's intervention in Georgia with a cheerleading tone and emphasis on its potential contribution to the decline of American hegemony (Qandil, 2008), media outlets with an Islamist bent have been more circumspect in their coverage. For example, in an article in *IslamOnline*, the popular Web forum associated with Yusuf al-Qaradawi, a commentator launched a scathing attack on Arab nationalists who conveniently disregard Russia's own imperial ambitions because of an all-consuming focus on the American presence in the region. Drawing on the historical parallel of short-term interest convergence between U.S. foreign policy and Islamist actors in combating the spread of communism, Shabib (2008) argues,

> Just as inattention to the nature of American hegemony during Moscow's invasion of Afghanistan was unacceptable, so too is the present day inattention to the nature of Russian hegemony . . . . Imperialism does not have an American identity or a European identity, but throughout the Tsarist period, and in the Communist and Post-Communist eras, the Russian state was and remains a colonial-imperial state.

In summary, the extent to which U.S. standing has fallen in the region has opened the door for Russia to present itself as a more-sympathetic, pro-Arab alternative to the United States. While Russia has made some gains among the region's more-strident critics of the United States, Russian ambitions are still viewed with wariness. Unlike China, Russia comes to the region with significant baggage from its World War II occupation of Iran, its direct presence in the region during the Cold War, and its invasion of Afghanistan. Thus, while

Russia may benefit from general antipathy toward the United States in the region, Russia's own history limits its ability to present itself as a kinder, gentler alternative to the United States.

Russian-Iranian Cooperation. The relationship between Moscow and Tehran is characterized by a mix of cooperation that reflects the countries' shared interests and competition that grows out of each state's ambitions and perception of its weight in regional affairs (Shaffer, 2001). Specifically, Russia is an important arms supplier to Iran and has shown reticence in confronting Tehran on the nuclear file. On the other hand, Moscow and Tehran compete for influence in the Middle East and Central Asia, particularly with regard to control over and future development of gas pipelines (Katz, 2008). While the internal decisionmaking of both regimes is notoriously opaque, it is logical to assume that the U.S. decision to invade Iraq and the ease with which it deposed the former regime contributed to threat perceptions in both Moscow and Tehran that would create incentives for closer alignment. On the other hand, recent developments suggest that the subsequent U.S. entanglement in Iraq has fueled greater competition between the two states, given its constraining effect on the U.S. ability to project force in the region. Put another way, growing self-assurance in Tehran and Moscow, and with it ambitions for expanded regional roles, can be observed in greater competition between the two states.

Over the past decade, Russia has become Iran's most important arms supplier (Kassianova, 2006). While Moscow contends that its arms sales to Tehran are defensive, they do include some advanced technology that has drawn protests from both the United States and Israel. Specifically, in 2005 Russia negotiated a $700-million U.S. sale of the Tor-MI air defense system to Iran, upgrading the latter's ability to deter any attack against its nuclear facilities. And in late 2008, there were conflicting reports over whether Russia would provide Tehran with the more-advanced S-300 air defense system.[21] That said, these arms sales are predicated on financial considerations and the nature of

---

[21] See, for example, "Russia Delivers S-300 Favorit to Iran," 2008, and Schwirtz and Fathi, 2008.

Russia's defense industry more than the state of security cooperation between the two states.

By way of cooperation, Russia has also done much to further Iran's nuclear program. This includes the supply of material, such as Russia's 2006 delivery of 82 tons of commercial-grade enriched uranium, to providing technical support, such as Russia's work on building the nuclear reactor at Bushehr. Of course, Russia has also used its leverage to help shield Iran from Western efforts to halt its nuclear program, first by delaying referral of the Iranian nuclear file from the International Atomic Energy Agency to the U.N. Security Council and later by working to soften the sanctions regime imposed on Tehran for incomplete disclosures and refusal to stop uranium enrichment and reprocessing (Katz, 2008, pp. 203–204).

That said, Russia has not completely broken with the United States and its European allies on this issue. Thus, while Russia (and China) have shown less resolve than their Western counterparts in confronting Tehran, Russia has voted numerous times in the Security Council for measures that called for a halt to Iranian enrichment and greater transparency from Tehran in disclosing its activities. This hedging is evidence of a more-complex strategy on the part of Moscow to use Iran as a point of leverage in its dealings with the United States. As Katz (2008) argued persuasively, Russia's on-again off-again support of Iran is consistent with a concerted effort to cultivate Iranian dependence on Russia. By serving as a deterrent to any preemptive use of force against Iran and providing the regime access to material and technology, Russia seeks to position itself for a payoff in any resolution of the Iranian nuclear issue. By positioning itself as the only actor capable of both enabling and halting Iran's nuclear program, Russia is maximizing its leverage vis-à-vis both Washington and Tehran.

However, Russia's capacity to play out this game assumes Iran's willingness to accept the role of dependent. While this may have been acceptable to Tehran in 2003–2004, when the United States appeared to have consolidated its strategic position in the region with the insertion of forces on Iran's border, there is evidence that the course of the war in Iraq and its eroding effect on U.S. power have emboldened Iran to aspire to a larger role in the Middle East and Central Asia than just Russia's junior partner (Ghali, 2007). Iran's growing assertiveness and aspirations for independent sources of power are apparent in its refusal to rely on Russia as its sole source of nuclear material but to pursue enrichment activities of its own. In another act of defiance, in 2006, Iran proposed partnering with French (and not Russian) firms for the monitoring of its uranium enrichment, and Tehran has showed its independence from Russia in its positions on the demarcation of the Caspian Sea as it relates both to drilling and the construction of Central Asian pipelines (Katz, 2008, pp. 206, 209–210).

Thus, in contrast to more-alarmist portrayals of Russian-Iranian alignment, evidence suggests that the relationship is far more nuanced. Russia and Iran do have shared interests that drive limited cooperation in the spheres of energy and security, however, the states also have competing visions of the balance of power in the Middle East and Central Asia. Russia sees itself as the natural hegemon and, while willing to carve out a supporting role for Iran, expects deference in return. For its part, Iran has astutely used its relationship with Russia as added leverage in its dealings with the West; however, it has bucked at accepting Russian dominance in regional affairs. Given Iran's self-assurance that it has become a serious regional power, tension in the Russian-Iranian relationship is likely to persist and prevent it from evolving into a full-fledged alliance.

Russia as an Extraregional Power in the Gulf: The Iraq Effect. Although Russia is not currently in a position to present itself as an alternative to the U.S.-led regional security order, its resurgence represents a significant challenge to U.S. strategic planners. In contrast to China, whose interests in the Middle East largely intersect with those of the United States, Russia and the United States have divergent interests on a number of key issues. Thus, while the United States (and China) have a strong stake in low energy prices, Russia seeks the opposite. Moreover, while the United States has a vested interest in regional stability both in terms of its contribution to low energy prices and to avoid the interventions that tax its resources and military readiness, Russia is content to see some measure of U.S. entanglement in the region insofar as it leaves Moscow a free hand in its dealings with the Caucasus and Central Asia. Finally, although neither the United States nor Russia would like to see Iran obtain a nuclear weapon (Oliker et al., 2009), Russia has shown a willingness to provide limited support to Tehran to reinforce the latter's dependence on it and maximize its payout from any future resolution of the Iranian nuclear issue.

Given this strong split in regional interests, Russia represents the strongest extraregional challenge to U.S. preeminence in the Middle East. However, since it is the perception of U.S. weakness that has opened the door to Russian influence more than Russia's own initiative, the United States has the means to reverse this decline. U.S. success in stabilizing its position in Iraq would greatly enhance the broader U.S. strategic position and serve as a counter to Russia's ascent in the region. As for Russia's calculus, the outcome of its recent aggressiveness in its "near abroad" will likely serve to inform Moscow's future engagement with regions farther afield.

Should Russia succeed in consolidating its influences in the Caucasus and Central Asia, this could embolden it to become more assertive in the Persian Gulf region. Russia's arms sales to Iran are of particular concern, including its supplying of Tehran with surface to air defense systems and upgrading Iran's Su-24 and MiG-29 aircraft (Oliker et al., 2009). That said, despite its recent resurgence, Russia still greatly lags the United States in the capacity to project power in the region. Going forward, Russia's posture toward the region will likely combine the selective use of hard power (arms sales) with economic leverage and soft power as the principal means of advancing its Middle East agenda.

Conclusion

The perceived erosion of U.S. power has created an opening for the expansion of extraregional roles in the Middle East. This can be observed both in the hedging strategies of traditional U.S. allies that are increasingly looking to China and Russia as a means of diversifying their security portfolios, as well as in the reactions of states that, like Iran and Syria, reject U.S. hegemony and see China and Russia as potential partners in returning the regional system to multipolarity. The future weight of these extraregional actors will depend on the trajectories of the states themselves—that is, on the degree to which China is able to translate its economic leverage into hard power and to which Russia is able to sustain its recent resurgence—as well as on the ability of the United States to consolidate its own strategic position.

However, given that these actors—China, in particular—could play a complementary role in the U.S.-led regional security order, the objective for U.S. planners is not necessarily to blunt their influence inasmuch as it is to engage these states to help shape their involvement in ways that support U.S. interests. With regard to China, shared interests in regional stability and the free flow of Middle East oil and gas create a natural basis for Sino-American cooperation. On the other hand, finding a foundation for cooperation with Russia may prove more vexing, given that the Russian Federation's regional interests do not align as neatly with those of the United States. Of particular import is Russia's interest in high energy prices and the continuation of U.S. entanglement in the region, to leave Russia greater maneuverability in pursuing its foreign policy objectives in the Caucasus and Central Asia. Nonetheless, both Russia and the United States have a strong interest in preventing Iran from becoming a nuclear power, even if Russia seeks to position itself for a payoff in the resolution of the issue.

With regard to China, the United States can strengthen incentives for cooperation by communicating a clear commitment to the protection of Chinese interests. This would likely involve discussions of energy security that provide the Chinese reassurances that, while the United States is committed to the efficient production and delivery of the region's oil and gas, it does not advance proprietary claims to these resources (Leverett and Bader, 2005–2006, p. 198). As for Russia, the United States may be better served by focusing on a consolidation of its own strategic position to increase its leverage vis-à-vis the Russian Federation. Finally, given Russia's focus on its near abroad and self-reliance on its own energy resources, projecting influence in the Middle East is less of a strategic imperative for Russia than for the United States. This factor, along with the United States' far superior hard power, limits the scope of the Russian challenge even if it remains the most capable challenger to U.S. regional preeminence.

CHAPTER FOUR

Domestic Reverberations of the War: Internal Challenges to Regime Stability

Aside from affecting the regional balance of power, the Iraq War has had significant reverberations *inside* a number of key states. These ripple effects can be roughly grouped into two categories: those that weaken the cohesion of the state and threaten regime stability and those that encourage increased acquiescence to or support for regimes.

In the wake of escalating strife in Iraq since 2006, most analyses have focused on the former, predicting the spillover of the war into neighboring societies marked by long-standing sectarian tensions or the presence of marginalized ethnic groups. The underlying argument is that violence in Iraq would have a cascading "demonstration" or "echo" effect across the region: historic sociocultural links between Iraq and the rest of the Middle East would accelerate the spread of the conflict or, at the very least, intensify local sympathies for the country's warring factions (Byman and Pollack, 2007).[1] Similarly, several analysts have asserted that the push for increasing provincial autonomy in Iraq, particularly among the Kurds, could inspire similar impulses among other ethnic groups or worsen existing center-periphery disputes.[2] Others have laid the blame more squarely on U.S. policy, assert-

---

[1] Byman and Pollack, 2006, expounds this argument succinctly; see also Terrill, 2005.

[2] The proliferation of transnational media coverage in Iraq underpins these dynamics. Accordingly, events in Iraq, such as the bombing of a Shiʻa pilgrimage, the U.S. siege of Sunni insurgents in Fallujah, and the hanging of Saddam Hussein, assume a heightened proximity and immediacy to regional viewers, hardening sectarian identities and forcing audiences to "take sides."

ing that the surge itself is "stoking forces that have traditionally threatened the stability of Middle Eastern states: tribalism and sectarianism" (Simon, 2008). Finally, some have even argued that U.S. policy should actually harness this momentum to redraw the Middle Eastern map along lines that would make it less predisposed toward conflict.[3]

This chapter explores these various pressures, assessing the threat from sectarian tensions, tribal mobilization, ethnic agitation, and Iraqi refugees. But we also highlight how these effects may have fostered the consolidation of regime control and the cohesion of the state. Nearly seven years after the invasion, the Middle East state system is intact. Iraq has inspired no explicit attempts at secession or increased autonomy by ethnic groups.[4] Sunni-Shi'a violence, even in the fractured state of Bahrain, has been largely contained. Indeed, our research indicates that, on balance, the war has probably strengthened the control of regional governments or at least encouraged domestic opponents to challenge the state more cautiously and within the system.[5] In addition, our fieldwork in a number of at-risk societies in the Gulf revealed a guarded optimism about the ability of local Sunni and Shi'a communities to weather the storm because of long-standing trade, familial and class ties and, in some instances, a renewed sense of national unity and loyalty to the state.[6]

---

[3] For a recent example, see Goldberg, 2008.

[4] Ironically, the state that has been universally declared the beneficiary of the Iraq invasion has been most afflicted with these phenomena: Iran. The Islamic Republic has, since the Iraq War, witnessed renewed attacks on its territory by Kurdish militants (PJAK), a low-grade ethnic insurgency within its Baluch population in the southeast province, and sporadic outbreaks of violence among ethnic Arabs in the southwestern Khuzestan province. For more on Iran's ethnic unrest, see Bradley, 2006–2007.

[5] The posture of various regimes on the Iraq War has provided new ammunition to their domestic opponents; in Egypt, the Muslim Brotherhood has turned Mubarak's acquiescence of U.S. policy on the war into a call for renewed political reform (interview with Muslim Brotherhood activist, Cairo, February 2008). In Turkey—prior to its intervention in northern Iraq—the military had mobilized public support against the ruling Islamic Justice and Development Party by pointing to its inaction on cross-border PKK attacks emanating from northern Iraq (Larrabee, 2007b).

[6] Interview with leading Shi'a and Sunni activists in al-Qatif, Damman, al-Ahsa, Eastern Province, Saudi Arabia, March 2007 and Manama, Bahrain, November 2006.

The Iraq War Is Not the Main Driver of Increased Sectarian Tensions

Across the region, our interlocutors saw the narrative of increased sectarian tensions stemming from Iraq as an ultimately artificial construct—a device Sunni Arab regimes used to bolster public support for the balance-of-power strategy against Iran or a strategy the United States used to divide and weaken Muslim solidarity. Similarly, in such countries as Egypt and Jordan, we observed frequently fantastic estimates of "hidden" Shi'a populations or massive conversions from Sunnism to Shi'ism. While these dynamics exist, there is also an element of urban folklore at play, and these warnings are most instructive for what they illuminate about perceptions of Arab political illegitimacy and economic disparities.[7] In other instances, particularly in the Levant, we found that Iraq was not the principal driver for domestic concerns and was frequently overshadowed by developments in the Arab-Israeli sphere, especially the aftermath of the 2006 Lebanon War.[8] We examine these dimensions of the sectarian issue in the following sections.

Sectarianism Has Spread in the Gulf, but Regimes Are Mostly to Blame

Internecine violence in Iraq and the perception of Iranian influence have certainly increased the prominence of Shi'ism and Sunnism as markers of identity and vehicles for political activism, particularly in the Gulf.[9] At the same time, discourse about the "rise of the Shi'a" can

---

[7]   Interview with Jordanian analysts and U.S. embassy official, Amman, February 2007.

[8]   For example, Lebanon—despite its long-standing sectarian issues—has proven largely immune to instability resulting directly from the Iraq War. The country enjoyed a period of relative tranquility and sectarian harmony from 2003 until 2005–2006, when it was undermined by local developments—the assassination of Prime Minister Rafiq Hariri in 2005 and Hizballah's war with Israel in the summer of 2006. "It is Iraq that is 'Lebanonizing,' not the other way around," noted one Lebanese analyst (interview, Beirut, March 2008). Noting Iraq's declining relevance to Egypt in light of renewed violence in Gaza, a former Egyptian foreign ministry official quipped, "Iraq is not our baby" (interview Cairo, March 2008).

[9]   Certainly, the divisions separating Shi'a and Sunnis are real, in terms of lived religious practice, ritual, and shared historical memory. But these distinctions have been frequently subsumed by other affiliations, such as tribal lineage, class, ethnicity, rural versus urban dif-

be considered a sort of code regimes deployed to express more deeply seated fears about challenges to the status quo. Shi'a in many countries are pressing for their rights via liberalization and democratization, which presents an explicit threat to the current authoritarian system (dominated by Sunnis). In our Gulf fieldwork, we noted that Shi'a have typically cooperated with other activists (both secularists and Sunnis) in demanding broad-based reforms; it becomes much easier for regimes to discredit these initiatives by painting them as "Shi'a- or Persian-inspired" or narrowly sectarian in character.

In addition, this sectarian-based discourse reflects fears of Iran's appeal to Arab popular opinion, as we discussed in Chapter Two. By supporting the Palestinian cause, adopting a rejectionist posture on the nuclear issue, and evincing a general hostility to the West, Iran has garnered sporadic applause from Arab publics, which stands in sharp contrast to the caution and immobility of Arab rulers.[10] If Iran's strategy, particularly under Ahmadinejad, can be characterized as highlighting *vertical* splits in the Arab world (between regimes and their publics), the response of some Arab regimes has been to emphasize the *horizontal* fissures (Shi'a versus Sunni) that separate Iran from the rest of the Middle East.

Taking this dynamic into account, events in neighboring Iraq have indeed stoked sectarian tensions at a number of flashpoints in the region. Bahrain offers the best illustration: The tiny island kingdom is arguably the region's epicenter for sectarian disenfranchisement. Shi'a comprise 70 percent of the population; are ruled over by the Sunni al-Khalifa family; and have long suffered from political exclusion, unemployment, housing shortages, and cultural discrimination.

---

ferences, political ideology, and membership in such state institutions as the officer corps. It is important to note in this regard that the earliest adherents of the Iraqi Ba'ath party were Shi'a. Regarding class affiliation, in mandate Iraq, British colonial administrators purposefully cultivated the elite class identity of Shi'a tribal shaykhs—forcing them to act in greater unity with Sunni and Kurdish tribal *aghawat* [chieftains], rather than advancing the interests of their Shi'a coreligionists. See Dodge, 2007, and Sluglett and Sluglett, 1993.

[10] It is important to note that public support for Iran fluctuates rapidly and is subject to rapid downswings, often due to perceptions of Iran's misdeeds in Iraq. See Kiernan, 2007, and Zogby International/Arab American Institute, 2007.

A key grievance is Shi'a nonrepresentation in the Bahraini security forces and army. To add fuel to the fire, activists point to a recent government policy of recruiting foreign Sunnis, from Yemen, Pakistan, Saudi Arabia, and Syria, into the army and then naturalizing them as citizens. This strategy is seen as a thinly disguised effort to tip the demographic balance of the island in favor of Sunnis. Moreover, several analysts pointed to this policy as effectively tribalizing the kingdom and creating hidden channels for importing al-Qa'ida ideology: Many of these foreign recruits hail from tribal areas in eastern Syria, northern Yemen, and the Baluch region of Pakistan, where al-Qa'ida has traditionally found support.

The Iraq invasion and ongoing strife have intensified tensions between Shi'a and Sunnis. Events in Iraq are frequently mirrored in contentious partisanship among the island's citizenry that has sparked vocal parliamentary debates and, increasingly, violent street protests.[11] In March and April 2004, there were Bahraini Shi'a protests in support of Iraqi coreligionists battling U.S. troops in Najaf; later in the year, Bahraini Sunnis made similar demonstrations in sympathy with Fallujah.[12] The February 2006 destruction of the revered Hadi al-Askari shrine in Samarra saw similar expressions of solidarity, spurring tensions

---

[11] On the Sunni side, there are long-standing familial ties linking Bahrain and Sunni communities in Basra and Zubayr, in southern Iraq. For Bahraini Shi'a, the reemergence of Najaf and Karbala as centers of Shi'a clerical authority and sites of pilgrimage has strengthened their links to Iraq. One important development emerging from the revival of Najaf has been the influence of Grand Ayatollah 'Ali al-Sistani on the kingdom's Shi'a: It was Sistani who advised that Bahraini Shi'a participate in the November 2006 parliamentary elections rather than boycott them to pursue more militant tactics. Another important example of the strong juridical and theological links between Bahrain and Najaf is the 2006 debate over the Law of Personal Status. Shaykh 'Isa al-Qasim, the leading Bahraini Shi'a cleric who lived for ten years in Iran, reportedly told Bahraini parliamentarians that his Shi'a constituents could not support changes in the Law of Personal Status unless they first received the endorsement of Shi'a authorities in Najaf. Interviews with Bahraini Muslim Brotherhood activist and Shi'a clerical representative of Grand Ayatollah Sistani, Manama, Bahrain, November 2006.

[12] A senior Sunni cleric in Bahrain was reportedly approached by Sunnis angered over the U.S. attack on Fallujah about receiving a fatwa to legitimate the murder of Shi'a or U.S. servicemen in Bahrain. Interview with senior Salafi cleric, Manama, Bahrain, November 2006.

with Bahraini Sunnis and provoking clashes with security forces.[13] In other instances, slander against Shi'a clerics or expressions of support for Saddam Hussein have triggered Shi'a ire, while Shi'a applause for Hizballah and Iranian Supreme Leader 'Ali Khamenei have sparked similar outrage among Sunnis.[14]

Our fieldwork suggests that many of these ripple effects remain manageable and contained. Ironically, it may be the al-Khalifa regime's overreaction to Shi'a demands that threatens long-term stability. Many respondents spoke of the November 2006 parliamentary elections as a turning point; if Shi'a participation within the system fails to yield any tangible improvements in their economic and social conditions, the ranks of more-radical factions will swell with increasingly frustrated Shi'a.[15] Similarly, the regime's "sectarian balancing" strategy—endorsing Sunni Islamists to counter the Shi'a—could backfire and ultimately undermine the regime; several analysts compared this tactic to "playing with fire," and one Bahraini politician likened it to the Saudi practice of creating a "Sunni Frankenstein" (as quoted in Daragahi, 2007).

Across the causeway, in Saudi Arabia's Eastern Province, the war has had a similarly chilling effect on Sunni-Shi'a relations and political reform.[16] Here, Shi'a comprise perhaps 10 to 15 percent of the total population and enjoy a somewhat better standard of living than their

---

[13] One telling example of these tensions is popular perceptions of the Bahraini media. A Bahraini sociologist noted that different transnational media outlets in Bahrain display a decidedly sectarian bias: Many Bahrainis regard it as a "Sunni channel," while the Lebanese Hizballah's popular TV station al-Manar helps promote Shi'a identity. Al Arabiya appears to be the most balanced in its sectarian orientation. More locally, *al-Watan* newspaper—dominated by a Salafi board of advisors—serves as a counterweight to the Shi'a-dominated *al-Wasit. Al-Watan* is heavily influenced by Saudi Arabia and, the sociologist asserted, frequently tries to inflame Sunni opinion. One example of this newspaper's purported indifference to Shi'a concerns was its failure to mention the February 2006 Samarra mosque bombing. Interview with Bahraini sociologist, Manama, Bahrain, May 10, 2006. See also Fattah, 2006a.

[14] Interviews in the suburbs of Manama: Sitra, Isa Town, Muharraq, November 2006.

[15] Interviews with al-Haq leaders, Manama, Bahrain, November 2006. See also al-Ekri, 2007.

[16] Interviews with Sunni and Shi'a reform activists, Jedda, Riyadh, and the Eastern Province, March 2007. See Jones, 2005, and Wehrey, 2007.

counterparts in Bahrain.[17] Among Saudi Shi'a, the ruling al-Saud also appear to enjoy greater legitimacy as mediators and advocates than do the al-Khalifa among Bahraini Shi'a. Yet unlike Bahrain, Saudi Shi'a confront the long-standing animosity of the vocal Salafi religious establishment, which, since the invasion of Iraq, has intensified its anti-Shi'a vitriol, exerting pressure on the al-Saud and forcing a subtle backtracking on reforms.[18] Many of the Salafi fatwas support Saudi Arabia's Sunni allies in Iraq, but it is Saudi Shi'a who frequently feel the backlash domestically.[19] In some cases, Shi'a perceive that the al-Saud are tacitly endorsing this Salafi venom as a sort of stick to induce greater Shi'a loyalty toward the ruling family.

Another important effect of the war has been the fraying of cooperation between Saudi Shi'a and reform activists from other sects across the kingdom; in light of the strife in Iraq, these parties have increasingly regarded one another with suspicion. Sunni reformists accuse their Shi'a counterparts of embracing a winner-take-all mentality and being overly zealous in their support for Muqtada al-Sadr. Sunnis, for their part, are increasingly regarded by their Shi'a allies as closet Wahhabis. The ultimate victor in this unraveling is the regime, which is likely to feel even less compelled to undertake reforms in the face of such a fragmented opposition. And like the al-Khalifa in Bahrain, the al-Saud may feel sufficiently empowered to balance and manipulate these substate tensions rather than address their underlying roots. Finally, as in Bahrain, the kingdom's backtracking on reform could ultimately empower more-militant Shi'a factions, such as the Iranian-backed Saudi Hizballah or Hizballah al-Hijaz, which, although dormant for many years, appears to be increasingly active.[20]

---

[17] Accurate official population estimates are difficult to ascertain, given the sensitivity of the issue.

[18] This includes the closure of Shi'a mourning houses, the desecration of cemeteries, the banning of books, and other measures.

[19] Interviews with Shi'a clerics and intellectuals, al-Qatif, Saudi Arabia, March 2007. They noted that Salafi figures in the kingdom were given greater media access to comment on Iraq's internecine conflict but invariably took aim at the Shi'a sect more generally.

[20] Interviews in al-Ahsa and al-Qatif, Saudi Arabia, March 2007.

Kuwait is another state in which preexisting sectarian tensions could have been worsened by the conflict in Iraq. Yet the country appears to have emerged as a success story, in which a long-standing tradition of participatory politics has arguably "inoculated" the populace against the spillover from Iraq (Pollock, 2007, p. 16). Kuwait's tribally based tradition of *diwaniyya* [consultation], emphasis on women's rights, and the political inclusion of its Shi'a population (one-third Kuwait's population of 1 million) have drawn applause from reformists in neighboring states—Bahraini activists frequently pointed to the Kuwaiti constitution as a model for emulation.[21]

In 2006, during interviews with Kuwaiti Shi'a lawmakers, Sunni clerics, and government officials, we noted that the Iraqi occupation from 1990 to 1991 was a turning point in Shi'a-Sunni relations. Kuwaiti Shi'a played a prominent role in the anti-Iraqi resistance and thus solidified their nationalist bona fides in the eyes of the ruling al-Sabah family, as well as the broader populace. We also noted that the doctrinal disposition of the country's Salafis is markedly less hostile toward Shi'a than other strands in Saudi Arabia and the Levant (see Blanford, 2006).[22]

Still, the country remains at risk to external shocks upsetting its political balance and societal relations.[23] Most recently, this has been demonstrated by a parliamentary fracas that erupted in the wake of the assassination of Hizballah commander 'Imad Mughniyah. Shi'a demonstrated in solidarity with Hizballah, provoking Sunni lawmakers to accuse prominent Shi'a of being part of a secret Hizballah cell.[24] There are also ominous signs that the country's stagnant economy has

---

[21] A comparative study of reform priorities in Gulf states is found in the work of the prominent Bahraini sociologist, 'Abd al-Nabi al-Ekri, 2006.

[22] Nonetheless, there are prominent radical voices that bear watching: most notably the Kuwaiti-born jihadist cleric Hamid al-'Ali who served as secretary general of the Kuwaiti Salafi Movement from 1997–2000 and later received a two-year suspended prison sentence for insulting the Kuwaiti emir.

[23] Relative to other Gulf states, Kuwait has made progress integrating its Shi'a. Still, problems exist—there are no known Shi'a in the Kuwaiti Security Services, and Shi'a are underrepresented in high levels of government.

[24] "Kuwait MPs Expelled . . . ," 2008.

fostered a sort of democracy fatigue that could bode poorly for future Shiʻa-Sunni relations.[25]

Fears of Sunni-to-Shiʻa Conversions Suggest Deeper Problems in the Levant and Egypt

In Jordan, Egypt, Syria, and Lebanon, sectarian pressures have also assumed prominence in the wake of Iraq but are further exacerbated by the more-local phenomena of the Lebanese Hizballah and its 2006 war with Israel. With the exception of Lebanon, the regimes have not wrestled with the challenge of Shiʻa political marginalization or opposition; a major concern has been the phenomenon of *tashayu*ʻ [Sunni conversion to Shiʻism].

Exact numbers are murky and hard to verify, but the issue is closely linked to popular acclaim for the Lebanese Hizballah after 2006 and the sense that Shiʻism is now the "winning" sect.[26] Our interlocutors in Jordan spoke about the growing appeal of "political" Shiʻism embodied in Hizballah as opposed to the "religious" Shiʻism that, as practiced in the Arab world, is often quietist and frequently hostile to Iran.[27] The noted Salafi-jihadist cleric Abu Basir al-Tartusi, whose website contains a litany of warnings against the spread of Shiʻism, has echoed this distinction, arguing that Iranian-backed proselytizing frequently uses "national revolutionary rhetoric" to obscure its religious hue and facilitate conversions (al-Tartusi, 2004; al-Tartusi, 2006). In Jordan, the debate over Shiʻa conversions appears closely tied to the influx of

---

[25] Kuwaitis appear increasingly frustrated by the fact that the Gulf's most thriving economies are those presided over by absolutist monarchies: Dubai, Abu Dhabi, and Qatar. See Worth, 2008b.

[26] The phenomenon appears particularly pronounced in Syria. For a report on Shiʻism by the Syrian opposition, see The Movement for Justice and Democracy in Syria, 2007. This report alleges that 70 percent of conversions to Shiʻism in Syria took place among the country's ruling Alawite sect, which is much closer doctrinally to Shiʻism than Sunnism. In reality, the likely numbers of conversions in Syria and elsewhere are quite small.

[27] Interview with Jordanian researcher, Amman, February 2008.

Iraqi refugees and the fear that these new arrivals could further upset the Hashemite Kingdom's delicate demographic balance.[28]

Even in Egypt, the internal Shi'a issue has sparked debate; the country has "rediscovered" its Shi'a population, which, according to a report on religious freedom, comprises less than 1 percent of the country's population of 83 million (U.S. Department of State, 2009). There have been sporadic reports of increased harassment and discrimination, and the issue of conversions has attracted criticism from noted Sunni clerics, such as Yusuf al-Qaradawi. For its part, the official religious establishment at al-Azhar has called for rapprochement between the sects.[29]

In both Jordan and Egypt, the issue of Shi'ism has spurred tension between various strands of Sunni Islamist currents, with more-doctrinaire Salafi elements accusing the Muslim Brotherhood of being too conciliatory toward the Shi'a. These debates were brought violently to the fore in the wake of the Saddam Hussein execution—an event that was widely interpreted in Arab circles as a blow to Sunni Arab identity, engineered by Iran and the United States (Slackman, 2007). Available polling following this incident showed precipitous decline in Arab views toward Iran (see Figure 2.1) and, more generally, Shi'a. The Muslim Brotherhood in Jordan took a more-tolerant view of Iran and the Shi'a, which provoked ire from both the government and other Sunni Islamists.

Ultimately, the Iraq War exacerbated tensions over Sunni-Shi'a conversions that themselves were symptomatic of deep fundamental structural problems: an illiberal political culture and nonacceptance of the internal "other." While these deficiencies do not present an imminent threat to regime survival, they are long-term challenges that will have a direct bearing on the growth of radicalism over the next decade.

---

[28] Our field research suggests that this is overblown; most Iraqi Shi'a refugees are settling not in Jordan but in Syria, in the Sayida Zaynab district of Damascus. Interview with Jordanian analyst, February 2008.

[29] Interviews with Egyptian researchers, Cairo, March 2008.

Local Dynamics, Not Iraq, Drive Most Sectarian Strife in Lebanon

Lebanon is a special case where sectarianism is indeed a very real threat to stability and state survival; the country's confessional political system has formalized religious divisions and the government has ceded its monopoly on violent force to factional militias—many of whom appear to be rearming since late 2007 and early 2008.[30]

Territorially, the reach of the government has long been circumscribed, and this problem appears to have worsened in recent years. In the northern Sunni strongholds of Sidon and Tripoli, for example, Saudi-backed Salafi groups have enforced strict moral codes, banning alcohol.[31] In the Jebel Druze, previously mixed schools have been purged of Sunni, Shi'a, and Christian students, while in the southern Beirut suburbs, Hizballah has functioned as a veritable ministate, providing electricity, sewage, and even its own telecommunications network.[32] As one long-time observer has noted, "old taboos" are slowly being broken, and ominous signs of a drift back toward "militia politics" are reappearing; sectarian banners are reappearing, as are roadblocks erected by party militiamen in full view of the "official" traffic police (see Malbrunot, 2007).[33]

---

[30] Interviews with Beirut-based analysts, Lebanon, March 2008. This problem is compounded by reported sectarian splits within the Lebanese security forces: the Internal Security Forces are generally regarded as more pro-Sunni and pro-Hariri, while the Lebanese Army is more sympathetic to Shi'a and Hizballah—many of the rank-and-file are lower-class Shi'a seeking upward mobility.

[31] A Beirut-based researcher appeared astonished by this transformation in the north, telling RAND, "Whenever I go to the north I feel I am among Bedouin or in Arabia." Interview with Lebanese researcher, Beirut, March 2008. A Salafi cleric in Tripoli lamented that Lebanon was infertile soil for the spread of Salafism; most of the country's Sunnis followed the Hanafi *madhhab* [legal school] and were relatively liberal in outlook, which contrasted sharply with Salafism's roots in the more doctrinaire Hanbali *madhhab*.

[32] It was the government's attempt to shut down this network that provoked Hizballah's temporary assumption of control over west Beirut and the flare-up of violence in early May 2008. Interviews with Lebanese analysts, scholars, and clerics, Tripoli and Beirut, March 2008. For background on Hizballah's state-building efforts in the 1990s, see Harik, 1994, and Wehrey, 2002.

[33] Added to these dynamics is the long-standing problem of the Palestinian refugee camps (known locally as "islands of insecurity"), which are effective no-go areas for the Lebanese army.

Taken in sum, this system would appear highly susceptible to an exogenous shock from the Iraq War. Yet our research suggests that the country's recent tribulations are rooted more in local dynamics than in any direct spillover from Iraq: The 2005 assassination of Prime Minister Rafiq Hariri, the 2006 war with Israel, and the ongoing presidential crisis are the key drivers.[34] That said, the Iraq War appears to be affecting developments in the Sunni-dominated north, albeit indirectly. Salafi-jihadist fighters returning from Iraq are a current and future concern, and several contacts spoke of the Iraq War radicalizing Lebanon's previously quietist Sunni population (Shadid, 2006; Fisk, 2006).[35]

Yet the threat of Salafi-jihadist blowback from Iraq should not be overstated and may over the long term be mitigated by indigenous factors. Shakr al-Absi, the commander of the Lebanese Salafi-jihadist group Fatah al-Islam, was indeed a lieutenant of Abu Mus'ab al-Zarqawi, the deceased head of AQI, and many of Fatah al-Islam's hardened fighters were Iraq veterans from other Arab states. But Fatah al-Islam was ultimately a *local* outgrowth of the Nahr al-Barid Palestinian camp. It thus enjoyed limited appeal among Lebanon's northern Salafi community, many of whom harbored deep animosities toward the Palestinians in their midst and were repulsed by the group's violent massacre of locally garrisoned Lebanese soldiers and were thus supportive when Lebanese forces stormed the camp.[36] This dynamic argues against the analytic projection of Iraq's sectarian divisions onto

---

[34] The Iraq War may have indirectly contributed to the worsening of ties between Syria and Hariri. The Lebanese prime minister's decision to challenge the Syrians may have been partly based on a perception of U.S. support for democratization and the anti-Syrian agenda of the Bush administration—and the Iraq War boosted his perception of both of these.

[35] The Ayn al-Hilwa refugee camp was a major way station for the recruitment and transfer of foreign Arab volunteers to Iraq. In previous civil conflicts, Lebanese Sunnis had remained largely aloof from the fighting; it was the Palestinian camp populations that had provided the Sunni "muscle" in internecine warfare.

[36] Even other jihadist groups, such as Asbat al-Ansar, failed to assist the group while it was pummeled by Lebanese forces for three months. Interview with Salafi cleric, Tripoli, Lebanon, March 2008. Also, "Fighting in Nahr . . . ," 2007. One contact in Tripoli noted that the Lebanese soldiers who attacked the camp hailed from the surrounding Sunni areas; those that died were feted as martyrs by local Salafis.

neighboring states.[37] In the case of Lebanon, Palestinian-Lebanese fissures appear to have undermined the prospect of any Sunni Islamist solidarity.[38]

In the wake of the Nahr al-Barid episode, the empowerment of Lebanon's Sunni Islamists has been facilitated through a deliberate strategy of co-option and support by the Future Movement under Sa'ad Hariri, as a counterweight to the pro-Syria March 8th coalition.[39] As in the Gulf, our local contacts saw this as a dangerous game of sectarian balancing that could ultimately backfire. Already, there are signs that Lebanon's Salafis are pulling out of the political "deal" with the Future Movement—a retreat that could pave the way for more-radical, militant factions. On the Shi'a side, the perception of Salafi ascendancy has reportedly strengthened support for Hizballah as a protector and guarantor.[40] "Many Shi'a are unhappy with Hizballah, with its provocations and the pace of reconstruction," noted one Shi'a activist in southern Beirut. "But they know that in the face of the Salafis, there simply is no other protection."[41]

---

[37] This point has been well-argued by Saab and Riedel, 2007. Our research, however, has shown that cross-sectarian solidarity for Hizballah has diminished since 2006, and we did not find as much evidence of support for Hizballah among Sunni Islamists.

[38] A critical debate on this issue is *tawtin* [granting of citizenship] to Lebanon's Palestinian refugees. Some of Lebanon's Salafi figures approve this, provoking tensions from both Hizballah and Christian Maronites, who perceive this is an attempt to tip the country's demography in favor of Sunni Muslims. According to one local observer, "If *tawtin* happens, the Maronites will disappear among Muslims and the Shi'a will disappear among Sunnis." Interviews with Lebanese analysts, Beirut, March 2008.

[39] Interviews with Lebanese analysts, Beirut, March 2008. *Tayyar al-Mustaqbal* [The Future Movement] is a Sunni political bloc led by Sa'ad Hariri comprising the largest party in the March 14th coalition. The Future Movement enjoys significant support from Saudi Arabia and has included a number of Lebanon's key Salafi factions among its core constituents. In the city of Sidon and in the Ayn al-Hilwa refugee camp, Sa'ad Hariri's aunt, Bahia, has been the main intermediary with these Salafis—to the point where armed Salafis are known as "Bahia's Army." Arrayed against the March 14th coalition is the pro-Syria March 8th, which includes Hizballah, the Afwaj al-Muqawama al-Lubnaniyya [Lebanese Resistance Detachments] (AMAL) movement, and the Free Patriotic Movement of the Christian politician Michel Aoun.

[40] For background on Lebanon's Salafis, see Abdel-Latif, 2008.

[41] Interview with Shi'a activist, southern Beirut, March 2008. Also, see Rougier, 2007.

Some of this can be considered an *indirect* effect of the Iraq War—the Lebanese Salafi movement is being underwritten by Saudi Arabia as part of a larger diplomatic strategy to roll back Iran's influence in the Levant while containing it in Iraq. Tehran, for its part, has intensified its financial involvement in the country's reconstruction via Hizballah. "The regional tug-of-war is definitely being felt here," noted one observer.[42]

The above sections have highlighted sectarian tensions in the wake of the Iraq War, exploring how conflict has exacerbated these dynamics in some cases and how the dynamics have arisen independently from it in others. In several instances, regimes have deliberately cultivated or exploited Shi'a-Sunni fissures as part of an anti-Iran strategy or to conceal more deeply seated insecurities over political legitimacy and authoritarianism. With the exception of Lebanon, sectarianism remains contained, and the threat of spillover appears exaggerated. All this argues against imposing a two-dimensional sectarian template on the region; a multitude of other loyalties coexist and, in some cases, take precedence over religious affiliation. The next section will survey some of these other substate identities and their links to the Iraq War.

Tribalism in Iraq May Animate Tribal Activism in Neighboring States

In light of the U.S.-backed Awakening Councils in al-Anbar, exploring the spread of tribal assertiveness in the Middle East appears especially salient.[43] It is probably too soon to tell whether this recent empowerment of tribes in Iraq is a direct driver for similar activism in neighbor-

---

[42] Interview with Lebanese researcher, Beirut, March 2008.

[43] The *Majalis al-Sahwa* [Awakening Councils] were tribal coalitions forged to combat al-Qa'ida in key Iraq provinces. Many members of these groups had direct or indirect ties to nationalist Iraqi insurgents but had agreed to ally themselves with the Iraqi government against the common foe of al-Qa'ida. This arrangement received strong support from the United States in the form of funding, advice, supply, and promises of reintegration and jobs training to prevent Sahwa members from drifting back to insurgency. The term originated with the effort by Shaykh 'Abd al-Sattar al-Rishawi (assassinated in September 2007) to form an anti-AQI coalition in Iraq's al-Anbar province.

ing states. One U.S. analyst noted that there was nothing "new" about the tribal dynamic; the United States has simply "rediscovered" a long-standing feature of the sociocultural milieu.[44] The strategy of employing tribal proxies against an Islamist militant threat or in a counter-insurgency environment is also not new. A former Egyptian general argued that the United States had effectively borrowed this paradigm from the Egyptian experience of "playing the tribal card" against insurgents from the *al-Gama'a al-Islamiya*, who typically recruited youth from prominent southern clans.[45]

The degree to which the Iraq War animates tribal sentiment in the region is contingent on existing tribe-state dynamics and is most likely to be felt among transnational tribes that straddle Iraq's borders to the west.[46] Thus, it appears Jordan has been particularly susceptible to tribal activism, especially in light of shifting regime policies. The most recent parliamentary elections were structured to give preference to rural tribes; intertribal clashes are becoming more common on university campuses; and employment is increasingly scrutinized for tribal affiliation, rather than the previous focus on Palestinian or trans-Jordanian affiliation.[47] Our fieldwork among a broad swath of Jordanian activists and analysts suggests that the government's recent appeal to

---

[44] Interview with Middle East analyst, Washington, D.C., January 2008. The postinvasion era has also seen a number of new tribal ethnographies by Arab authors, some of which impart balance to Ba'athist-era studies that had more explicit political agendas in mind; these include al-Zubaydi, 2005; al-Athim, 2005; al-Handal 2005; al-Wa'ili, 2002; and al-Athim, undated.

[45] Interview with a retired Egyptian general, Cairo, Egypt, February, 2008.

[46] The Dulaym, for example, have long resided along the key smuggling route of the Amman-Baghdad highway; to the north, the Jabbur inhabit a strategic zone at the edge of Mosul, giving them trilateral access to Turkey, the Kurds, and Syria. In Saudi Arabia, the Shammar confederation spans the northern Jawf region, across historic trade routes into Fallujah. In many cases, these ties are solidified by an overlay of religiosity; the influential clerical family of Banu Tamim in Saudi Arabia (which includes both regime-supported clerical families, such as the al-Al Shaykh, and oppositionists, such as Sa'ad al-Faqih) helped establish the Sunni pocket of al-Zubayr in southern Iraq. The Salafi current uniting these tribes is now known as the Khat al-Zubayr (the Zubayr Line). Interviews with Saudi analysts and clerics, Riyadh and the Eastern Province, March 2007. Also, see al-Rashid, 2007, p. 269, fn. 16.

[47] Interviews with Jordanian researchers and a UN official, Amman, February, 2008.

tribal interests is tied to a general backtracking on participatory governance and a return to patronage politics; the parliament is increasingly seen as a mere provincial council that caters to the needs of rural Bedouin, rather than legislating in the broader service of the citizenry.[48]

In Kuwait, tribal identity and the government's response appear to be undermining the aforementioned experiment in democracy. Tribes have long been a feature of Kuwait's power structure, even organizing their own "primaries" to select candidates for the national parliamentary elections. Beginning in 1998, the state outlawed these tribal voting forums, arguing that they would reduce the chances of nontribal candidates in national voting.[49] As of May 2008, this ban has been a significant and ongoing source of contention between the government and tribes; the imprisonment of prominent tribal organizers of these primaries sparked rioting and an assault on a police station. Aggravating this discord is the perception of electoral gerrymandering to reduce tribal clout in the run-up to the May 17, 2008 elections.[50] Several commentators, however, counted the election returns as a victory for tribalism and sectarianism: In at least two of Kuwait's five electoral districts, tribal loyalties decided the outcome, and tribal candidates also fared well in the remaining districts (Brown, 2008).[51]

In Yemen, where tribes have traditionally filled a vacuum left by the state, tribal political influence is becoming more formalized. In July 2007, the paramount shaykh of the powerful Hashid tribe set up the "National Solidarity Council," specifically in response to parliamentary paralysis and the weakness of the state.[52] This body pro-

---

[48] Interview with former Jordanian official, Amman, February 2008.

[49] Tribes have attempted to circumvent this restriction by calling these primaries *consultations*. "Kuwait: Thousands Demonstrate . . . ," 2008.

[50] For more on tribal dynamics in Kuwait, see Crystal, 2005, p. 177; "Kuwait Tribes Storm Police Station . . . ," 2008; and Izzak, 2008.

[51] Brown also wrote, "Most post-election punditry in Kuwait focused on the triumph of tribalism and sectarianism, and for good reason" (Brown, 2008, p. 5).

[52] The exact power of this body remains unknown, but it includes members of the ruling General People's Congress, as well as oppositionists. A Yemeni academic has called it a sign of the "failure of civil society" (al-Alaya'a, 2007).

voked a strong response from the Hashid's traditional rivals, the Bakil, who were not included and subsequently formed their own bloc as a counterweight (al-Ashmouri, 2007). This tribal tit-for-tat presents significant challenges for the Salih government, which has also had to contend with a rebellion in the northern Saada province by followers of Zaydi Shi'a revivalist leader Husayn al-Houthi, an increased threat from al-Qa'ida, and a reinvigorated southern secessionist movement.[53]

In Saudi Arabia, tribal activism remains strong, with some observers noting a prominent tribal undercurrent to voting patterns in the 2005 municipal elections. Many Islamist candidates received strong endorsement from prominent tribes; this is particularly evident in the Hijaz, where notable merchant families have lent their support to more Muslim Brotherhood–inspired strains of Salafism.[54] A Riyadh-based political reformer told RAND that these dynamics illustrated how the Iraq War had unleashed "centrifugal forces" in the kingdom—what he further described as intensified challenges to the homogenizing nationalist narrative the state had constructed.[55]

It is important to note, however, that, in many cases, the specter of tribal parochialism is often used by opponents of political liberalization. This theme has emerged quite frequently in Saudi Arabia, with regime defenders asserting that the citizenry is too rooted in familial loyalty, too immature, and "not ready for democracy." Similarly, there are those who argue that, unless nontribal civil society institutions are

---

[53] The Zaydis are a sect within Shi'a Islam that recognizes the authority of the fifth imam, Zayd ibn Ali. Its members are often called "Fiver Shi'a." In this respect, they are distinct from the majority of Shi'a in Iraq, Iran, and Lebanon, who follow 12 imams and are known as "Twelver Shi'a." Some observers have noted that the Zaydis are doctrinally closer to the Hanafi school of jurisprudence within Sunni Islam than they are to mainstream Shi'sm. The rebellion was reportedly triggered in late 2004 by Zaydi alarm that the government was playing "sectarian politics," i.e., co-opting radical Salafi factions against the marginalized northern Zaydi tribes (Phillips, 2005). Although the Saleh regime has frequently made reference to Iranian involvement, the conflict is rooted in center-periphery tensions, a movement by Zaydi figures to revive Zaydism as a political identity, and the politicoeconomic marginalization of the northern Saada province.

[54] Interview with a Saudi analyst, Jeddah, March 2007. These families included the Bayt Hanif, Bayt Nasif, and Jamjum.

[55] Interview with a Salafi legal reformer, Riyadh, March 2007.

first in place, elections are bound to be tainted.[56] "If we held parliamentary elections tomorrow," a Saudi academic argued, "power would shift from the urban centers to the Bedouin periphery."[57]

This brief survey of tribalism in a number of key states suggests that the Iraq War and, in particular, the empowerment of the Awakening Councils, has increased the salience of tribal identity as both a bedrock and a potential challenge to regime legitimacy. Given the presence of transnational tribal links that straddle Iraq's borders, it is logical to assume that various tribal trajectories in Iraq—increased political activism, quietism, repression by the central regime, or intratribal conflict—will have an echo effect on political stability in neighboring states. While the full scope of these effects has yet to be felt, they highlight an important post-Iraq pressure that regional states will have to contend with.

Developments in Iraq Have Inspired Kurdish Ambitions in Turkey, Syria, and Iran

Aside from tribal influence, ethnic activism presents another post-Iraq challenge to state stability. As in the case of sectarian tensions, it is important to distinguish the actual processes of ethnic mobilization from regime rhetoric, which is often designed to fracture opposition coordination and stoke fears of a domino effect.[58] Many ethnic oppositionists do not seek to mirror Iraq's federalized system, but are rather aiming for greater civil and social rights as part of a broad-based reform platform. If regimes can portray these initiatives as being fueled by ethnic particularism or provoked by "outside forces," they stand a better chance of combating or discrediting them, as they have done

---

[56] Other scholars have argued that tribal organizations do represent civil society, albeit not along Western lines. See Antoun, 2000, and Carapico, 2007.

[57] This observer argued that the winning tribes would be drawn from the al-Mutayr, al-Shammar, al-Qahtan, and al-Utayba. Interview with a Saudi political scientist and newspaper columnist, Riyadh, March 2007.

[58] In Egypt, for example, we encountered fears that the push for a federated Iraq was inspiring activism by southern Copts. Interviews with Egyptian analysts, Cairo, February 2008.

with Shi'a. The Kurdish populations in the region have drawn the most attention in this respect.

The events in Iraq have indeed animated Kurdish aspirations, and Kurdish insurgents, empowered by the availability of safe haven in northern Iraq, present an ongoing security threat to Syria, Turkey, and Iran. Iran, in particular, offers a useful illustration of these postwar echo effects. Following the election of Jalal Talabani as Iraqi president, spontaneous celebrations erupted among Iranian Kurds in at least two border cities, prompting clashes with Iranian security forces and a subsequent crackdown (see Samii, 2005).

The war has also indirectly led to escalated attacks on Iranian security forces by the anti-Iranian Kurdish group PJAK, which reportedly fields over 30,000 combatants in northern Iraq (Brandon, 2006).[59] Since 2006, a cycle of Kurdish demonstrations, Iranian repression, and Kurdish counterattacks has ensued, with sporadic incursions of Iranian troops into northern Iraq (see Oppel, 2007). According to the Iranian government, PJAK killed at least 120 Iranian soldiers in Iran in 2005, and the same number again in 2006 (see Global Security, 2007). In March 2006, Kurdish media reported that Iranian soldiers had killed 10 Kurdish militants in Maku. As a result, PJAK raided three army bases in Kurdish-populated areas of Iran. One PJAK official claimed to have killed hundreds of Iranian officers in these offensives.[60] Other PJAK sources advanced a more-realistic figure of 24 officers killed (Global Security, 2007). Since June 2007, the Iraqi border region of Bashdar, in Sulaimaniya, has been subject to periodic artillery bombardments from the Iranian Army, which claims that the area harbors PJAK fighters allied to the PKK.[61]

As noted in Chapter Two, Turkey has seen a resurgence of PKK militancy, using northern Iraq as a base. Attacks on Turkish soil have inflicted extensive casualties and provoked a cross-border Turkish mili-

---

[59] For further background on PJAK, the principal antiregime Kurdish insurgent group in Iran, see Wood, 2006.

[60] Zanar Agri, a member of PJAK's coordinating committee, made this claim. See Wood, 2006.

[61] "Iran Tujadid Qasfuha . . . ," 2007. Also see "Iranian Forces Shell . . . ," 2008.

tary incursion into Iraq in December 2007 (see Tank, 2005). The real effect of the Kurdish spillover, however, may be felt more in the political realm. PKK-associated violence has prompted a renewed drift in Ankara toward solving the Kurdish dilemma via security measures, not reform, with the result that the Turkish military has been handed increased leverage in its clash with the Justice and Development Party (see Larrabee, 2007a). More ominously, the military's impetus for external intervention against the PKK has been mirrored by a parallel drift toward internal repression, potentially sabotaging Turkey's diplomatic efforts to join the European Union (see Barkey, 2005).

It is in Syria that Iraqi Kurdish autonomy has had its most direct and explosive effect, sparking eight days of rioting by Syrian Kurds in March 2004—the country's worst outbreak of ethnosectarian violence in two decades. It is important to note that the demonstrations (known today among Syria's Kurds as "the uprising") came amidst growing anticipation about events in neighboring Iraq. Aside from the aforementioned election of Talabani, March 8, 2004, saw the ratification of the Iraqi Transitional Administrative Law, which gave the Iraqi Kurds substantial autonomy, including the right to their own police forces and to levy taxes (Lowe, 2006). Subsequently, there was widespread euphoria among Syria's Kurds during the 2004 *Nowruz* [New Year] celebrations, and there were expectations about pushes for similar initiatives in Syria (Lowe, 2006). In this charged atmosphere, a melee between Arab and Kurdish soccer fans erupted in the northeastern city of Qamishli on March 12. Supporters of a visiting Arab soccer team shouted pro-Saddam slogans and ethnic slurs, and Kurdish fans responded with praise for President Bush. Security forces opened fire on the Kurdish demonstrators, killing eight and sparking the spread of the violence. The turbulence left 40 people dead and spread to Lebanon, where security forces arrested several Kurdish activists.[62]

As of 2008, however, it appears that the threat of Kurdish activism in Syria had subsided. Kurdish-regime relations have improved, with one observer noting that a mutual fear of Sunni Islamists has pushed

---

[62] "Clashes Spread in Northeast Syria . . . ," 2004.

many Kurds to rally behind the government for support.[63] The Kurds themselves are also divided, with as many as 12 Kurdish political parties jostling for primacy.[64] Finally, prominent Iraqi Kurdish leaders are reportedly sympathetic to the Assad regime for hosting them in exile during the Saddam era (Rubin, 2007, p. 9).

Iraqi Refugees Present One of the Most Significant Long-Term Challenge

The influx of Iraqi refugees to neighboring states presents one of the most significant yet often misinterpreted effects of the Iraq War. Much of the focus thus far has been on either the immediate humanitarian challenge this crisis poses or on refugees as imminent security risks, with some analysts seeing them as vectors for radicalization, terrorism, sectarianism, and disease.[65] Our research certainly captures this dynamic but also suggests that the most worrisome consequences of this population transfer may be longer-term, political, and economic. Gauging this, however, is somewhat difficult, given the tendency of host regimes and their publics to scapegoat, misrepresent, and exaggerate the consequences of the refugee flow.

There is a dearth of accurate data on the refugee crisis.[66] Although estimates vary, it is generally believed that 2 million Iraqis have fled to neighboring states and that over 2.5 million are internally displaced within Iraq, making this refugee flow the largest in the region since 1948, which it already surpasses in numbers. Of those who have left the country, over 1 million are estimated to be in Syria, and half that

---

[63] Author telephone discussion with a European scholar of Syria, January 2008.

[64] Author telephone discussion with a European scholar of Syria, January 2008.

[65] See the discussion of refugee "catch basins" in Byman and Pollack, 2007, pp. 22–27.

[66] Iraqi refugee numbers are unreliable and difficult to estimate for many reasons. For instance, Iraqis in neighboring countries illegally fear discovery; not all estimates count Iraqis who left the country before 2003; some Iraqis travel to Jordan and Syria regularly for business and personal reasons, and it is difficult to disaggregate their numbers from those fleeing conflict; most Iraqis who have fled do not wish to be referred to as "refugees."

number in Jordan. Fafo, a Norwegian research group, has estimated that there are approximately 450,000 to 500,000 Iraqi refugees in Jordan.[67] Others are in Lebanon, Egypt, various Gulf states, Iran, and Turkey. Figure 4.1 portrays a country breakdown of Iraqi refugees, drawing on data from the United Nations High Commissioner for Refugees (UNHCR).

Jordan is a special concern on the refugee issue, given its turbulent history. The country's stability has long been buffeted by the exogenous shock of Palestinian refugees, spurred by chaos in neighboring states. By the late 1960s, Palestinians in Jordan had coalesced into an autonomous parastate, fielding their own army and boldly defying the monarchy's will. The echoes of the government's showdown with these fighters in 1970 continue to shape the regime's current policy toward Iraqi refugees. This is particularly true concerning its reluctance to erect any "parallel structures"—hospitals, camps, water supply, and other services—for Iraqi refugees that might become the incubus for Iraqi statelets in the kingdom ("little Baghdads") or encouragement for the population to stay.[68] Indeed, Iraqi refugees in Jordan and elsewhere largely live in rented housing, not refugee camps.

The added population strain has affected Jordan in a number of ways. The influx has cost the government over $1 billion U.S. per year, Iraqis have begun to compete for jobs with Jordanians. Public schools, which started accepting Iraqi students in July 2007, have become increasingly overcrowded.[69] Even though children are allowed to attend school, most do not because parents fear that attendance may compromise illegal or quasi-legal presence in the country and because many children work illegally to keep their families housed and fed.

More dangerous, perhaps, are the long-term societal tensions and the potential for radicalization. Iraqis in Jordan have increasingly

---

[67] For background on Iraqi refugees in Syria, Jordan, and Lebanon, see al-Khalidi, 2007; "Rot Here or Die There . . . ," 2007; FAFO, 2007; Bruno, 2007; Fagen, 2007; and Chamberlin, 2008.

[68] Interview with U.S. official, Amman, February 2008.

[69] Interviews with Jordanian analysts, Amman, February 2008. The $1 billion U.S. figure is from the Jordanian Ministry of Interior. See Hindi, 2007.

Figure 4.1
Regional Distribution of Iraqi Refugees as of March 2008 (000s)

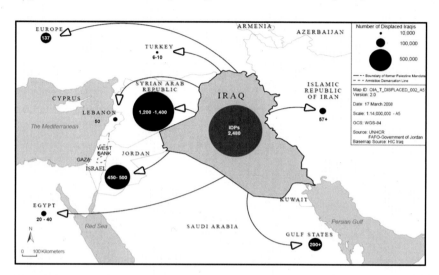

SOURCE: UNHCR
RAND MG892-4.1

become a scapegoat for larger economic problems in the kingdom, such as the end of fuel subsidies, unemployment, inflation, and a housing shortage.[70] "Services to Iraqis are now viewed as a threat," noted one Jordanian researcher.[71] A UN official argued that the problem could be further compounded by the demographic of young Iraqi males who have graduated from college but now sit idly unemployed—a profile that many analysts have identified as being susceptible to radicalization.[72]

In contrast to these worries, some observers argue for a less-alarmist view of the influx and have actually highlighted its economic

---

[70] Fagen, 2007, p. 13, notes that "[e]very Jordanian encountered in the research singled out the rapidly accelerating cost of housing and most blamed wealthy Iraqis for having purchased or rented available space." A major cause for escalating prices in oil and fuel has been the end of subsidies from Iraq after the invasion.

[71] Interview with Jordanian researcher, Amman, February 2008.

[72] Interview with UN refugee official, Amman, February 2008. This is echoed by Syrian officials, who reportedly consider unemployed Iraqi males a "time bomb." See Laipson, 2009.

benefit.[73] Many Iraqis who initially moved to Jordan were from a middle- or upper-class background, especially from the former Ba'athist elite. The capital influx from their savings reportedly fueled Jordan's mortgage market, helping new buyers from the lower and middle classes.[74] A Georgetown University study noted that Iraqis in Jordan

> do not make large demands on public health facilities. They do, however, purchase very large quantities of Jordanian goods and services, and they employ Jordanian construction workers, doctors, concierges, technicians. (Fagen, 2007, p. 12)

Our fieldwork appeared to echo some elements of the Georgetown study's findings on popular inflation of the ill effects of the refugee presence. However, as the resources of Iraqi refugees dwindle and as their conditions become more dire, friction with the local population is likely to increase over time. But the destabilizing sectarian dimension of the problem in Jordan appears overstated to date; in contrast with Salafi warnings about an Iraqi Shi'a influx, most refugees are Sunni or Christian, with little interest thus far in political agitation. "Iraqis just want jobs and money," noted one U.S. diplomat to RAND.[75] "For the serious bad guys, Jordan is not the place," noted this U.S. official.[76]

In Syria, our research identified a similar mix of alarm, caution, and pragmatism about refugees. Syria's initial opening of its borders to the refugees appears to have been driven largely by ideology, to boost its pan-Arab bona fides on the regional stage, with little regard for the economic consequences. As in Jordan, the state bears most of the burden of accommodating this influx, yet the situation in Syria is more serious because its Iraqi population is generally poorer than those who fled to Jordan (Wilson, 2005). Eighty to ninety percent of Iraqi refugees have clustered in Damascus, resulting in overcrowding and increasingly unsanitary living conditions (Fagen, 2007, p. 19). Many

---

[73] For a Jordanian view of the benefit of Iraqi influx, see Saif and DeBartolo, 2007.

[74] Interview with independent Jordanian analyst, Amman, February 2008.

[75] Interview with U.S. official, Amman, February 2008.

[76] Interview with U.S. official, Amman, February 2008.

women have been forced into prostitution to support themselves and their families. Like Jordanians, the Syrian populace has begun blaming Iraqis for the escalating costs of housing, goods, and services.[77] Lower-class Syrians and those on fixed incomes are especially at risk. This is an important constituency for the regime and could result in a future hardening of the country's policies toward Iraqis. Despite these detrimental effects, some analyses point to the benefits of the influx. International Monetary Fund (2007), for example, asserted that the country's rebound from a decade of slow economic growth was due in part to the pressures placed on the government by the refugees.

As in Jordan, sectarian tensions accompanying the Iraqi influx have been muted thus far. Few areas of refugee settlement in Damascus are explicitly communal, with the exception of Sayida Zaynab, an important Shi'a shrine and pilgrimage site (al-Khalidi, Hoffmann, and Tanner, 2007, pp. 23–26).[78] In predominately Iraqi neighborhoods, Sunni ex-Ba'athists coexist alongside representatives of Muqtada al-Sadr; sect and ideology are less-important markers in exile than class, wealth, and nationality. One contact related the story of an Iraqi Christian who sought refuge among Syrian Christians but was rebuffed and found shelter instead among Iraqi Shi'a in the Sayida Zaynab district.[79]

Despite this commonality, an emerging source of tension is the changing demographic complexion in areas that were formerly Syrian and are now Iraqi. The suburb of Jarmana is a good example; the area was predominantly Syrian Druze and Christian before the war but now has a distinctly Iraqi feel to it—to the point where one section is nicknamed "Fallujah." (al-Khalidi, Hoffmann and Tanner, 2007, p. 25).

In both Syria and Jordan, the refugee influx has had mixed economic effects but has generally not yet undermined security and sta-

---

[77] Telephone discussion with a European researcher on Syria, February 2008. This has been buttressed by official figures citing a spike in demands for subsidized goods, such as water, bread, and cooking gas.

[78] Interview with a UN refugee official, Amman, February 2008. Neighborhoods in Damascus are not organized along sectarian lines as they are in Baghdad. Class and piety, however, are important markers; in more-conservative Syrian areas, these populations have stirred animosity by selling alcohol.

[79] Telephone discussion with a European researcher on Syria, February 2008.

bility. Nonetheless, it has placed long-term stresses on the state that stem principally from public linkages of the refugees with worsening domestic ills. Syrian views in particular bear watching; many citizens continue to credit their government for its generosity toward refugees and fidelity to pan-Arabism, but there is growing unease about the economic opportunity costs of this benevolence (al-Khalidi, Hoffmann, and Tanner, 2007, p. 42). Much will depend on how Amman and Damascus manage both the needs of refugees and the expectations of their citizenry. This, in turn, will ultimately hinge on an effective prioritization of resources and on increased international support.

The U.S. drawdown in Iraq also has the potential to exacerbate the long-term negative implications of this crisis if it is accompanied or followed by increased violence in Iraq. In such a situation, more refugees may attempt to flee, but Jordan, Syria, and others are not likely to accept them as they have done to date (Jordan has already largely closed its doors to Iraqis), which could lead to the development of refugee camps. A large Iraqi diaspora combined with continuing conflict in Iraq has the potential to spread conflict to neighbors because Iraqis living abroad funnel support to Iraqi groups, are recruited to fight, or lobby governments to provide aid to combatants. If camps are indeed set up, these risks increase because camps have often been primary sources of militant recruiting for fighting and unrest in the home and host countries.

Even if new refugee flows do not emerge in the context of drawdown, the existing refugee populations pose significant long-term challenges to host states. Given that many, if not most, Iraqi refugees are unlikely to return home even with improved security conditions in Iraq, the Iraqi refugee challenge may prove to be the most enduring effect of the Iraq conflict. Previous refugee crises hold important lessons for how this situation could evolve.[80] First, the humanitarian crisis will worsen unless host countries take steps to integrate the displaced and thus accept at least some long-term presence. Poverty will grow, as

---

[80] For an overview of literature linking security and refugee crises and a detailed discussion of such linkages in Iraq, see Lischer, 2008.

will numbers, through natural increase even if no more refugees leave Iraq. Lack of education will make future generations of Iraqi refugees even less competitive for jobs. Even if camps do not develop, poverty-stricken enclaves will.

And it is well known that humanitarian crises have security implications. Poverty and resentment can feed radicalization among the displaced and host populations. Poor education may make refugees more vulnerable to extremist recruitment. Economic strains caused by displacement can also contribute to resentment and anger between refugee and indigenous populations, with each seen by the other as privileged or taking away goods and services. As discussed above, this is already taking place in Jordan and Syria. If displacement actually shifts demographics in these countries, these problems may be politicized and create instability in the years to come.[81]

Conclusion: The Iraq War May Ultimately Strengthen Neighboring Regimes but Not the State

This chapter has surveyed domestic dynamics in a number of regional states, identifying the stresses and pressures that were either caused by the war or exacerbated by it. The threat of immediate spillover appears to have abated, although sectarian tensions, tribal identity, ethnic mobilization, and the refugee influx remain key concerns that are tied to developments in Iraq—but only partially. In many cases, regime policies themselves are what ultimately aggravate sectarianism or reassert other substate identities. Much of this stems from deliberate tactics of manipulation, co-option, and exploitation of these affiliations in lieu of more-meaningful and long-term structural reforms.

The most significant effect of the war in the domestic sphere may therefore be a sort of authoritarian adaptation and learning that has

---

[81] This is already an issue in Bahrain, where some Shi'a leaders allege that the government is offering citizenship to Sunnis from Iraq. Interview with Shi'a activist, Manama, Bahrain, November 2006.

entrenched *regimes*, without necessarily fortifying the *state*.[82] Regional governments have skillfully cultivated a perception of external siege, portraying themselves as "buffers" against Iraq's sectarian furies and mediators over an immature citizenry that is prone to tribal and ethnic loyalties. Our research shows that public acquiescence may be partly facilitating this consolidation. Across the region, there is a premium on *wahda* [unity], *watan* [homeland], and *nitham* [system] as an antidote to *fitna* [strife], *fawda* [chaos], and *ta'ifiya* [sectarianism]. Commenting on Saudi Arabia, a state that some have viewed as ripe for fragmentation, Bernard Haykel noted that

> The dissolution in Iraq has further confirmed to ordinary and elite Saudis the wisdom of clinging to the present system, convincing most people that no alternative exists to a unified Saudi Arabia. (Haykel, 2007)[83]

In many instances, support for the reassertion of the "security state" has been aided by domestic attacks by al-Qaʻida and the resulting public backlash. One Jordanian analyst noted that the November 2005 Amman hotel bombings by Zarqawi's network improved public perceptions of the Jordanian security services; they were no longer seen as purely "monitoring" but rather "protecting" the citizenry.[84]

The net effect has been a deferral of any "domestic experiments" that might weaken regime authority. In this, local governments have been aided by an apparent decrease in U.S. pressure for political liberalization since 2003. Reformists and democracy activists in a number of states told us that their governments had been effectively granted a reprieve on reform because of Washington's preoccupation with Iraq and, more recently, building a regional coalition against Iran. In other cases, democratization appears to have lost its luster among certain

---

[82] Heydemann, 2007, explores this dynamic of calibrated reforms and authoritarian "learning."

[83] Haykel was responding to a January 2008 article in *Vanity Fair* in which Kenneth Pollack, Daniel Byman, David Fromkin, and Dennis Ross were asked to redraw the political map of the Middle East according to underlying socioethnic contours (Pollack et al, 2008).

[84] Interview with Jordanian activist, Amman, February, 2008.

population segments because it is seen as a "U.S. project" and as the catalyst for the ongoing strife in Iraq.[85] Whether or not this battening down of the hatches genuinely qualifies as a new nationalism is debatable. Public coalescence behind undemocratic rulers may prove temporary and cyclical—what one scholar has aptly termed a "winter of autocracy" (Brumberg, 2006).

There are indeed a number of worrisome trends in the region, many of which predate the Iraq War, but were exacerbated by it: the perceived legitimacy deficit of hereditary rulers, stagnant economies, an illiberal political culture, and draconian judicial systems. Taken in sum, these internal maladies do not portend the imminent failure of the state, but neither are they favorable to long-term U.S. interests and regional stability. Many were identified after September 11, 2001, as the wellsprings of radicalization, and their persistence today argues for a renewed focus on domestic reform as a pillar of future U.S. security strategy in the region.

---

[85] Interviews with Saudi and Egyptian reform activists in, respectively, Riyadh and Cairo, March 2007 and February 2008. Decreased U.S. pressure for democratization was also noted because Washington belatedly recognized that the "wrong people" can win—HAMAS and Hizballah.

The Iraq War and the Future of Terrorism: Lessons Learned and New Strategic Trends

The effect on terrorism trends among Iraq's neighbors and beyond is one of the most widely discussed, yet least understood, ripple effects of the conflict. In line with the recommendations of the NIE and the *Iraq Study Group Report* (Baker et al., 2006),[1] prevailing views focus on Iraq's role in directly causing an upsurge in global terrorism, amplifying terrorist successes without fully assessing their causes or highlighting vulnerabilities and weaknesses. Our findings suggest a more-mixed picture, the true colors of which are unlikely to clarify themselves for a number of years. This chapter examines some of the data substantiating claims that events in Iraq have exacerbated terrorist threats and explores the theories in circulation that the war and its aftermath have boosted terrorist recruitment and public support for Salafi-jihadist movements, furthered al-Qa'ida's ideological and strategic goals by opening up new fronts for jihad, and created a new laboratory for terrorist training and tactical innovation.

In the sphere of recruitment and strategic communications, although al-Qa'ida has capitalized on the emotive message of Iraq as the central outlet for defensive jihad, it has lost public support as a result of its brutal tactics in Iraq. Ideologically, the trajectory of events in Iraq has reduced the perceived legitimacy of al-Qa'ida's key theological tenets and exposed a mismatch between its ideological aspirations

---

[1] National Intelligence Council, 2006, provides an unclassified list of key points of the NIE.

and strategic possibilities. In practical terms, Iraq has indeed provided a training ground for both Sunni and Shi'a insurgents and a military laboratory for the development of terrorist TTPs. Salafi-jihadist tactics perfected in Iraq are already manifesting themselves elsewhere, but Iraq cannot be held solely accountable for this. In the meantime, while Shi'a militants have been the greatest beneficiaries of new technologies, the capacity for proliferation elsewhere is limited by Iran's own interests and by the objectives of the Shi'a.

In short, the immediate blowback from Iraq may not be as severe as commonly assumed. However, judging by the Afghan model, in which mujahidin who fought the Soviets in the 1980s went on to campaign in central Asia in the 1990s, it may be a decade or more before the full effects of Iraq on terrorism are felt. Before this happens, the United States and regional partners should focus on exploiting weaknesses in the information operations of the jihadi movements, on better understanding the most novel and prevalent TTPs and strategies being used in Iraq, and on encouraging preventative policies in the most vulnerable states.

Existing Reports Present Contradictory Evidence on the Net Effects of the Iraq War

The majority of statistical studies indicate that terrorism levels worldwide rose sharply after the Iraq War. However, the data presented to identify Iraq as a *causal* factor are inconclusive. Starting with official reports, the U.S. Department of State's "Patterns of Global Terrorism" annual reviews indicated a rise in international terrorist acts, from 198 incidents in 2002 to 208 in 2003.[2] In 2005 the U.S. National Counterterrorism Center unveiled a more-comprehensive Worldwide Incidents Tracking System. While the center cautioned against purely quantitative analysis, this system recorded a jump in the number of terrorist

---

[2]   These reports are available on the department's website. The 2003 findings do not include the majority of attacks on Coalition Forces in Iraq during Operations Iraqi Freedom and Enduring Freedom.

incidents worldwide from 3,255 in 2004 to 11,088 in 2005, subsequently rising to around 14,500 in both 2006 and 2007.[3] In November 2007, two law professors complied a "Report Card on the War on Terror" using the Memorial Institute for the Prevention of Terrorism (MIPT)–RAND Terrorism Knowledge Database. They reported that annual worldwide terrorist incidents had increased from 1,732 in 2001 to 6,659 in 2006 (Cole and Lobel, 2007).

Adding to this, Peter Bergen and Paul Cruickshank used MIPT-RAND Terrorism Knowledge Database statistics to compare the periods between 9/11 and the start of the Iraq War in March 2003 and March 2003 to September 2006 to focus more intently on the Iraq effect.[4] Grounding their analysis specifically on jihadi militant groups, the authors acknowledged that increased attacks by jihadi groups might not be attributable to Iraq. Nonetheless, they maintained that the most direct test of the Iraq effect was whether the United States and its allies had suffered more jihadi terrorism after the invasion than before and found that attacks on Western interests and citizens around the world (outside of Iraq and Afghanistan) had risen by roughly 25 percent.

Not all academic studies conform to these findings. At the other end of the spectrum, a study conducted by Simon Fraser University in Canada in May 2008 indicated that, Iraq aside, terrorism had actually gone down since 2003 and pointed out that according to both MIPT-RAND and Study of Terrorism and Responses to Terror (START) data, non-Iraq deaths from terrorism had declined by more than 40 percent since 2001.[5] The disparity of these findings highlights one of the fundamental difficulties involved in providing quantitative

---

[3] These findings emerged from searches using the tracking system in December 2009.

[4] The authors later clarify that they are referring specifically to terrorism committed by jihadi groups (Bergen and Cruickshank, 2007).

[5] Mack, 2008, and Zakaria, 2008. Similarly, Dreyfuss, 2006, responded to the leaked NIE judgments with an article affirming that he did not believe there was much evidence to suggest that Iraq was creating more terrorists: "It is a long leap from anti-Americanism to terrorism." Anti-American Arabs had, Dreyfuss said, expressed their ill feelings toward America in other ways—for instance, by voting for HAMAS or Hizballah or by joining the insurgency in Iraq—but not by turning to terrorism. This highlights the highly disputed nature of the term terrorism.

analysis detailing terrorist attacks: the disagreement over what should be counted as terrorism. The polarization between results pointing to a massive increase in terrorism and those indicating a static, or declining, level is often indicative of whether or not the studies included attacks committed within Iraq.[6] Those who reject these do so on the grounds that Iraq is a war zone; as such, it is misleading to include attacks there, particularly when violent attacks committed in other war zones have not been identified as terrorism in government-funded terrorist databases. Those who include attacks in Iraq imply that discounting the violence jihadi groups in Iraq perpetrate is nonsensical when Iraq was, for a time, the principle territory for defeating terror.

An accurate reading of the immediate Iraq effect on Salafi-jihadist terrorism is further impeded by the intensification of counterterrorism efforts of Western security apparatuses after 9/11 and the heightened sensitivity to threats, which have mitigated effects that would otherwise have been felt as a result of Iraq. The opportunistic policy of regional governments to recategorize domestic violent dissent motivated by preexisting grievances as Salafi-jihadism is another complicating factor. True, there is no shortage of data connecting terrorist attacks throughout the Middle East to Iraq; whether the connection is an emulation of strategy, the sourcing of weapons, or the perpetrators' prior experience in Iraq. However, Iraq's high profile increases the temptation to attribute all terrorism Muslims commit to the Iraq effect, and analysts should be wary of doing so, even when perpetrators of terror attacks cite Iraq as a motivating factor.

If the findings from databases and incident reporting prove unsatisfactory, they also fail to address questions relating to the war's longer-term effect as a symbolic vehicle for radicalization and recruitment, a

---

[6] National Counterterrorism Center, 2008, claims that, of the 14,499 reported terrorist attacks for 2007, almost 43 percent occurred in Iraq. Bergen and Cruickshank, 2007, maintain that, even excluding Iraq and Afghanistan, terrorist attacks rose 35 percent between March 2003 and September 2006. But again, their definition of terrorism is debatable. They discount Palestinian attacks on the grounds that "they depend largely on factors particular to the Israeli-Palestinian conflict," although Gaza now plays host to a collection of self-proclaimed Salafi-jihadist groups. On the other hand, they include attacks in other countries, such as Algeria, presumably because these have no basis in local grievance.

jihadi case study informing future strategy development, and a laboratory for the development of new asymmetric tactics.

The Iraq Conflict Has Boosted al-Qa'ida's Recruitment but Reduced Its Long-Term Base of Popular Support

Iraq Has Offered an Attractive Narrative of Resistance to Aggrieved Muslims

The Iraq War has provided an anti-Western motivational focus and consolidated preexisting grievances, which encourage Muslims worldwide to join terrorist groups. As a *cause célèbre*,[7] the conflict, particularly from 2003 to 2006, offered a narrative of resistance to occupation that proved intensely attractive to multiple audiences across the region whose immediate local grievances may have been unrelated to Iraq itself but who nonetheless may have been inspired toward violence by the war. Many of these volunteers did not adhere to the "typical" terrorist profile; instead, they are students and professionals attracted to a cause, much as the Spanish Civil War proved a magnet for young professionals and intellectuals. Iraq became the focus for anti-American, anti-Western sentiment. Author interviews in Jordan revealed that young Jordanians went to Iraq because it was an easy target; if Gaza were easier to access, they would have gone there. The same sentiment was reflected in the citation of a Palestinian in the Lebanese 'Ayn al-Hilwa refugee camp interviewed by Al Arabiya:

> Most of the Muslim youths in Lebanon wanted to go to Iraq for jihad. As you know, the situation in Lebanon does not allow us to go to Palestine to fight, even though the Palestinian cause is the core issue and Palestine is worthier than all the Arab countries . . . . Therefore, we felt Iraq was closer to us than Palestine because it is easier to go to Iraq. Everybody is ready to open the way to Iraq and close the way to Palestine . . . .[8]

---

[7]   The NIE used this phrase in reference to Iraq.

[8]   "Al-Arabiyah Net Interviews . . . ," 2007.

Many volunteers are young; Muhammad Hafez recounts a story of the recruitment of almost an entire Saudi soccer team of 17- to 25-year-olds. In July 2004 (Hafez, 2007), three Kuwaiti teenagers were sent home from Syria en route to Iraq (Spencer, 2004), and in January 2005, Mohsen al-Fahdli—a Kuwaiti al-Qaʻida suspect—was arrested on suspicion of recruiting youths to attack U.S. forces in Iraq (see Janardhan, 2005).

The general unpopularity of the conflict contributed toward local regimes intermittently turning a blind eye to nationals making their way to Iraq to fight,[9] in a bid to deflect violence from the home front. Added to this, al-Qaʻida's ideologues and strategists have successfully portrayed Iraq as the most striking example of an infidel invasion of an Arab Muslim land, drawing historic parallels to Mongol invasion of the ʻAbbasid caliphate in Baghdad in the 13th century. In doing so, they appeal not only to those who consider their time in Iraq as a surrogate battle against the rulers of their own countries but also to Muslims who view Iraq as a legitimate site of *jihad al-dafʻa* [defensive jihad] but who do not subscribe to the more-aggressive Salafi-jihadist interpretation of *jihad al-talab* [offensive jihad],[10] although their attitudes may evolve as a result of involvement in Iraq. The greatest Salafi-jihadist strategic communication successes within the Sunni Muslim world appear to rely on the simple message that Iraq represents an opportune front for performing jihad against foreign occupation and expunging its attendant humiliation. The conflict provides a compelling, universalizing narrative that transcends boundaries by incorporating themes of occupation, honor defiled, brave resistance, and redemption. That emotive message travels well and is easily conveyed through the mass media.

---

[9]   In July 2006, Yemeni courts acquitted 14 Yemenis and five Saudis accused of plotting to attack Americans in Yemen. Prosecutors claimed that the men had returned from Iraq to Yemen on the instruction of Abu Musʻab al-Zarqawi to undertake the attacks, and some of the men admitted to having fought in Iraq, but the chief judge declared that Shariʻa law did not prohibit the men from going to fight jihad.

[10]   The majority of Islamic scholars (of all Islamic schools of law) maintain that defensive jihad is an individual and thus compulsory duty for all Muslims, whereas offensive jihad is a collective duty, which may be carried out by some, thus relieving the burden on others.

But al-Qa'ida Has Failed to Translate Popular Support for Resistance in Iraq into Broad Backing for Its Global Jihad Bid

While al-Qa'ida has been able to exploit the Iraq conflict to reinvigorate its narrative following demoralizing setbacks with the 2002 fall of the Taliban in Afghanistan, its efforts to create a long-term base of ideological support by using Iraq as the crux of a hearts-and-minds media campaign have been far less successful. The centrality of an attractive mass-media campaign has not escaped the al-Qa'ida central leadership or its regional franchises, including AQI.[11] As Ayman al-Zawahiri noted in a letter to Abu Mus'ab al-Zarqawi in July 2005,

> More than half of this battle is taking place in the battlefield of the media. We are in a media battle in a race for the hearts and minds of Muslims.[12]

A scan of Salafi-jihadist Internet forums, particularly the al-Boraq online forum dedicated to AQI's self-declared "Islamic State of Iraq" (ISI),[13] reveals the level of attention AQI accords its ideological outreach in the form of detailed treatises addressing the *Umma* [Islamic nation] and conveying AQI's version of events.[14] For some time in 2005, AQI's own online magazine—*Zurwat al-Sanam* [*Tip of the Camel's Hump*]— was distributed over the forums, boasting a collection of rallying cries, success stories, ideological treatises, and vitriolic attacks against the coalition (Rageh, 2005). In early 2007, in an apparent communication strategy designed to trump the recently announced U.S. surge, ISI declared the initiation of the *Karama* [Dignity] Plan within its terri-

---

[11] Increasingly, al-Qa'ida central, composed largely of the movement's original leadership and headed by bin Laden and al-Zawahiri, is distinguished from al-Qa'ida "franchise" operations established in many places by field commanders.

[12] U.S. forces intercepted the letter.

[13] ISI was declared in October 2006 by AQI's "legal" entity, the Mujahidin Shura Council. This nominal state allegedly comprised Baghdad, Anbar, Salah al-Din, Ninawa, Kirkuk, Diyala, and parts of Babil.

[14] The hard-core, password-protected *al-Ekhlaas* and *al-Hesbah* online forums, among others, broadcast AQI publicity, but were suspended during 2008, apparently because of hacking.

tories. Essentially, the plan consisted of nothing more than attributing ongoing attacks to a coordinated strategic program with a high-profile title. Since then, reports of the Karama Plan's *Hissad* [Harvest of Successful Operations], as the AQI/ISI refers to them, have been faithfully disseminated by the AQI-endorsed media outlet, *al-Furqan*, over the forums.

And yet, despite the premium placed on the strategic communications campaign, the Salafi-jihadist camp itself assesses its media operation as an area of vulnerability. In view of the limited access of the Arab world in general to the Internet,[15] the investments jihadi forum participants have made may not be paying satisfactory dividends. Links between Internet usage and radicalization have been established but are insufficiently understood, and the Internet appears to have had a limited role within Middle East countries in motivating foreign volunteerism in Iraq. Using evidence from the Sinjar records, a collection of profiles of over 600 foreign fighters who entered Iraq via the Syrian border between August 2006 and August 2007 (Felter and Fishman, 2007; Fishman et al., 2008), Clinton Watts (2008) states that,

> Although the Sinjar records do not explain how young men are radicalized, they do eliminate the Internet as a major factor for three reasons. First, Sinjar recruits rarely mention utilizing the Internet to reach Iraq. Second, many North African and Middle Eastern countries have limited access to the Internet. Third, most North African and Middle Eastern countries producing large numbers of foreign fighters access militant Web sites with less frequency than Western countries that produce far fewer foreign fighters.

He further points out that only 3.4 percent of those who gave details on how they had made contact with their coordinators had done so via the Internet. The vulnerabilities of al-Qa'ida's own strategic communications campaign are compounded by unfavorable portrayals of

---

[15] United Nations Conference on Trade and Development, 2007, pp. 25–26, considers Internet use in the Arab world.

AQI's conduct in Iraq by both the Western and pan-Arab media, where al-Qa'ida really needs to make inroads. A September 2007 ISI statement bemoaned this fact (al-Furqan Foundation, 2003):

> Let us discuss the deceitful crusader media that spreads its lies and hides its losses. It is clear, dear brothers, that the various media outlets of today are controlled by America—thus, matters that are pro-American are broadcast, while all other matters are kept hidden.

And while the West harbors deep suspicions toward the pan-Arab channel Al Jazeera and to a lesser extent, Al Arabiya, so do Salafi-jihadists. While Al Jazeera is famed for being the first to air bin Laden audiotapes, its stance on AQI is also much maligned among al-Qa'ida affiliates, who accuse it of being a secret tool of the U.S. administration. In September 2007, al-Fajr Media Center produced a tract for the mujahidin, in which it noted,

> We have seen how Al Jazeera did manipulate the speech of our Sheikh Osama bin Ladin . . . . Al Jazeera directors have shamefully chosen to back the crusaders' side, and the defenders of hypocrites and the thugs and traitors of Iraq.

Similarly, in November 2008, an Iraq-centric jihadi Internet media outfit, Ansar Media Group, produced a video attacking Al Arabiya, Al Jazeera, and the U.S.-funded al-Hurra channels for their "distorted" anti-jihadi slant, drawing particular attention to Al Arabiya's high-profile "Death Industry" series on militant Islam (Ansar Media Group, 2008).

Al-Qa'ida in Iraq's Violent Tactics Have Alienated Muslim Publics

AQI has pursued a calculated policy of publicizing its brutal tactics within Iraq, but this is proving a double-edged sword for the al-Qa'ida movement as a whole, which faces a basic tension between the need to recruit radicals and the need to prevent a mainstream public backlash against it. If the psychological effects of its graphic portrayals of violence enhance al-Qa'ida's fearsome reputation and appeal to radicals, its execution policies, targeting of Muslim civilians manifestly uncon-nected to the "occupation," and inability to cooperate with nationalist resistance groups in Iraq have cost it mainstream Muslim public sym-pathy.

On the whole, regional polls reinforce the theory that public sup-port for al-Qa'ida has fallen in inverse relationship to the movement's use of horrific tactics in Iraq and elsewhere. A 2005 Pew Survey that polled views on Islamic extremism in the Muslim world found that, in Lebanon, support for suicide bombings "often or sometimes" had fallen from 73 percent in summer 2002 to 39 percent,[16] and in Morocco, support fell from 40 percent in 2004 to 13 percent (Pew, 2005). Con-versely, in Jordan, support rose from 43 percent in 2002 to 57 percent in 2005, and while confidence in Osama bin Laden fell noticeably in most Arab countries between 2002 and 2005, support rose in Jordan from 55 percent to 60 percent. But on November 9, 2005, a triple suicide bomb attack staged by Abu Mus'ab al-Zarqawi, then leader of AQI, targeted three hotels in Amman, killing 59 people, the majority of whom were Jordanian. Two years later, support for bin Laden had dropped to 20 percent (U.S. Department of State, 2007).

A decrease in mainstream public support for the use of terrorist tactics does not necessarily reflect a recruitment drought for the ranks of terrorist groups: Revulsion toward terrorism often occurs in commu-nities that are falling victim to it, even if they had previously applauded it from afar.[17] Even so, the loss of a base of public support facilitates local regimes in striking Salafi-jihadist movements with an iron fist. Among Iraq's neighbors, this backlash, coupled with the inhospitality that existing nationalist opposition movements have shown the move-ment, has weakened the credibility of al-Qa'ida's key ideological mes-sages and, in turn, further eroded the movement's perceived legitimacy.

---

[16] This may have been more closely connected to the assassination of Rafiq Hariri in Febru-ary 2005 than to the Iraq War.

[17] Illustrating this, a poll the Terror Free Tomorrow organization conducted in late 2007 indicated that, in Saudi Arabia, 40 percent of respondents had a favorable view of the United States (the highest of any Arab country), and only 10 percent had a favorable view of al-Qa'ida. This reflects that Saudi Arabia has been one of the hardest hit in terms of Salafi-jihadist attacks with traceable connections to Iraq.

Al-Qa'ida's Experience in Iraq Has Exposed Its Ideology and Strategy

Scholars debate the salience of ideology in terrorism, but its priority among al-Qa'ida's higher echelons is demonstrated by a major post-Iraq treatise, "Iraqi Jihad, Hopes and Risks: Analysis of the Reality and Visions for the Future, and Actual Steps in the Path of the Blessed Jihad."[18] That document is a follow-up to a seminal text by a major Saudi-born al-Qa'ida strategist, Yusuf al-Ayiri, titled "The Future of Iraq and the Arabian Peninsula After the Fall of Baghdad," which states that

> a jihadist group that does not hold a clear ideology or a legitimate, intellectual, and practical perspective is always exposed to division, penetration, and is threatened with extinction. At one stage, it will become unable to maintain its achievements, let alone win new members. (al-Ayiri, 2003)[19]

Although connected, the operational successes of al-Qa'ida and associated Salafi-jihadist groups are distinct from the organization's ideological strength as a coherent movement. While many of the movement's own members may not grasp the finer details of its ideological core, that ideology remains a central unifying factor and simultaneously legitimizes al-Qa'ida's existence in the greater Muslim world as something more than a purely anarchistic collection of terrorists. Operational conditions and the need for strategic flexibility have always influenced al-Qa'ida's portrayal of its ideology, but in Iraq, the movement's targeting of Shi'a, refusal to cooperate with nonaligned nationalist resistance groups, and rhetorical focus on prioritizing new fronts have stretched its ideology to the breaking point.[20]

---

[18] Written by The Media Commission for the Victory of the Iraqi People (The Mujahidin Services Center), 2003.

[19] For further details, see Paz, 2004b. al-Ayiri was killed by Saudi authorities in June 2003.

[20] Hegghammer, 2006, highlighted some of the debates that had already become apparent within Salafi discourse as a result of Iraq. Notably, Iraq had been identified as the most important front for jihad, and this had diverted attention away from other fronts; the use of

The ideological underpinnings of al-Qa'ida are grounded in Salafi tenets that include the restoration of the legendary Islamic Caliphate; *jihad* [struggle], which, according to Salafism, is violent; *takfir* [excommunication], which by extension also means the killing of Muslims who do not adhere to the Salafi vision of Islam; and *al-wala' wa-l-bara'* [loyalty and disavowal], which by extension requires *wahdat al-suf* [unity of the ranks among the faithful]. Strategically, al-Qa'ida has traditionally aimed to pursue these goals by initially targeting the "far enemy" (i.e., the West) in preference to the "near enemy" (secular or corrupt Arab regimes); by rejecting nationalist interests and denouncing political participation; and by focusing on a tight-knit structure headed by key ideologues. But in bringing the global jihad to the Arab heartlands, the Iraq conflict has in some cases forced it to change strategy and in other cases has exposed the counterproductive nature of its doctrinaire behavior. By acting as a principal protagonist in a "Muslim on Muslim" civil war, al-Qa'ida has emphasized a focus on the near enemy—"collaborationist" Shi'a, Sunni tribes allied with the coalition, and neighboring lands. By refusing absolutely to engage in the political process, the movement has alienated nationalist Sunni resistance groups. Equally, though, AQI's role in Iraq has allowed battlefield jihadi leaders to rise to the fore at the expense of the core leadership of al-Qa'ida central—for whom ideology is the legitimizing trumpet.

The blow dealt to the credibility of al-Qa'ida's key ideological tenets plays out not only in Iraq, but in neighboring countries where al-Qa'ida's aspirations to open new fronts for jihad are also being undermined. Symbolically, Iran and Palestine are perhaps the most important of these fronts, and in both countries, al-Qa'ida's options are limited.

Al-Qa'ida's Demonization of Iran and the Shi'a World Is Backfiring

The sustained presence of coalition armies in an unstable Arab country enabled al-Qa'ida to capitalize on the charged theme of an infidel invasion, in addition to providing a geographical territory accessible to

---

brutal tactics and the targeting of Shi'a played badly in the public relations campaign; and strategic studies were becoming increasingly important in Salafi-jihadist thought.

volunteer foreign fighters. But this apparently ideal scenario has created unrealistic expectations among al-Qaʻida's followers about the movement's capabilities, and its long-standing rhetorical refrain that Iraq will serve as a springboard for attacks against neighboring countries has precipitated the expectation of full-scale jihad in Arab lands as opposed to periodic attacks on Western interests. Similarly, al-Qaʻida's traditional insistence that the greater enemy is the foreign entity has become difficult to maintain when the vast majority of victims of al-Qaʻida's attacks are Iraqis. This is forcing the movement to adopt a different posture toward identifying its enemies internally and externally.

Where al-Qaʻida central prioritized the far enemy, the former AQI leader Abu Musʻab al-Zarqawi deliberately focused on the near enemy; one of his strategies was to play on the minority status and fears of the Iraqi Sunni population to stir up sectarian warfare against the Shiʻa majority.[21] This shift in al-Qaʻida's targets introduced the theologically murky questions of targeting Muslims, and civilians at that, as legitimate subjects of *takfir*. The bombing of the Hadi al-ʻAskari mosque in Samarra in February 2006 was a point of no return. Al-Zarqawi justified these tactics theologically by citing the 13th-century Salafi authority Ibn Taymiya, who affirmed that the Shiʻa consistently betrayed the Arab Muslim nation to invaders throughout history, and strategically, by arguing that "If we succeed in dragging them into the arena of sectarian war, it will become possible to awaken the inattentive Sunnis as they feel imminent danger."[22]

Justifications for targeting Shiʻa within Iraq have been matched by genuine fears about Iran's expansionist plans, which appear all the more realistic in the light of Iranian political, cultural, and religious influence in Iraq. Within Salafi-jihadist Web forums, some maintain that Iran has become an even greater threat than America,[23] but periodic suggestions that the mujahidin should temporarily pair with either America or Iran to defeat the other side have met with no consensus. The "Safavids" are a more problematic enemy than the "Crusaders" and

---

[21] Fishman, 2006, explores the dynamics of this strategy.

[22] Text from al-Zarqawi letter to bin Laden, 2004.

[23] See, for instance, a SITE-translated forum posting, "al-Sabeel5," 2008.

"Zionists"; their Muslim status complicates attempts to vilify them, as does their backing of Hizballah, possibly the organization with the greatest pan-Islamic appeal in the Arab world.[24] Nonetheless, in December 2007, Ayman al-Zawahiri responded to a question on why al-Qaʿida would not unite with Iran to defeat the United States, saying,

> we used to concentrate on confronting the American-led Zionist-Crusader alliance in its contemporary crusade against the Muslim *Umma*. But all of a sudden we discovered Iran collaborating with America in its invasions of Afghanistan and Iraq. (al-Sahab Media, 2007)

By contrast, in March 2008, the prominent Kuwaiti Salafi-jihadist cleric Hamid al-ʿAli, for whom verbal attacks on Iran are a frequent occupation, insisted that, with respect to the Arabian Gulf,

> The true contest is between the American project and the Iranian project. The weak and disintegrated Gulf States are nothing more than a stage for this contest. (al-ʿAli, 2008)[25]

The lurch toward anti-Iranian rhetoric is not purely a result of Iraq and is not solely cultivated by al-Qaʿida. Rather, it plays into the greater debate over Shiʿa ascendancy in the region (discussed in Chapter Two). The popularity of HAMAS and Hizballah, two Iranian-backed clients, has stoked Salafi, especially Saudi, fears that Iran and Shiʿism have usurped the mantle of anti-Western and anti-Israeli resistance—traditionally the purview of Sunni Arab states.

However, sectarian warfare in Iraq, exacerbated by al-Zarqawi's anti-Shiʿa strategy, has pushed anti-Shiʿism to the forefront of ideological rhetoric in al-Qaʿida and the wider Salafi-jihadist community. In August 2007, Shiʿa media outlets erupted with indignation after reports that influential Saudi Salafi scholars had issued fatwas

---

[24] *Safavids* is a pejorative term for Iranians, referring to the expansionist dynasty that ruled Iran from 1502 to 1722 AD.

[25] Hamid al-ʿAli espouses the Salafi-jihadist doctrine but is not directly connected to the al-Qaʿida movement and remains critical of the movement's pursuit of ISI.

sanctioning the destruction of Shiʻa shrines in the aftermath of the al-'Askari mosque bombing in Samarra, Iraq.[26] In Jordan, an article by Sayf al-Din al-Zubaydi condemns the Jordanian government's tolerance of the Iraqi Shiʻa migration from Iraq into Jordan, warning that Sunnis in Jordan could face the same fate as their brothers in Iraq at the hands of the Shiʻa (al-Zubaydi, undated).

Despite this inflammatory rhetoric, the operational reality is that Iran is no easy target for al-Qaʻida, and so far, the anti-Shiʻa shift remains more evident in word than in deed. There are indications that al-Zarqawi had considered how best to target Iran. However, a document allegedly discovered at the emir's hideout after his death in 2006, which discussed ways of igniting a war between the United States and Iran, suggests that he recognized the impracticality of al-Qaʻida directly infiltrating Iran from abroad (Yacoub, 2006). In April 2008, a local jihadi group—"The Jihadi Movement of the Sunni People in Iran"—claimed the bombing of the Rahpuyan-e Vessal religious center in Shiraz in southern Iran was in retaliation for what they cited as the Iranian government's torture and execution of two Sunni scholars.[27] Further attacks undertaken by al-Qaʻida affiliates against Iran were announced on the al-Minbar forum in May 2008.

On the whole, however, Salafi-jihadist attacks on Iran and indeed the wider Shiʻa community in the region remain conspicuous in their absence.[28] In fact, many suspect that al-Qaʻida's central leadership regards Iran as a short-term ally, as well as a long-term enemy. Up to 30 senior al-Qaʻida figures, including Saʻad bin Laden, have spent the past 6 years in Iran, supposedly under house arrest, but sheltered from the reach of U.S. counterterrorist operations (Miller, 2009).

Rhetorical hostility toward Iran and the Shiʻa may win al-Qaʻida converts in areas where Sunnis have preexisting grievances against Shiʻa communities (and this is what the movement has been trying to achieve in Lebanon and Saudi Arabia) but seems unlikely to raise its

---

[26] "Fatwas in Saudi Arabia . . . ," 2007.

[27] "Sunni Iranian Jihadist Groups . . . ," undated.

[28] Al-Qaʻida's rivals in Iraq, and particularly the Army of Islam, often taunt al-Qaʻida for not targeting Iran.

profile as a champion of pan-Islamic causes in the region as a whole. As long as Hizballah and HAMAS continue to be perceived as the most effective (and territorially based) anti-Zionist bulwarks, al-Qaʻidaʼs outspoken hostility toward these movements will limit the extent of its appeal among the broader Muslim public. At the same time, the mismatch between the movementʼs stated intentions toward Iran and the Shiʻa and its actions, or inactions, is frustrating its supporters.[29]

Al-Qaʻida Is Losing the Battle Between Nationalist and Transnationalist Agendas

Al-Qaʻidaʼs difficulties in competing with Hizballah and HAMAS spring not only from a sectarian or political basis but also from the fact that latter groups are territorially based and have an established nationalist agenda. Al-Qaʻidaʼs transnational agenda is its indefatigable pursuit of an Islamic Caliphate. That ideal that appeals to many foreign volunteers but dictates a doctrinal inflexibility that refuses absolutely to engage in any nationalist agenda. In some places, al-Qaʻida has successfully forged a partnership with existing domestic Islamic groups; in others, it has procured the *baya* [oath of allegiance] from them. Such partnerships are, however, only liable to last so long as domestic groups perceive the realization of their nationalist goals to be impossible. Where this is no longer the case, a rift is likely to spring up between those with nationalist interests and those rather more interested in perpetuating jihad ad infinitum, pursuing the ephemeral end-state of caliphate.[30]

In Iraq, this is precisely what has happened. In 2003, foreign volunteers entering Iraq under the banner of al-Qaʻida allied themselves with existing Sunni resistance groups and tribes in the Sunni

---

[29] This frustration is amply demonstrated by questions al-Qaʻida leaders receive from participants in extremist Salafi-jihadist Web forums. In March 2008, for instance, when Ayman al-Zawahiri invited forum participants to submit questions to him, a great number of those posed related to al-Qaʻidaʼs failure to act against Iran (al-Zawahiri, 2007).

[30] In February 2008, in a surprising affirmation of nationalism that enraged al-Qaʻida supporters, the Taliban leader Mullah ʻOmar, al-Qaʻidaʼs closest ally outside of Iraq, reportedly declared that the Taliban sought positive and "legitimate" relations with all neighboring states. See Schemm, 2008.

Triangle. Over time, these alliances deteriorated to the point that the Islamic Army in Iraq and allied forces of the Jihad and Reform Front affirmed their firmly nationalist credentials and started to attack foreign al-Qaʻida fighters.[31]

The proclaimed U.S. breakthrough came with the establishment of the first of many Awakening Councils in Anbar with the objective of encouraging tribes in Ramadi, which had previously allied themselves with al-Qaʻida in fighting the coalition, to eject foreign fighters. Conscious of the upsurge of infighting among Sunni resistance groups, Ayman al-Zawahiri told the al-Sahab Media foundation in December 2007 that his most important piece of advice to the mujahidin in Iraq was "unity around *tawhid* [Islamic monotheism]" and backing for ISI. *Wahdat al-suf* [unity] has been a common refrain for AQI, but al-Zawahiri was probably in fact aware that many of the Iraqi mujahidin to whom he appealed had never been committed to al-Qaʻida's vision of *tawhid* and had joined forces only until their interests in Iraq diverged (al-Zawahiri, 2007).

The length and intensity of the conflict in Iraq have reinforced the national-transnational rift. While that rift may not have hitherto become so apparent in other countries, al-Qaʻida's loud proclamation that its presence in Iraq heralds the launch of major offensives against neighboring Arab lands suggests that such clashes are more likely to emerge elsewhere in the future.

In Lebanon, rumors abound that al-Qaʻida has tried to exploit preexisting sectarian tensions between Sunnis and Shiʻa rhetorically; most worrying is the rumor that Hariri's Sunni Future Movement sanctioned the creation of the Salafi group Fatah al-Islam as a counterweight to Hizballah to serve as a bargaining chip that might persuade Hizballah to disarm. Fatah al-Islam, which carried out the Nahr al-Barid massacre in May 2007, contained a number of foreign fighters on their way into or out of Iraq. However, a RAND interview with a

---

[31] The Islamic Army in Iraq is one of the largest Iraqi nationalist resistance groups. In mid-2007, it joined with the Jaysh al-Mujahidin and the Shariʻa Commission of Ansar al-Sunna to form the Jihad and Reform Front. The front opposes the coalition, Iraqi government, and al-Qaʻida. It favors the imposition of Shariʻa law in Iraq, but opposes al-Qaʻida's ISI and its severe interpretation of *takfir* against fellow Muslims.

prominent Lebanese Salafi representative revealed that most preexisting Salafis had been co-opted into the Future Movement and did not employ the language of *takfir* or *taghut* [tyrant] against the government.[32] The same interviewee also speculated that Fatah al-Islam was a mere fringe refugee group that enjoyed little to no backing in the larger Salafi community in Tripoli, Sidon, Kuba, Bekaa, and elsewhere.

In Palestine, where al-Qaʻida comes face to face with HAMAS, its long term prospects are bleaker still. Al-Qaʻida's leadership has undermined its chances for a partnership with HAMAS in Gaza by issuing blazing condemnations of the party for its sellout to the political process and its signature on the Mecca Agreement, which bound it and Fatah to a national unity government in February 2007. In March 2007, al-Zawahiri claimed that "nobody, be he Palestinian or not, has the right to relinquish a grain of Palestinian soil" (Ulph, 2006b). Then, in February 2008, in an ironic twist to the nationlist-transnationalist debate and a strategic misstep for al-Qaʻida, the putative (and probably fictional) leader of ISI—Abu ʻUmar al-Qurayshi al-Baghdadi—exhorted the mujahidin to take the fight to Palestine (al-Baghdadi, 2008a). In the light of accusations that AQI comprised foreigners with no interest in the fate of the Iraqi people, al-Baghdadi, with his consummately Iraqi Sunni name, had represented a bid to give the movement an Iraqi face. Instead, he took the opportunity to lay a claim on Palestine.

Palestine as al-Qa'ida's Misguided New Raison d'Être

Since early 2007, as al-Qaʻida's former Sunni allies in Iraq turned against it and as its fortunes there became increasingly uncertain, the movement has built up its rhetorical focus on Palestine. On May 16, an audiotape was released of Osama bin Laden addressing the West and claiming, as he had never done before, that Palestine was "the main root of the Conflict between Our Civilization and Your Civilization" (bin Laden, 2008). Two days later, he exhorted Islamic audiences to

---

[32] Interview with a prominent Lebanese Salafi representative, Tripoli, February 28, 2008. *Taghut* is used frequently in Salafi-jihadist terminology to refer to the oppressive rulers of Arab countries.

liberate Palestine through Jihad against the Zionists and crusaders, and called on the Muslim youth to be on hand in the arenas of jihad near Palestine, ready to fight the governments and forces that prevented them from getting to the Jews (bin Laden, 2008). The narrative of this appeal was compelling and universal: Palestine as the ultimate front for jihad; the symbolic land epitomizing Western and Zionist oppression of the Islamic Umma.

Bin Laden's call followed a January text by a well-known Web ideologue, Assad al-Jihad2, "The Timing of the Entrance of the Al-Qa'ida Organization to Palestine" (Global Islamic Media Front, 2008), which half appeased and half spurred on the growing impatience of Salafi Web forum participants about launching the campaign in Palestine. In it, Assad al-Jihad2 announced that al-Qa'ida had reached the third of four phases in its "plan," scheduled to last from 2007 until 2010, which included the objective of completing al-Qa'ida's preparations for direct confrontation with the Jews in occupied Palestine. Iraq, he suggested, was the base for launching future attacks, and he asserted that "Undoubtedly, Palestine will be the main destination of Al-Qaida."

In February 2008, in the tract "Religion Is a Sincere Advice," ISI leader al-Baghdadi suggested that ISI's purpose was to fight for the liberation of Palestine, and concluded that

> We are willing to help you with the little money we have, and to train your fighters [in everything], from preparing explosive charges to manufacturing rockets. (al-Baghdadi 2008a)

In reality, as previously discussed, Palestine presents limited opportunities for the movement. While some Palestinian and Egyptian intelligence suggests that the Rafah border breach in January 2008 occasioned an influx of hundreds or thousands of foreign jihadi fighters into Gaza to join the offensive against Israel, in general, tight security around the occupied territories makes infiltration very difficult.[33]

---

[33] Egyptian security authorities estimated that 2,000 people had infiltrated Gaza via the Rafah border crossing with Egypt during the January 2008 border breach, some of whom were suspected to have gone to join the jihad against Israel. See "al-Mukhabarat al-Misriya . . . ," 2008, and di Giovannangeli, 2008.

Internal Salafi-jihadist groups in Gaza have made partially successful attempts to garner endorsement from al-Qaʿida central so that they might represent the al-Qaʿida franchise for Palestine. However, these efforts have been marred by accusations within the Salafi community that they represent little more than criminal gangs or splinter groups that have fallen out with either HAMAS or the Fatah command. HAMAS's intolerance of what it clearly sees as upstart Salafi-jihadist "pretender" groups in Gaza has become patently obvious since late 2008. In September 2008, HAMAS security forces conducted a violent raid on the headquarters of the largest Palestinian Salafi-jihadist group, the Army of Islam, eliminating a number of the Daghmash clan who led the group.[34] The following year, a declaration of the creation of an Islamic State of Palestine by Abu Nur al-Maqdisi, ideological leader of the Jund Ansar Allah Salafi-jihadist group, was rapidly met with fierce suppression. In August 2009, HAMAS staged a seven-hour bloody assault on the Ibn Taymiya Mosque in Rafah where al-Maqdisi was preaching, killing scores including the cleric himself (BBC News, 2009).[35]

Condemnation of HAMAS has confused and angered many of al-Qaʿida's former supporters who see the Palestinian group as one of the most successful counters to Zionism, in contrast to al-Qaʿida, which, for all its incendiary speeches, has so far been unable to establish a tangible presence in the area. Most recently, support for HAMAS on the Arab street and, indeed, within Salafi-jihadist echelons during the Israeli war against Gaza has further demonstrated the extent of al-Qaʿida's miscalculation with regard to Palestine, where the movement has been deprived of a rhetorical platform. In the meantime, HAMAS continues to capitalize on the phrase that al-Qaʿida would have liked for itself: "Islam is the solution." Al-Qaʿida has been left to

---

[34] The most notorious achievement of the Army of Islam was its kidnapping of the BBC journalist Alan Johnston in March 2007 ("Demands Issued on Johnston Tape," 2007). Despite its espoused Salafi-jihadist objectives, the Army of Islam was commonly accused within Gaza of being a criminal racket.

[35] "Deadly Gun Battle in Gaza Mosque," 2009.

backpedal by letting the focal point of the Islamic Caliphate slide and refocusing attention on Iraq as the primary theater of jihad.

AQI's Franchise Model Has Arguably Sidelined the Role of Ideology

The preceding paragraphs indicate some of the ideological shifts or stumbling blocks either created or exposed by the jihadi misadventure in Iraq. In the light of the AQI experience, however, the importance of the ideological concerns that elite strategists (whom some jihadis have scathingly referred to as *al-qa'idun* [those who sit]) have advanced has been questioned. Some commentators suggest that these concerns are taking a back seat to operational and tactical imperatives, and that it is better to look more toward the theater or battlefield emirs, Abu Mus'ab al-Zarqawi and Abu Yahya al-Libi, for clues on the jihadi trajectory than toward the grand strategists, such as Abu Bakr Naji and Abu Mus'ab al-Suri. As fighting becomes a reality, rather than simply a cause, practical advice becomes paramount. On the strategic front, some of the seminal texts on Iraq have been written not by the ideologues of al-Qa'ida's leadership but by strategists lower down the command chain.[36]

However, it was the ruthless leadership of the former Jordanian *Takfir wa-l-Hijra* member Abu Mus'ab al-Zarqawi that illustrated the ascendancy of the on-the-ground battlefield emir over the strategists of al-Qa'ida and so-called "armchair jihadists." Seen as al-Qa'ida's most successful franchise, AQI has also proved the most unruly. The establishment of al-Qa'ida franchises is now the easiest way for al-Qa'ida central to diffuse its influence and the call to global jihad, but it is also certain to dilute direct authority. The sense that ideology is subordinating itself to tactics and battlefield charisma echoed elsewhere in responses to the publication of "The Rationalization of Jihad in Egypt and the World" (or simply, "The Revisions"), by former Zawahiri mentor and Egyptian Jihad leader, Sayyid Imam (2007). The self-declared leader of al-Qa'ida in the land of Kinana [Egypt],

---

[36] Al-'Ayiri (2003), an undated tract from the Media Commission for the Victory of the Iraqi People, and such Web strategists as Assad al-Jihad2 have significantly influenced jihadi views on Iraq.

Muhammad Khalil al-Hakaymah, downplayed the import of the Revisions. Sayyid Imam forfeited his religious authority when he broke off his ties with al-Zawahiri in 1993 (Brachman, 2007).

Nonetheless, in the aftermath of al-Zarqawi's death, AQI is thought to be aligning itself more closely with al-Qa'ida central.[37] This could be attributable either to the lack of a charismatic leader or to al-Zarqawi's successor, Abu 'Ayyub al-Masri, having closer links with al-Zawahiri. In a rebuttal to Sageman's (2008) theories on "Leaderless Jihad," Hoffman (2008) argues, with recourse to the 2007 NIE findings (National Intelligence Council, 2007a), that

> The unmistakable message is that al Qaeda is a remarkably agile and flexible organization that exercises both top-down and bottom-up planning and operational capabilities. It is not exclusively focused on the grass-roots dimension that is Leaderless Jihad's sole preoccupation.

It is too soon to say whether a move away from the center represents a long-term trend that will significantly decrease the core leadership's prominence, but it is clear that, in either case, Salafi-jihadist ideologues will be hard pressed to keep up with the pace of change in evolving fronts for jihad. Is al-Qa'ida stronger in the region as a result of Iraq? For those who believe that the movement is primarily a short-term catalyst for terrorist attacks, the answer is, yes, almost certainly. For those who maintain that the movement's success relies on the long-term propagation and fulfillment of fixed ideological objectives, the answer is, definitely not.

Iraq Has Provided Sunni and Shi'a Militants with Tactics, Techniques, and Procedures for Asymmetric Warfare

The Iraq conflict may have had an ambiguous and problematic effect on jihadi recruitment, symbolic discourse, and strategy formulation, but its contribution to terrorists' tactical adaptation has been more explicit.

---

[37] Peter Bergen makes this argument in Chapter 5 of Fishman et al., 2008.

Six years of sustained conflict in Iraq, initially driven by pockets of Sunni resistance and foreign fighters against the coalition and more recently converted into sectarian warfare, have given rise to a proliferation of TTPs. Most of these are not entirely new to the Arab theater: The most common forms of attack—firearms, IEDs, vehicleborne IEDs (VBIEDs), suicide bombings, and kidnapping—appeared during the Lebanese civil war and later in confrontations between HAMAS and Israel. At present, there is as much evidence of trends being transferred into as out of Iraq. Yet the diversity of targets, objectives, and fighting conditions within Iraq has created the environment of a military laboratory: a training ground for combatants and a test-and-development-site for techniques. It is highly probable that these TTPs will spread widely in the future; in certain instances, this is already in evidence.

From an ideological perspective, al-Qa'ida presents the greatest terrorist threat because its global expansionist ambitions and exclusionary Salafi doctrine intrinsically dictate the exportation of its campaign of violence, as foreshadowed in an infamous quote from the putative emir of ISI, Abu 'Umar al-Baghdadi (2008b):

> One of their enemy devils was right in saying that if Afghanistan was the School for Terrorism, then Iraq is the University of Terrorism.

Nonetheless, not all, or even most of the violence in Iraq is instigated by al-Qa'ida; nationalist Sunni-resistance movements, adherents of the former regime, Shi'a militants, and criminal groups all contribute to insecurity on the ground, and all these elements have learned lessons about guerrilla warfare and staging complex attacks. By August 2007, Iranian-backed groups were thought to account for roughly 50 percent of attacks on coalition forces (Kagan, Kagan, and Pletka, 2008), In practical terms, Shi'a militias are increasingly making the most headway with military technology, perfecting ingenious adaptations (the explosively formed projectiles and improvised rocket-assisted mortars [IRAMs]) with the help of a state sponsor.

While Salafi-jihadist and Shi'a militia groups in Iraq employ some of the same strategies and tactics, their objectives differ, and this becomes apparent when considering evidence of a tactical spillover throughout the region. The next section considers some of the novel and most prevalent technologies and tactics in evidence.

Improvised Explosive Devices

While firearms remain the most prevalent form of attack in Iraq, IEDs have been the most lethal weapon among both Sunni and Shi'a militants. Both sides use roadside IEDs, triggered by a remote control device or mobile phones, to target coalition forces, but Sunni groups use VBIEDs and suicide VBIEDs more commonly to target coalition and Iraqi forces, as well as civilians. Between March 2003 and November 2008, 40.4 percent of U.S. forces personnel killed in Iraq (1,700) were killed by IEDs.[38]

IEDs can be cobbled together in the backyard with household chemicals or forged in factories in Iran. Insurgents have developed their use of IEDs considerably, progressing from relatively basic pressure-detonation models based on U.S. manuals to shaped charges and sophisticated models impervious to U.S. electronic jamming systems. They have equally learned to combine low-grade and more-sophisticated IEDs (Cordesman, 2005) and have improved their targeting by predicting popular enemy transport routes and by hiding roadside bombs so that they are virtually undetectable, to the extreme of concreting over planted IEDs.

Indirect Fire

Shi'a militants in Iraq have been the most lethally proficient in using indirect fire against coalition forces. In the summer of 2007, British forces in the remaining Basra city bases were subjected to months of sustained indirect fire in the form of mortars and rockets from Jaysh al-Mahdi–affiliated groups. In March 2008, rockets fired on the International Zone in Baghdad as part of a sustained attack displayed pictures of the Hizballah commander Imad Mughniya assassinated in

---

[38] As a measure of comparison, during the second Palestinian intifada, 147 suicide bombs and three roadside bombs were recorded in over five years. In Iraq, 75 suicide bombers; 550 suicide car bombs; 1,300 car bombs; and 16,500 roadside bombs were recorded in nearly three years (Eisenstadt, 2006).

Damascus a month before, clearly pointing to the affiliations of the assailants.

A recent technological development used around Baghdad is the IRAM, a multiple-launch rocket system. While it is not clear that Iran is directly providing IRAMs to Shi'a militias, the sources of expertise required to adapt IRAMs are limited. As the principle external provider of technology for IEDs (including shaped charges), rockets, and mortars, Iran is the main suspect. Shi'a militias are the main beneficiaries, although there are indications that Sunni insurgent groups also acquire equipment from Iran.[39] Shi'a militants have been discovered holding C-4 explosives with labels allegedly identifying them as Iranian military. In February 2007, U.S. military officers asserted they had evidence that Iran had supplied armor-piercing, explosively formed projectiles to Shi'a militias. In August 2007, a U.S. general reported that Iran had supplied Shi'a militias with 122-mm mortars they used to fire on the Green Zone in Baghdad.[40]

Since the IRGC-Quds Force is the principal source of the expertise and technologies for Shi'a militants, the dispersal to and migration of TTPs among Shi'a groups outside Iraq is likely to be more disciplined and regulated than they are with Sunni jihadists. The IRGC-Quds Force has a history of attempting to calibrate the distribution of highly lethal technology to Shi'a groups based on its reading of their reliability, controllability, and Tehran's calculus of the risks and gains. Iran's own Basij units, Hizballah in Lebanon, and HAMAS in Palestine will likely be the main beneficiaries of IED and IRAM technology refined in Iraq. Nonetheless, Iran may be focusing increasingly on enforcing targeting discipline among its militant allies after the mid-2008 anti-Iranian backlash in Iraq that was due to the popular Iraqi perception that the Quds Force was inciting intra-Iraqi conflict by providing lethal aid to Shi'a groups.

---

[39] Kagan, 2007, names Ansar al-Sunna as one of them.

[40] Maj Gen Richard Zahner, September 2006, quoted in Katzman, 2007.

Snipers

The use of snipers has become prevalent among insurgent groups, particularly AQI and the nationalist Sunni Islamic Army, which have capitalized on the strategic communications potential of producing hundreds of videos recording sniper attacks on coalition forces for dissemination among extremist forums and, eventually, on YouTube.[41] According to Multi-National Force–Iraq data, there were 386 sniper attacks on coalition forces in 2006 (Vandenbrook, 2007). Insurgents have learned to wait until entire U.S. convoys have passed through a zone to fire on the last vehicle so that the rest of the convoy will not be aware for some time of the contact. In the early days, the development of signals and communications for sniper tactical operations, the acquisition of new rifles, antiarmor ammunition, and body armor from outside of Iraq suggested support from Islamist extremists outside Iraq. Lately, the snipers have developed their own techniques, which include hiding in vehicles and firing through a small hole cut into the trunk of the vehicle (Cockburn and Taylor, 2006).

Foreign Volunteerism and Suicide Bombing

In the early years of the Iraq War, foreign volunteers sustained one of the most shocking tactics among Salafi-jihadis: suicide bombing. Muhammad Hafez concluded, on the basis of 2005 data, that only 10 percent of all insurgent fighters in Iraq were foreign, but that foreigners comprise 90 percent of suicide bombers (Freedberg, 2007). According to figures from the Washington Institute for Near East Policy on attacks undertaken between April 2003 and March 2007, suicide bombing as a proportion of total attacks rose from 2.4 percent in 2003 to 8.2 percent in 2007, peaking in 2005 with 9.5 percent.

Suicide attacks are by no means new to the Middle Eastern–Islamic scene; Islam forbids suicide, but proponents of the practice portray it as martyrdom, a venerable practice, and cite early Islamic precedents. The cult of martyrdom has traditionally been the preserve of

---

[41] In January 2009, ISI released a video entitled "The Power of Sniping" which discussed the effectiveness of sniping compared to suicide bombing. Subsequently, detailed instructions on shooting were issued on forums. See "Al-Qanasa wa Assas . . . ," 2009.

the Shi'a but has become more widely practiced by Sunnis, particularly HAMAS. The difference is that, in Iraq, the vast majority of suicide volunteers are foreigners, willing to sacrifice themselves in the name of jihad rather than their concept of the nation.

Trends in suicide bombing have already been rising outside Iraq, particularly in Afghanistan, North Africa, and Yemen, but martyrs cannot propagate jihadi cells elsewhere—this can only be done by seasoned fighters. Al-Qa'ida propaganda has unabashedly petitioned for weapon experts and military engineers, as well as those with media and managerial skills.[42] To this end, it must tap into pools of expertise. Hafez describes how four preexisting Salafi-jihadist networks were vital for the growth of volunteerism in Iraq (Hafez, 2007, p. 166): the Jordanian network associated with al-Zarqa and Salt; Saudi and Kuwaiti networks associated with al-Qa'ida in the Arabian Peninsula; Syrian and Lebanese networks associated with Salafis in Hums, Dayr al-Zayr, and al-Ladhikiyah; the Ayn al-Hilwa refugee camp and Majdal Anjar in Lebanon; and European networks led by North African dissidents from Morocco and Algeria. All four networks have direct links to the second generation of jihadists trained in Afghanistan and Pakistan in the 1990s. This gives us a picture of how the military expertise foreign volunteers have demonstrated in Iraq is itself a product of another military laboratory—Afghanistan.

Recruiting Women and Children

In an open question-and-answer session in 2008, Ayman al-Zawahiri told a questioner that al-Qa'ida has no female members.[43] Nonetheless, women are good candidates for suicide bombings because they can act without arousing suspicion. Iraq has seen a rising trend in the use of women as suicide bombers by Salafi-jihadist groups. This began in 2005, when Abu Mus'ab al-Zarqawi announced the death of the first woman and was closely followed by an attempt by Sajida al-Rishawi,

---

[42] See, for example, Bakier, 2008.

[43] Al-Zawahiri, "Selected Questions and Answers . . . ," 2008.

who was also involved in the Amman bombings.[44] According to a researcher in Islamist Groups, Hasan Abu-Hamiya, speaking on Al Arabiya, an estimated 11 suicide attacks were committed by women in 2005 and 2006, in comparison to 12 attacks in the first three months of 2008. Children are also recruited. Between January 2007 and May 2008, al-Qaʻida is thought to have used six children to carry out major operations.[45] In February 2008, Al Arabiya aired a video that showed footage of an al-Qaʻida training camp for children under 13.[46] In May, Iraqi soldiers rounded up six youths in Mosul who were being forcibly trained as suicide bombers.[47]

Targeting Economic Assets

Targeting a fragile state's infrastructure to prevent the provision of basic services is a mainstay tactic of civil war, used to great effect by Sunni and Shiʻa insurgents. As the main potential source of income, oil facilities and pipelines are the favorite target in Iraq, but power and water facilities have also been targeted. In southern Iraq, the main Shiʻa political groupings—the Sadrists, the Islamic Supreme Council of Iraq,[48] and the Jamiʻat al-Fadhila—have all exploited their political leverage to siphon off oil revenues. As a jihadi strategy, however, economic sabotage is relatively new. In December 2004, a day after Osama bin Laden had exhorted his followers to sabotage the West's key supplies, there were five attacks on the Iraqi oil infrastructure in Sunni areas of northern Iraq, one of which was claimed by al-Qaʻida in Mesopotamia (Kabbara, 2004).

---

[44] Additionally, the Iraqi government claimed that the two women who triggered the explosions on February 1, 2008, in Baghdad that killed 98 people and injured 200 were mentally handicapped, although this claim was later questioned. ("Iraqi Security . . . ," 2008.)

[45] Al Arabiya's Panorama program on May 7, 2008, presented by Maryam al-Rayyis, discussed Iraqi women suicide bombers.

[46] "Al-Qaʻida Video . . . ," 2008.

[47] "Officials: Teens Trained . . . ," 2008.

[48] Until 2007, this organization was known as the Supreme Council for Islamic Revolution in Iraq. The name change was intended to reflect new political circumstances.

Kidnapping, Torture, and Assassinations

With the development of intersectarian strife, both Sunni and Shi'a have resorted to kidnapping, torturing, and assassinating members of the other sect, particularly high-profile personalities. For al-Qa'ida–affiliated groups, the kidnapping and assassination of Westerners is a policy calculated to shock the outside world, in an attempt to drive an unbridgeable wedge between Salafi Islam and Western values. They do not court negotiation or financial incentives from the coalition.

By comparison, Shi'a militias have kidnapped relatively few foreign nationals. For the main part, Sunnis and, indeed, other unfortunate Shi'a are the targets of the Shi'a militia. The Badr Corps carried out a notorious program of hunting down and assassinating ex-Ba'athists (Sunni and Shi'a), while Jaysh al-Mahdi has used kidnapping as a mainstay for revenue by demanding ransom for the return of captives.

Strategic Communications

If al-Qa'ida and other Salafi-jihadist groups have not garnered the level of public support they might have wished for through mass messaging, they have nevertheless gained unique expertise in Iraq by employing strategic communications to amplify the tactics described above, some of which are only effective because they are publicized. As practitioners of asymmetric warfare, Salafi-jihadis rely more heavily on the psychological effects of media attention to sow fear than on the actual damage they inflicted on the enemy. A jihadi website ran an article by 'Abd al-Rahman al-Faqir (2008) on the "The Real War and the Symbolic War," in which he stated:

> The war conducted by the mujahidin today is more a symbolic war than it is an actual war. In the symbolic war, we seek to give an appearance of force more than we seek to acquire that force and that is the practice with most guerrilla warfare or non-governmental wars.

Among Sunni groups, al-Qa'ida has run by far the most high-profile propaganda campaign. Media manipulation comprises propaganda by insurgents for outside audiences; communicating new techniques and weapon construction manuals to other members over the

Internet; and exploiting the relative transparency of international media coverage of Iraq. Insurgents have rapidly learned to procure video footage of their attacks; a U.S. army officer recounted how, in 2003, within moments of coming under IED attack, his convoy was surrounded by a camera team disguised as press who came to film the aftermath of the attack (Freedberg, 2007). Insurgents have also prolifically produced tips on how to maintain good operational security; conduct successful kidnappings and assassinations; manufacture IEDs, mortars, and rockets; and what equipment to bring to Iraq.

The Greatest Effects on Terrorism May Be Felt After the Conflict, and Outside of the Region

The Impact of Volunteers from Iraq Is Lower Than Anticipated

At a Senate hearing in February 2008, Director of National Intelligence Mike McConnell discussed his fears that al-Qaʻida would shift its focus to attacks outside of Iraq but added that fewer than 100 al-Qaʻida terrorists have moved from Iraq to establish cells in other countries (Hess, 2008).

While we do know that the number of foreign fighters going into Iraq has fallen dramatically,[49] it is harder to gauge their rate of return. Given what is known about the top nationalities of volunteers and assuming that some will survive the Iraq experience, Saudi Arabia, Kuwait, Syria, and North Africa (primarily Libya and Algeria, but also Morocco) will likely see the greatest returns of Salafi-jihadist fighters— although it should not be assumed that they will go on to target their own countries; rerouting to Afghanistan could be more probable.[50]

---

[49] "Iraq Index . . . ," 2008, stated that the estimated number of foreigners illegally entering Iraq to support the insurgency had fallen from 80 to 90 per month in January–May 2007, to fewer than 20 per month in June 2008.

[50] Reports of al-Qaʻida leaders redirecting fighters from Iraq to Afghanistan are already in evidence. In May 2008, jihadi forums released a statement by Mustafa Abu Yazid, head of al-Qaʻida in Afghanistan, announcing the "martyrdom" of Shaykh Abu Suleiman al-Oteibi, a former Shari'a court judge in ISI who had been removed from the post in August 2007 in Paktia province, Afghanistan. See SITE Intelligence Group, 2008.

Most of Iraq's neighbors have experienced attacks that can be traced back to Iraq veterans, but despite reports warning of waves of returning jihadi hordes, the consequences of returnees in terms of propagating terrorist trends have thus far been less than predicted.

There are a range of reasons for this. As noted, in many cases, Iraq is a black hole for foreign volunteers, from which they never return. For those who do, some have no further interest in terrorist activities. In spring 2006, a senior Saudi diplomat in the Gulf affirmed that, unlike volunteers to Afghanistan, Saudi volunteers to Iraq were not acquiring sophisticated logistical and tactical expertise; instead, indigenous Iraqi resistance elements were using them as "cannon fodder," which was a discouraging factor.[51] Added to this, as the dispute between Iraqi and foreign resistance groups demonstrated, local Iraqi fighters ultimately have a domestic agenda and are unlikely to join the global jihad in the long term.[52]

Nonetheless, it only takes a few well-trained individuals to spread knowledge of techniques with mass effect, and when Iraq loses its appeal as the central front for jihad, numbers could multiply.

In the case of the Shi'a, a small number of IRGC-Quds Force and Lebanese Hizballah members have operated in Iraq to assist Shi'a militants, and it can be anticipated that they will take any evolutionary lessons learned in guerrilla warfighting back to Iran and Lebanon. For the most part, however, it is they who offer the expertise to Iraqi Shi'a, not vice versa. According to U.S. intelligence reports in late 2006, up to 2,000 members of the Mahdi Army and other Shi'a militias have been trained in Lebanon by Hizballah in weapon-handling, bomb-making, intelligence, and assassinations. Some of these were present in Lebanon over the Israeli-Hizballah war in the summer of 2006. Similarly, a Mahdi Army Commander asserted that 300 of his fighters had been trained in Lebanon (Gordon and Filkins, 2006). Sadrists see in

---

[51] Interview with senior Saudi diplomat in the Gulf, February 2006.

[52] Paradoxically, however, in the medium to long term, one of the greatest terrorist threats emanating from Iraq may not come from foreign fighters with training experience gained in Iraq but from young Iraqi refugees who have fled to neighboring countries. See "Iraq Refugees Present the Most Significant Long-Term Challenge" in Chapter Four of this monograph.

Hizballah a model for emulation, incorporating armed resistance with social services and political participation. At the same time, while capitalizing on assistance offered by Iran, most Jaysh al-Mahdi members are profoundly nationalistic and have little affinity with Iranians.

Tehran has played a precarious balancing game by supporting various Shi'a militias in Iraq. The later focus on Jaysh al-Mahdi's activity should not obscure the fact that the Badr Corps (later renamed Badr Brigades) was Iran's first Iraqi client and, for many years, the principal recipient of its military aid. Even so, it is difficult to envisage how Badr would directly contribute toward the spread of terrorist trends unless it is, at some stage, called on to offer paramilitary support to a besieged Iran itself.

The Most Promising New Jihadi Fronts May Not Be Iraq's Neighbors

As indicated in our discussion of waning ideological credibility, the most promising new post-Iraq fronts are not necessarily those of al-Qa'ida central's choosing. The spread of tactics and technology depends on a range of factors, including the nature and locations of terrorist networks, available expertise, and a suitable domestic environment. Knowledge of new TTPs could be stored passively until the optimum circumstances arise.

As a comparable war zone and theater for jihad, it is not surprising that Afghanistan has witnessed the most direct transfer of technology from Iraq, in the form of IEDs. Techniques for making and using remote-controlled devices and timers for IEDs have been transferred. Afghan groups are thought to have gleaned this information from Iraq veterans, either via the Internet or in face-to-face visits with the Taliban and Hizb-i-Islami (Jones, 2008, p. 35).[53] Interviews with senior Afghan government officials in 2006 indicated that Taliban commanders received information from Iraqi groups on improving

---

[53] As early as September 2005, a *Newsweek* article described the experience of a Taliban commander and his team that had been invited to Iraq to learn about fighting tactics by bin Laden's representative to insurgents in Iraq, 'Abdul Hadi al-Iraqi. As a result of their on-the-job training, they had successfully adopted the "TV bomb"—a shaped charge mechanism that can be hidden under brush or debris on a roadside and set off by remote control from 300 yards or more. See Yousafzai and Moreau, 2005.

the construction of armor-penetrating weapons by disassembling rockets and rocket-propelled grenade rounds, removing the explosives and propellants, and repacking them with high-velocity shaped charges (Yousafzai and Moreau, 2005).

In the tactical realm, jihadi groups across the region have adopted many of the same practices seen in Iraq, although in many cases it is difficult to identify Iraq as *the* causal factor. Like Iraq, Afghanistan has also seen a marked increase in suicide bombing—the number of suicide attacks increased from one in 2002 to 140 in 2007—and the attempted recruitment of children by the Taliban (Theyab, February 2008). In Algeria, national intelligence sources have reported the recruitment of over 50 children under 16 years of age into al-Qaʻida in the Islamic Maghreb (AQIM) between December 2006 and April 2007.[54] In September 2007, a 15-year-old boy carried out a suicide attack against the barracks of the Algerian Navy in Dellys, killing 35 and wounding 46. The boy's *nom de guerre* was allegedly "Abu Musʻab al-Zarqawi, the Algerian."[55] AQIM also initiated a series of attacks in 2006–2007 against police stations and Western oil targets and claimed responsibility for an attempted assassination of the Algerian president in September 2007. The decision of AQIM (then GSPC) to join forces with al-Qaʻida in 2006 was a public relations coup for al-Qaʻida central and has been identified by commentators and by al-Qaʻida itself as the hub for Salafi-jihadist activity in North Africa and a key recruiter of youthful volunteers for Iraq.

In the Gulf, the hub of Salafi-jihadist activity is shifting from Saudi Arabia to Yemen. In 2003, al-Qaʻida in the Arabian Peninsula (QAP) ran a high-profile bombing campaign in Saudi Arabia.[56] On June 18, 2004, QAP filmed the beheading of Paul Johnson, carried out by the QAP's "al-Fallujah Brigades," in what appeared to be a conscious emulation of al-Zarqawi's tactics and a gesture of solidarity

---

[54] "Algeria: Al-Qaeda . . . ," 2007. AQIM was originally known as the Groupe Salafiste pour la Predication et le Combat [Salafi Group for Preaching and Combat] (GSPC). In January 2007, GSPC changed its name to reflect its merger with al-Qaʻida.

[55] "The al-Qaʻida Organization in the Islamic Maghreb . . . ," 2007.

[56] For a detailed assessment of this campaign, see Hegghammer, 2008.

with Iraq. Since then, however, the Saudi security services have rigor-ously pursued the group, crippling its activities. There have been several attempted attacks on oil infrastructure, including a foiled attack on the Abqaiq oil refinery in February 2006 by the Osama bin Laden bri-gades, in which weapons smuggled in from Iraq were used. This, how-ever, was more likely a response to Osama bin Laden's call for sabotag-ing economic assets rather than a direct imitation of attacks in Iraq. Iraq has diverted volunteers who might previously have contributed to the QAP program, and when the focus on Iraq has abated, there will doubtless be a renewed focus on the Arabian Peninsula—although more probably in Yemen than in Saudi Arabia.

In 2004, the Yemeni Prime Minister 'Abd al-Qadr Bajammal claimed that Yemen's security apparatus had purged the country of 90 percent of its al-Qa'ida activity, but as al-Qa'ida's presence in Iraq is indeed gradually purged, Yemen's uncontrolled tribal lands will continue to provide a potential safe haven or "land of savagery" for al-Qa'ida affiliates. Since 2006, Salafi-jihadist activity in Yemen has surged under the auspices of two groups: "al-Qa'ida in the Southern Arabian Peninsula" and "al-Qa'ida in the Arabian Peninsula–Yemen Brigades." Both adopted the slogan of the now defunct Saudi al-Qa'ida group—"Evict the polytheists from the Arabian Peninsula"—and their focus on suicide bombing and targeting economic interests (primar-ily oil instillations), particularly in the Hadramawt province, resem-bles al-Qa'ida's activities in Iraq.[57] In January 2009, al-Qa'ida in the Arabian Peninsula, having apparently subsumed the second group, announced a merger with al-Qa'ida in Saudi Arabia, signifying the shift of attention to Yemen.

In the meantime, two countries that, perhaps surprisingly, appear not to have suffered greatly from a terrorism spillover from Iraq are Egypt and Syria. The Director of the Center for Terrorism Studies at Cairo University suggested to RAND interviewers that this was

---

[57] Zadi al-Taqwa, 2008, put forth the argument that al-Qa'ida has strategically attacked U.S. oil interests since 1998 because oil is vital to the U.S. economy, citing the May 30, 2008, attack on Yemeni oil infrastructure in Aden, which al-Qa'ida senior leaders had embraced, and the subsequent rise in price to $122.80 per barrel as evidence of a strategic scheme.

because Egypt, unlike other regional states, had distanced itself from cooperation with the United States on Iraq.[58] What is certain is that the Egyptian security services have rigorously hunted down jihadis and dissidents. Syria too, although intermittently accused by the new Iraqi government and the coalition of sponsoring terrorism in Iraq, has intensified its security measures to avoid a blowback. These measures include erecting an earth barrier along its border with Iraq, demanding that estate agents provide the identity details of any foreigners staying on their premises, establishing new counterterrorism branches, enforcing strict surveillance of Internet cafes, and controlling the sale of Sim cards (Ulph, 2006a). A January 2009 tract issued on an extremist Web forum that discussed the reasons for the flagging fortunes of Salafi-jihadism there suggested among other things that Syrian activists had mistakenly hinged their hopes on AQI succeeding in its bid to take over Iraq before proceeding to overthrow the Syrian 'Alawi regime, and thus neglected consolidating their movement internally.[59]

Terrorism emanating from Iraq has affected both Kuwait and Jordan. In January 2005, there was a shoot-out between Kuwaiti police and the "Peninsula Lions" jihadi group, some of whose members had trained in Iraq; eight suspects and four policemen were killed.[60] In Jordan, al-Zarqawi's November 9, 2005, triple suicide bombing of three hotels in Amman was a shocking wake-up call. As a result of these events, both countries have taken strenuous security measures to avoid the full force of a terrorist blowback and, so far, their efforts appear to have been successful.

In December 2007, Osama bin Laden announced that al-Qa'ida's operational objective of creating a launching pad in Iraq for future

---

[58] Interview with university research director, Cairo, February 24, 2008. According to the same source, the Tawhed wa Jihad group that attacked in Sinai was a result of radicalization in Gaza and unemployment and marginalization of Bedouin in Sinai, not an effect of the Iraq War.

[59] "Lamhat 'an Inba'ath . . . ," 2009.

[60] Six other members were subsequently sentenced to death. See "Six Al-Qa'ida Men Awarded Death Penalty in Kuwait," 2005.

campaigns in the region had been achieved,[61] increasing expectations of an imminent onslaught against neighboring countries. But what emerges from the trends of targeting discussed is that the worst terrorist effects of the Iraq conflict may not in fact be felt by Iraq's immediate neighbors, whose regimes have braced themselves for a terrorist blowback by heightening security and, in Saudi Arabia's case, by initiating a reconciliation process.[62] The prime targets are also not countries that, for ideological reasons, have great symbolic resonance for the movement (Iran and Palestine). In fact, the most immediate threats—in Afghanistan, Pakistan, and Somalia—are not even in Arab lands. In the near term, AQIM and al-Qa'ida in Yemen appear to be sustaining the most vigorous al-Qa'ida franchise movements. This choice of territories was reiterated by the well-known London-based jihadist cleric Hani al-Siba'i, who noted in June 2008 that the "human forest [of individuals sympathetic to al-Qa'ida] and rugged geography . . . in Pakistan, Afghanistan, Yemen and Algeria," make those areas conducive to attacks on American interests (al-Siba'i, 2008).

Conclusion

Our assessment is that the immediate terrorist effects Iraq has generated are not as dramatic as commonly supposed but that the long-term effects have yet to be determined. In years to come, training and tactical development in Iraq will likely be one of several factors contributing toward the growth of terrorist movements, the others being determined primarily by domestic circumstances. If there is a silver lining to this debate, it is that the United States has time to assess its own

---

[61] For a full discussion of this, see Scheuer, 2008.

[62] In 2003, the Saudi Minister of the Interior announced his country's intention to construct a security fence that would extend for 840 km along its borders with Iraq from the Al-Rafaei outlet in the east to Toreif city in the west. This followed Kuwait's September 22, 2006, announcement of its own intention to establish border fences in the form of a ring road stretching along its border with Iraq to Saudi Arabia through Kuwait territory at 500 m from the borders between the two countries.

vulnerabilities; those of its allies; and indeed, those of its enemies and to take action accordingly.

Notwithstanding the initial boost Iraq gave al-Qa'ida and its message, the longer-term public appeal and ideological vision of al-Qa'ida have suffered gravely as a result of its conduct in Iraq. From this point forward, the movement will face similar targeting dilemmas wherever it operates in the Arab world. As long as its image as defender of the Muslims remains discredited, al-Qa'ida will struggle to regain popular standing. As the spread of tactics demonstrates, however, this has not prevented jihadists from undertaking devastating attacks periodically throughout the region. However, as the contradictions in the agenda of transnational jihadists and nationalist groups have become increasingly apparent, the movement's prospects for gaining a long-term foothold in the region are limited to "lands of savagery," where confidence in the state structure has collapsed, or to lands that provide access to training grounds with relative impunity. Al-Qa'ida's strategy of stoking an insurgency within Iraq may ultimately have backfired, but the movement has still been able to maintain a vigorous campaign against its enemies.

As al-Qa'ida deliberates its next course of action against the "near enemy," its most accessible havens continue to be lands where violence is endemic and where it does not face overwhelming competition from preexisting territorially based Sunni religious groups. At present, these are not primarily Iraq's immediate neighbors but the more-distant lands of Afghanistan and Pakistan and, to a lesser extent, Yemen and North Africa.

CHAPTER SIX

Conclusion: Managing the Aftershocks of Iraq and Seizing Opportunities

This monograph has surveyed the implications of the Iraq conflict for the Middle East strategic landscape, showing how the full effects of the conflict are more expansive yet also more nuanced than is commonly assumed. Previous analyses of the "Iraq effect" have used a conventional balance-of-power lens that divides the new regional map too neatly between an ascendant Iran and an opposing bloc of Sunni Arab states. Others have overstated the potential for a contagion of sectarian conflict and increased terrorist incidents resulting from the conflict. We found that, while elements of these trends are certainly present, they do not reveal the full complexity of regional developments. They also at times miss more-subtle perceptual shifts among neighboring regimes, Arab publics, and nonstate actors.

Although these perceptual shifts are less tangible from a conventional security perspective, they are nonetheless important for U.S. policy. One of the most significant is what can best be termed a sense of Iraq fatigue among neighboring states—the belief that, while the conflict and Iranian influence in Iraq are certainly alarming, they have been superseded by more-pressing "local" concerns, particularly in the Levant. Threat perceptions of Iran also vary significantly, both across different subregions and countries and between governments and their publics. The perception of eroding U.S. credibility and influence is also resulting in tangible outcomes, including growing responsiveness to other extraregional actors, particularly Russia and China.

On the domestic front, societal conflict in the broader region resulting from the war has not yet materialized to the extent forecast; rather, state power has strengthened and tolerance of domestic political opposition has decreased. Specifically, Iraq's instability has become a convenient scarecrow neighboring regimes can use to delay political reform by asserting that democratization inevitably leads to insecurity. And while the entrenchment of U.S.-allied regimes may be deceptively reassuring in the short term, it does little to address the more deeply rooted problem of regime illegitimacy or to mitigate the wellsprings of radicalism. Finally, and on a more-positive note, the war's appeal as a draw for terrorist recruitment has been offset by declining public support among Arabs of al-Qa'ida's goals, operations, and tactics.

Taken in sum, these dynamics present both challenges and opportunities for U.S. regional policy. Understanding gaps between U.S. and regional views of the conflict's consequences and implications will therefore be paramount—particularly for gauging the willingness of neighboring states to cooperate on U.S. objectives. Similarly, the United States must be attentive to how the post-Iraq environment, especially altered views of U.S. power and credibility, have opened up possibilities for new paradigms of regional security cooperation, involving traditional Middle East allies but also extraregional states, such as Russia or China.

Key Findings

With the above policy prerogatives in mind, the monograph's key findings are the following:

The removal of Saddam Hussein upset a traditional balance of power in the region. From the perspective of Sunni Arab regimes, the 2003 invasion overturned a long-standing paradigm of regional security by removing Iraq as a buffer between a seemingly expansionist and predatory Iran and its vulnerable neighbors to the west. According to this narrative, Iran has been handed increased latitude to project its influence across the region, upstaging Arab governments on traditional pan-Arab concerns, such as Palestine. It is important to note, however, that much of Iran's activism predates the 2003 invasion. Tehran has long supported nonstate actors, such as HAMAS, the Palestinian Islamic Jihad, and the Lebanese Hizballah. Moreover, it is doubtful that Saddam's Iraq ever really served as a viable balancer against Iran, given that the preponderance of Tehran's strength has been exerted in the naval, asymmetric, and ideological realms, while Iraq has traditionally been a land power and even this was considerably weakened by sanctions following the 1991 Gulf War. Nevertheless, the ousting of the Iraqi leader created the perception of increased vulnerability on the Arab side, resulting in a tendency to exaggerate the specter of Iran and its associated nonstate allies.

Iran *is* seizing strategic gains afforded to it by the Iraq War but faces greater obstacles to expanding its influence in the region than is commonly assumed. There is no doubt that Iran has skillfully exploited the strategic openings presented by the aftermath of the Iraqi invasion and the resulting shake-up in regional order. Buoyed by windfall oil profits for several years following the invasion and imbued with the nationalistic outlook of Ahmadinejad's "new conservatives," Iran has endeavored since 2003 to safeguard not just its near abroad in Iraq but also to assert its primacy on the wider regional stage and to erode U.S. credibility. This momentum was accelerated by the concurrent ascendancy of its Levantine allies, particularly the electoral victory of HAMAS in Gaza and Hizballah's battlefield performance against the Israeli Defense Forces in 2006. Although largely unrelated to Iraq, these events heightened the post-Saddam view in Arab capitals of Iran's inexorable rise and created the impression among Arab publics that Iran, and by extension the Shi'a, were now the winning side. The internal turmoil within Iran following the 2009 presidential election is likely to erode this image of invincibility somewhat, but Iranian links to nonstate actors and its continued nuclear ambitions continue to generate widespread concern.

Even before the 2009 election, Iran faced limitations to its regional influence. The post-2006 groundswell of popular support it garnered among Arab publics proved fleeting and was effectively reversed by widespread perceptions of its misbehavior in Iraq. Tehran's policy in Iraq became even more of a liability for Iran's standing following revelations of its support to Sadr's Jaysh al-Mahdi's fratricidal campaign against opposing Shi'a factions and the resulting anti-Iranian backlash within the Maliki government and among the Iraqi public. Inside Iran, Ahmadinejad's bellicose posturing on Arab issues has provoked criticism from multiple Iranian factions along the ideological spectrum, particularly in light of the country's deteriorating economy.

The perceived "rise" of Iran has not produced a consensus of opposition from Sunni Arab regimes; Arab states' responses to Iran have blended engagement, hedging, and balancing. The alarmism and fear of Iran among Arab rulers have not resulted in a coherent strategy to confront the expansion of Iranian influence. Rather, Arab regimes have responded to the rise of Iran in diverse and often contradictory ways, reflecting a more-nuanced appreciation of the Iranian challenge than the common refrain in Washington, as well as the different geostrategic imperatives of individual Arab states.

Among states of the Levant and in Egypt, for example, our research identified a preference for viewing Iranian influence in Iraq as a secondary concern to Tehran's more-threatening activities "next door," i.e., in Gaza and Lebanon. Yet the GCC at times has accused Egypt of being too rhetorically belligerent against Iran because its geographic location separates it from Iranian retaliation. Within the GCC itself, there is frequently intense disagreement, with some smaller states adopting a more-accommodating stance toward Iran and pointing to Saudi Arabia's dominance of GCC affairs as the more-proximate and worrisome concern. This preference for hedging on Iran has been further encouraged by what some Arab states perceive as inconsistent and ambiguous U.S. policies on Iran.

Even if consensus existed, there is currently no viable Arab state "balancer" to Iran. The result is that the emerging regional powers are now non-Arab states: the United States, Iran, Turkey, and Israel.

Uncertainty about U.S. intentions and capabilities in the region has increased local states' receptivity to assistance from China and Russia. Postinvasion disarray in the Arab world was accompanied by a corresponding erosion of confidence in the United States as a security guarantor, stemming from the perception of U.S. entanglement in Iraq. The effect has been the increased willingness of traditional U.S. Arab allies to consider patronage from other extraregional powers, most notably Russia and China.

The foreign policy of these two powers since 2003 has been marked by a new assertiveness and interest in the Middle East. Russia appears to be particularly active in challenging traditional domains of U.S. influence, claiming to be a more-balanced mediator on the Arab-Israeli front and through such symbolic gestures as its engagement with HAMAS. Yet the full potential of Russian influence is constrained by Moscow's historical "baggage" in the region and its frequent strategic blunders, such as its decision to brand the Muslim Brotherhood a terrorist organization. For its part, China appears more narrowly focused on energy security and it remains much more economically significant than politically or militarily influential in regional affairs.

Our fieldwork suggests that, while some Arab voices may welcome Moscow and Beijing's activism as checks against unrestrained U.S. hegemony, Arab regimes ultimately see Russian and Chinese assistance as a way to supplement, but not supplant, the traditional U.S.-led regional security order.

The war has heightened awareness of Shiʿa and Sunni identity, yet in many cases, regimes have cynically exploited these loyalties to discredit oppositionists and blunt Iranian influence. Iraq's descent into sectarian strife in 2006 reverberated inside a number of states in the region, creating new pressures on regimes and stoking societal tensions. Although the threat of a direct spillover of the fighting did not materialize during the height of violence in Iraq, Sunni-Shiʿa and tribal divisions have sharpened as forms of substate identities. The effects of the war in this area are felt strongest in states marked by authoritarianism and/or a fractured body politic: Bahrain, Saudi Arabia, and Lebanon. Kuwait provides an important case in which the negative consequences of the war for Sunni-Shiʿa relations were mitigated by a more-liberal and participatory political culture.

Warnings of increased Shiʿa activism, however, have emanated from regimes that have relatively little to fear from Shiʿa agitation, such as Egypt and Jordan. This dynamic illustrates the political utility of fear-mongering on the sectarian issue. In many cases, authoritarian rulers have skillfully exploited the fear of Shiʿa ascendancy to counter Iranian populist appeal at home, discredit and divide the political opposition along sectarian lines, and portray themselves as the only viable "buffers" against the chaos and uncertainty unleashed by the war.

The war has stalled or reversed the momentum of Arab political reform; local regimes perceive that U.S. distraction in Iraq and the subsequent focus on Iran have given them a reprieve on domestic liberalization. In tandem with sectarian tensions, the war has produced stalling or backtracking on reform, however halting and incomplete. Author interviews with activists and reformists in the Gulf and the Levant yielded a near consensus that 2003 was a turning point in reform, with authoritarian rulers sensing reduced U.S. interest in their domestic affairs and a subsequent return to Cold War–style balancing politics against Iran. Similarly, preemptive counterterrorism measures against returning jihadists provided a convenient pretext for the dragnet arrests of a broad spectrum of domestic opponents.

In several instances, the war appears to have increased toleration and even the support of Arab publics for unpopular rulers who, whatever their faults, are still preferable to the unknown. Some of this may stem from the declining cachet of democratization, given its image as a "U.S. project" whose forcible implementation in Iraq was widely blamed for sowing the seeds of the country's descent into sectarian violence. In other cases, Iraqi violence and the specter of spreading terrorism have encouraged a new public acquiescence in the security services as "protectors" rather than "monitors."

Increased Kurdish agitation in Syria, Turkey, and Iran is the war's most pronounced and visible spillover effect. The 2003 invasion and the subsequent push by Iraqi Kurds for increased autonomy has animated Kurdish activism in neighboring states, offering both inspiration and more-tangible support, such as a physical safe haven. Such events as the election of Kurdistan Workers' Party (PUK) leader Jalal Talabani as Iraqi president and the signing of the Transitional Administrative Law sparked celebratory rioting among Iranian Kurds and a serious uprising in Syria that left 40 dead. Violent Kurdish groups, such as the PKK in Turkey and the PJAK, have enjoyed increased sanctuary in postinvasion northern Iraq, posing new threats to domestic stability in Turkey and Iran. This challenge is spurring tripartite intelligence and operational coordination between Damascus, Ankara, and Tehran that will complicate U.S. diplomacy to pry Syria from Iran's orbit and solicit meaningful Turkish cooperation against Iran, although the United States also began assisting Turkey in its counterterror operations in northern Iraq. In Turkey, the effects are particularly worrisome as intensified PKK activity threatens to undermine many of Turkey's recent gains in human rights, undermining its efforts at European Union accession.

The influx of an estimated 2 million Iraqi refugees has created socioeconomic stress in Syria and Jordan; the resulting public discontent and demographic changes could challenge stability in these states over the long term. The Iraq War created the largest refugee crisis in the Middle East since the 1948 Arab-Israeli War, potentially jeopardizing the long-term stability of Jordan; Syria; and, to a lesser extent, Lebanon. At least in the short term, the refugee challenge has not transformed into a security risk to the degree anticipated. Indeed, some studies have pointed to beneficial effects, such as the injection of capital by the mostly middle-class refugee population in Jordan, which reportedly fueled Amman's housing boom in the years following the war. That said, as resources run out for these refugees, their situation is becoming more dire, particularly since most are unable to find legal work and are reportedly charged inflated rates for housing. Prostitution and female trafficking have become significant problems, particularly in Syria. Still, the Iraqi refugees have not yet carried Iraq's political and sectarian violence to neighboring soil. Most Iraqi refugees in neighboring states appear more concerned with surviving than with fomenting instability in their host countries.

But there is a tendency to scapegoat the refugees in both Jordan and Syria. The refugees are increasingly blamed for the end of fuel subsidies, unemployment, inflation, and housing shortages. The net effect over the long term may be pressure on regimes from key constituents to curtail and reduce services for Iraqis. The Jordanian and Syrian governments have already toughened their policies, and Jordan has largely closed its doors to new refugees. After significant international pressure, children have been allowed to go to school in some host countries (including Jordan and Syria), but few do because parents fear that attendance may compromise their illegal or quasi-legal presence in the country and because many children work illegally to keep their families housed and fed. Another worrisome trend is the presence of unemployed college-age Iraqi males whose profile of displacement and anomie could make them vulnerable recruits to Salafi-jihadism. Previous refugee crises in the region and globally suggest that poverty and resentment can feed radicalization among the displaced and host populations.

Finally, the long-term urban demographics of refugee settlement bear watching; thus far, the Syrian and Jordanian governments have avoided constructing any parallel institutions—schools, clinics, and camps specifically for Iraqis—to prevent a repeat of the Palestinian camp experience. But certain urban areas are nevertheless becoming increasingly Iraqi in character, displacing indigenous populations and possibly sowing the seeds of future discord. Moreover, if future instability in Iraq led to renewed refugee flows, Jordan and Syria would be unlikely to accept them as they have done to date, and refugee camps could develop. A large Iraqi diaspora, combined with continuing conflict in Iraq, has the potential to spread conflict to neighbors because Iraqis living abroad funnel support to Iraqi groups, are recruited to fight, or lobby governments to provide aid to combatants. If camps are indeed set up, these risks increase because camps have often been a primary site for militant recruiting for fighting and unrest in other cases (e.g., Lebanon).

The war has offered a universalizing narrative of resistance to occupation that has proven attractive to potential jihadist recruits, but AQI's abhorrent tactics in Iraq have undermined this appeal. The invasion was an initial boon to al-Qa'ida, offering a compelling arena for conducting defensive jihad against an occupying force that was seen as having defiled Muslim honor, even if the original grievances of many of its recruits were of a more local and parochial nature.

While initially receiving applause from Arab publics and even tacit approval from the media, al-Qa'ida's battlefield emir in Iraq, Abu Mus'ab al-Zarqawi, squandered this capital through the negative publicity generated by his abhorrent tactics and, in particular, the fallout in public opinion from the Amman hotel bombings. Populations that had previously cheered al-Qaʿida from afar now turned against it when afflicted with its violence firsthand, as in the cases of Saudi Arabia and Jordan, or when forced to live under its stifling social mores, as were the Anbar tribes. Although this downturn in public opinion may not significantly affect potential recruits, it has bolstered the ability of neighboring regimes to absorb and mitigate the threat from veterans returning from Iraq.

Iraq has served as a laboratory for innovating new asymmetric tactics that may migrate; al-Qaʿida may also try to apply lessons learned from its Iraq misadventure to new fronts. Five years of combat in Iraq against a conventionally superior opponent have invariably functioned as a crucible for terrorist learning, aiding the development of new tactics and the creation of worrisome social networks.

Yet several features of the Iraqi arena militate against precise comparisons to the 1980s Afghan jihad. First, despite the presence of strong foreign fighter facilitation networks linking the Levant, North Africa, and the Gulf, the training camp presence in Iraq has not been as robust as the one ʿAbdullah Azzam's *Maktab al-Khidamat* [Office of Services] provided during the Afghan jihad. Moreover, many foreign jihadists have returned to their home countries, reportedly disillusioned, or are subjected to an increasingly deliberate, if not entirely transparent, reindoctrination and reintegration program sponsored by regimes in Yemen, Saudi Arabia, and elsewhere.

Nevertheless, the potential exists for the migration of tactics and techniques developed in Iraq to other fronts. IEDs, female suicide bombings, increased sniper proficiency, and improved indirect fire techniques are all trends that will require security adaptations in neighboring states and U.S. force posture adjustments in the region.

Shiʿa insurgents have proven the most proficient at using technological innovations against the United States because of the provision and training Iran's Quds Force has provided, yet the potential for widespread migration is offset by Tehran's control. Much of the focus on terrorist spillover from Iraq has focused on Sunni jihadists, but Shiʿa Iraqi insurgents have actually been the most adept at utilizing technological innovations against U.S. and Iraqi forces. These groups have benefited from strong external links to Lebanese Hizballah and Iran's IRGC-Quds Force. U.S. forces accused the Lebanese Hizballah of training Iraqi insurgents in IED ambush techniques and imparting technology that it had honed during its campaign against the Israel Defense Forces during the 1990s. In tandem, the Quds Force has provided training and supplies of explosively formed projectiles and rocket-assisted mortars that have penetrated U.S. armor and challenged the best defenses of coalition air bases and other facilities.

A cyclical sharing network has likely emerged, with Iraqi Shi'a groups honing techniques Hizballah imparted, then briefing Hizballah and Quds Force about the battlefield applications, and then transferring these lessons back to Quds Force training camps inside Iran, whence they migrate eastward to the Taliban. Yet the potential for truly widespread and unregulated dispersal of these TTPs is partially offset by Tehran's sensitivity to crossing certain redlines, i.e., giving the United States an unequivocal pretext to attack Iran or provoking an intolerable anti-Iranian backlash among Arab audiences—as was the case in Iraq following the mid-2008 violence by Muqtada al-Sadr's Jaysh al-Mahdi and its splinter militias known as "special groups."

Policy Implications

Our findings have underscored the complex and diverse effects of the Iraq conflict on the regional landscape, both at the inter- and intra-state levels. Realistic readings of the regional environment are critical to the formulation of U.S. policy, given the magnitude of remaining challenges to U.S. interests emanating from this region. The U.S. Air Force should have a particular interest in understanding the shifting regional environment and views on U.S. policy because of its long-standing partnerships with local militaries and its important role in future contingencies. The picture that emerges from this monograph suggests both challenges and opportunities and requires a fresh set of policy options:

Pursue a U.S. regional security strategy that recognizes local preferences for hedging and that seeks to encourage more-positive

Iranian behavior. In terms of adapting to regional strategic shifts, particularly to Iran's growing influence in regional affairs, the United States faces the challenge of regional allies more interested in hedging and even accommodating Iran than balancing it. Arab regional allies (particularly governments) no doubt worry about and dislike Iran, but they will not unequivocally antagonize and provoke Iran. Indeed, many of our closest allies, particularly Turkey, have found new reasons to expand their ties to Tehran in the years following the Iraq War. U.S. policy should thus steer away from efforts to forge an anti-Iranian regional alliance of Arab "moderates" (e.g., the GCC states, Jordan, Egypt) to counter Iranian influence.

Such an alliance is not only unrealistic, but it may also backfire and escalate regional tensions by bolstering Iranian hard-liners—particularly during the unprecedented factionalism emerging in the wake of the 2009 elections. And the focus on Arab states, particularly the Saudis, as bulwarks against Iran misreads regional capabilities and interests. While the United States should continue to demonstrate support for key regional allies through continued security cooperation activities and exercises, such cooperation should remain low key and bilateral to avoid the impression that the United States is attempting to create a broad Cold War–style collective security organization arrayed against Iran.

Explore multilateral security and confidence-building measures between Iran and its neighbors. That said, the United States can engage in efforts to create multilateral regional security structures that leave the door open to Iran and that focus on confidence-building measures and dialogues in areas of common interest, such as counterterrorism, narcotics trafficking, and maritime security. Regional security dialogues involving military personnel, including Air Force officials, can allow the airing of threat perceptions and help avoid unintended conflict. They can also open up an indirect line of communication between Iran and Israel to avoid an unintended military confrontation, particularly if Iranian nuclear capabilities remain ambiguous. Although Iranian involvement in regional security discussions will prove more difficult in the aftermath of the contested 2009 election, such options should be developed and available for when political conditions in Iran improve. If substantive security dialogues eventually transpire and do not lead to a change in Iranian behavior, the United States will still gain important insights into Iranian decisionmaking and garner greater regional and international support for tougher actions against Iran, should they become necessary. If they do succeed, such dialogues can lead to enhanced security cooperation and a less-threatening regional security environment, reducing the potential for armed conflict.

Strengthen U.S. relations with Turkey, leveraging its unique role as a geopolitical bridge to mediate between Syria, Iran, and the Arab world. Another policy focus at the regional level that flows from our analysis is the need to strengthen U.S. relations with Turkey. Turkey can serve as a bridge for improving relations and modifying the behavior of current adversaries, such as Iran and Syria, because Turkey's relationship with both countries has strengthened thanks to common concerns over Kurdish separatism and terrorist acts within their nations. Turkey has already demonstrated an interest in regional mediation by facilitating indirect dialogue between Israel and Syria, and the United States should encourage such efforts. Rather than force our allies into rigid boxes—"you're either with the United States or against it"—we should view regional allies' relationships with such countries as Iran and Syria as an opportunity and leverage their roles to the extent possible.

Turkey's interests in and extensive economic ties with northern Iraq also present an opportunity for assisting in U.S. efforts to rebuild Iraq. Indeed, unlike Iraq's Arab neighbors, Turkey has proven far more forthcoming in contributing to Iraqi stability and reconstruction, even though, like Iraq's other neighbors, it still opposed the war. As a consequence, the Air Force should continue assisting the Turkish military with counterterrorism operations in Northern Iraq and should increase security cooperation activities and training with the Turkish air force. In the current threat environment, U.S. security cooperation with Turkey may be as or more important than security cooperation with America's Arab allies.

Continue the policy of encouraging responsible stakeholder involvement from China and, to the extent possible, Russia; har-

ness these countries' respective "niche" interests to promote regional economic growth and stability. In the same vein, the United States should avoid alarmist reactions to Chinese or Russian influence in the region, particularly their economic activities because many of these activities are more likely to complement than to supplant U.S. regional interests. For example, China and the United States share a strong interest in creating a stable regional security order conducive to the flow of the region's oil and gas. U.S. policy should also distinguish between extraregional powers' pursuit of their economic interests and more-aggressive attempts to move the regional system toward multipolarity, which is a greater concern in the case of Russia than with China.

Encourage Arab regimes to adopt incremental yet meaningful political reform as part of a long-term push to counter radicalization and to ensure the viability of key U.S. partners. To mitigate the war's effects inside key regional states, U.S. policy should focus both on ensuring that governing regimes do not abuse their newly entrenched power to crack down excessively on domestic opposition, while taking measures to prevent weakening state conditions from evolving into failed states (with all the accompanying problems that involves— shelter for extremists, a magnified proliferation danger, greater potential for massive human rights abuses). This suggests that U.S. policy should recognize the long-term security implications of continued repression and avoid putting regional reform on the back burner, even if the focus shifts from holding elections to strengthening democratic institutions and practices. Judiciary reform, increased media freedom and bolstering the legislative and oversight abilities of existing parliaments and consultative councils are key priorities to build public confidence in regime intentions. While the U.S. ability to influence what are largely indigenous processes is limited, U.S. attention to reform measures and sustained pressure can provide critical impetus for continued efforts among key allies. Ultimately, sustained and genuine reform processes will strengthen, not weaken, such key allies as Jordan, Egypt, and Bahrain. Backtracking on promised reforms and civil liberties weakens regime legitimacy and can increase the prospects for political violence, just as delaying political reform can lead to a build-up of dissent until regimes are forced to open precipitously, leading to instability.

Continue to provide U.S. assistance for Iraqi refugees and encourage more regional support to mitigate the potentially destabilizing consequences of the influx. While the Iraqi refugee influx into Jordan and Syria may have produced some short-term economic advantages, the refugee population ultimately places a strain on these countries' domestic infrastructures, particularly their education systems. The long-term political ramifications of the Iraqi refugee community are still unclear but could prove destabilizing to such key allies as Jordan. Rather than ignore the extent of this problem because of political sensitivities (the Jordanian government refuses to use the term *refugee*, for example, preferring *guest* because the latter assumes an eventual return to Iraq), the United States should actively address this new regional challenge.

The United States can continue to support efforts to relocate Iraqis to other countries (including the United States[1]) and provide and marshal significant financial assistance (particularly from Arab Gulf allies) to improve housing and education opportunities in both Syria and Jordan. The GCC states can offer direct financial support to the Jordanian government for this purpose. For Saudi Arabia, particularly, this can help its global image and aspirations to Sunni leadership. Because the GCC would be unlikely to provide this sort of direct assistance to Syria, the United States should also encourage sizeable financial contributions through UNHCR and other international organizations. That way, the funds can be justified as helping all fellow Muslims while avoiding support to less-than-friendly governments.

The United States can also improve its bilateral relations with Syria by focusing more attention on this issue. Syria has been generous

---

[1]   Although the United States has increased the number of Iraqi refugees it accepts, it continues to face criticism for the remarkably low numbers. For example, UNHCR estimates that there are between 80,000 to 100,000 "extremely vulnerable Iraqi refugees in the Middle East in need of resettlement"; the United States accepted only 1,608 Iraqi refugees in fiscal year (FY) 2007. The numbers went up to 13,823 in FY 2008, and 1,443 had been accepted in FY 2009 as of November 2008. For an account of refugees admitted to the United States, see U.S. Department of State, 2009.

and hosts more Iraqi refugees than any other state. It reports significant strain on its economy as a result. Yet Jordan, which hosts fewer refugees, has received the bulk of assistance. The United States should work cooperatively with Syria and UNHCR to raise additional funds and facilitate the ability of the Syrian government to improve its social services. This can be a helpful first step toward rebuilding a cooperative relationship with Syria, which could also improve the prospects for long-term stability in Iraq and the region and reduce Syrian incentives to intervene in Iraq in ways that counter U.S. interests.

Such policies would capitalize on this otherwise negative development and humanitarian crisis by improving long-term infrastructure and human development needs in key Arab states, reducing the possibility for future radicalization and challenges to friendly regimes, such as Jordan, and gaining regional and international goodwill by seriously addressing this humanitarian challenge.

In partnership with local allies, use strategic communications to broadcast al-Qaʿida's failures in Iraq across the region, to further discredit the jihadist movement in the eyes of public audiences. The terrorist trends emerging over the last six years also suggest a number of U.S. policy actions that can enhance opportunities for U.S. influence. The United States should exploit al-Qaʿida's failure to appeal to some of its target audiences, in particular the Sunni tribes and nationalist Islamic groups. Forging better regional intelligence sharing, tracking Iraq War veterans, and identifying recruitment networks are also important policy initiatives that can capitalize on the declining cachet of al-Qaʿida following its brutal tactics in Iraq. Other policy actions include encouraging greater involvement of women in regional security services to conduct female searches in the light of the growing trend of female suicide bombers and refocusing efforts on the potential establishment of Shiʿa militant networks outside of Iraq, such as TTP transfers by the IRGC-Quds Force to Hizballah in Lebanon.

Bibliography

Abdel-Latif, Omayma, "Lebanon's Sunni Islamists: A Growing Force," Washington, D.C.: Carnegie Endowment for International Peace, January 2008. As of August 6, 2009:
http://www.carnegieendowment.org/publications/index.cfm?fa=view&id=19882

———, "The Shia-Sunni Divide: Myths and Reality," *Al-Ahram Weekly*, March 1–7, 2007. As of August 6, 2009:
http://www.carnegieendowment.org/publications/index.cfm?fa=view&id=19047

al-'Abidi, Salam, "Russia wa Talab al-Indimam ila Munazhamat al-Mu'atamar al-Islami [Russia and the Request to Join the Organization of Islamic Conference]," Al Jazeera (in Arabic), March 10, 2004. As of October 5, 2009:
http://www.aljazeera.net/NR/exeres/10446E22-0287-4DDA-92C6-7DCE5A91A0AA.htm

Ahadi, Afsaneh, *Iran and the United States: Interaction in Iraq*, Tehran: Center for Strategic Research, Research Bulletin 15, September 2008. As of April 19, 2009:
http://www.csr.ir/departments.aspx?lng=en&abtid=05&depid=74&semid=277

al-'Alam, Akhbar, "Khalid Mish'al Yu'yid Mawqif Russia min al-Sir'a al-Georgi–al-Ositi [Khalid Mish'al Supports Russia's Position on the Georgian-Ossetian Conflict]," *World Bulletin* (in Arabic), August 19, 2008. As of October 5, 2009:
http://www.akhbaralaalam.net/news_detail.php?id=15197&uniq_id=1221281533

al-Alaya'a, Zaid, "Tribes Should Be Social Entities not Political Participants, Says al-Dhaheri," *Yemen Observer*, September 22, 2007.

"Algeria: Al-Qaeda 'Recruited Over Fifty Under-16s from Dec–April,'" WarIntel posting, Internet Anthropologist Think Tank blog, September 14, 2007. As of August 13, 2009:
http://warintel.blogspot.com/2007/09/al-qaeda-recruits-15-kids-under-16-yrs.html

Alhomayed, Tariq, "American Withdrawal and the Second Stage," *Asharq Al-Awsat*, October 9, 2007. As of July 31, 2008:
http://www.asharqalawsat.com/english/news.asp?section=2&id=10491

al-'Ali, Hamed, "al-Khalij bayn Mutraqa al-Sara'a al-Irani al-Amriki wa Sindan Da'afi Tafakakihi [The Arabian Gulf Between the Rock of the Iranian-American Contest and the Hard Place of Its Own Weakness and Disintegration]," Ana al-Muslim website (in Arabic), March 14, 2008. As of January 2009: http://www.muslm.net/vb/showthread.php?t=285888

'Aloush, Ibrahim, "al-Nufudh al-Amiriki fi al-Sharq al-Awsat [American Influence in the Middle East]," video, YouTube (in Arabic), July 31, 2007. As of October 21, 2009: http://www.youtube.com/watch?v=Z_ys1hgGQyE

Alterman, John B., and John W. Garver, *The Vital Triangle: China, the United States, and the Middle East*, Washington, D.C.: Center for Strategic and International Studies, 2008.

al-'Anani, Khalil, "al-Ikhwan al-Muslimun fi Misr: al-Shaikhukha Tusari' al-Zaman [The Muslim Brotherhood in Egypt: Old Age Fighting Time]," Cairo: Maktabat al-Shuruq al-Dawliya, 2007.

Ansar Media Group, "al-Shashat al-Butlan wa-l-Khadhlan [False and Deceptive Television Screens]," in Arabic, November 30, 2008. As of January 2009: http://www.muslm.net/vb/showthread.php?t=320219.

Antoun, Richard, "Civil Society, Tribal Process, and Change in Jordan: An Anthropological View," *International Journal of Middle East Studies*, Vol. 32, 2000, pp. 441–463.

AQI—*See* al-Qa'ida in Iraq.

Al Arabiya, report on poll, February 26, 2007. As of August 2007: http://www.alarabiya.net/Articles/2007/02/26/32078.html

"al-Asad Tujahal Tamaman fi Khitabih Ihtilal Iran lil-Juzur al-Imaratiya [In his Speech, al-Asad Completely Ignores Iran's Occupation of the UAE Islands]," Al Arabiya (in Arabic), March 29, 2008. As of August 6, 2009: http://www.alarabiya.net/articles/2008/03/29/47611.html

al-Ashmouri, Saddam, "Ash-Shayif Accuses National Solidarity Council of Treachery," *Yemen Times*, Vol. 15, No. 1077, August 15, 2007.

al-Athim, Mahmoud Firdaws, *Nasb Ma'ad wa al-Yaman al-Kabir [Ancestry of Greater Yemen]*, Damascus: Maktabat al-Yaqatha al-'Arabiya, undated.

————, *al-Qaba'il al-'Arabiyya fi al-Sham [The Arab Tribes of the Levant]*, Vol. 1 Damascus: Maktabat al-Yaqatha al-'Arabiya, 2005.

Atwan, Abd-al-Bari, "Paradoxes in the Corridors of Damascus," *al-Quds al-'Arabi*, March 31, 2008.

'Awad, Mahmoud, "Burkan bila Nihaya fi-l-'Iraq [A Volcano Without End in Iraq]," *Dar al-Hayat* (in Arabic), April 20, 2008. As of October 7, 2009: http://www.iraqshabab.net/index.php?option=com_content&task=view&id=1609 &Itemid=39

al-Ayiri, Yusuf, "Mustaqbal al-'Iraq wa al-Jazirah al-Arabiyah ba'd Suqut Baghdad [The Future of Iraq and the Arabian Peninsula After the Fall of Baghdad]," unpublished, 2003. As of December 5, 2009: http://www.tawhed.ws/a?a=cfmaghvc

al-Baghdadi, Abu 'Umar, "al-Din al-Nasiha [Religion Is a Sincere Advice]," Hanein Forum Network (in Arabic), February 2008a. As of June 21, 2008: http://hanein.info/vb/showthread.php?t=54556&page=2

———, "Al-Qa'ida: al-'Iraq Jami'at al-Irhab [al-Qa'ida: Iraq Is University of Terrorism]," Middle East Online (in Arabic), April 17, 2008b. As of November 2008: http://www.middle-east-online.com/?id=47152

Baker, James A., III, Lee H. Hamilton, Lawrence S. Eagleburger, Vernon E. Jordan, Jr., Edwin Meese III, Sandra Day O'Connor, Leon E. Panetta, William J. Perry, Charles S. Robb, and Alan K. Simpson, *The Iraq Study Group Report*, December 6, 2006. As of October 19, 2009: http://www.usip.org/isg/index.html

Bakier, Abdul Hameed, "Jihad Wants You: Al-Qaeda Seeks Skilled Recruits in Iraq," *Terrorism Focus*, Vol. 5, No. 7, February 20, 2008. As of October 21, 2009: http://www.jamestown.org/single/?no_cache=1&tx_ttnews[tt_news]=4737

Barkey, Henry J., "Turkey and Iraq: The Perils (and Prospects) of Proximity," in Scott Lasenksy, ed., *Iraq and Its Neighbors*, Washington, D.C.: United States Institute for Peace, Special Report 141, July 2005. As of May 13, 2008: http://www.usip.org/resources/turkey-and-iraq-perils-and-prospects-proximity-0

Barnett, Michael, *Dialogues in Arab Politics: Negotiations in Regional Order*, Irvington, N.Y.: Columbia University Press, 1998.

Barzegar, Kayhan, *Conflicting Roles: A Study on the Roots of Iran and U.S. Disputes After September 11*, Tehran: International Relations Research Division, Expediency Council, 2006. As of December 26, 2006: http://www.csr.ir/departments.aspx?abtid=07&&semid=34m

Beehner, Lionel, "Iraq's Meddlesome Neighbors," backgrounder, New York: Council on Foreign Relations, August 31, 2006.

Bergen, Peter, and Paul Cruickshank, "The Iraq Effect: War Has Increased Terrorism Sevenfold Worldwide," *Mother Jones*, March/April 2007. As of August 4, 2009: http://www.motherjones.com/politics/2007/03/iraq-101-iraq-effect-war-iraq-and-its-impact-war-terrorism-pg-1

Bhadrakumar, M, K., "Energized Iran Builds More Bridges," *Asia Times*, May 06, 2008. As of December 7, 2009:
http://www.atimes.com/atimes/Middle_East/JE06Ak01.html

Blanchard, Christopher M., Kenneth Katzman, Carol Migdalovitz, Alfred Prados, and Jeremy Sharp, *Iraq: Regional Perspectives and U.S. Policy*, updated, Washington, D.C.: Congressional Research Service, April 4, 2008.

Blanford, Nicolas, "Among Kuwait's Salafis, a Rejection of Violence," *Christian Science Monitor*, October 20, 2006.

Brachman, Jarett, "Leading Egyptian Jihadist Sayyid Imam Renounces Violence," CTC Sentinel, Vol. 1, No. 1, December 2007, p. 13. As of December 5, 2009:
http://www.ctc.usma.edu/sentinel/CTCSentinel-Vol1Iss1.pdf

Bradley, John R., "Iran's Ethnic Tinderbox," *Washington Quarterly*, Vol. 30, No. 1, Winter 2006–2007, pp. 181–190.

Brandon, James, "Iran's Kurdish Threat: PJAK," *Jamestown Terrorism Monitor,* Vol. 4, No. 12, June 2006.

Brannen, Samuel, "Turkish Airstrikes in Northern Iraq," online article, Center for Strategic Studies, December 19, 2007. As of August 13, 2009:
http://csis.org/publication/turkish-airstrikes-northern-iraq

Brown, Nathan J., "Kuwait's 2008 Parliamentary Elections: A Setback for Democratic Islamism?" online commentary, Carnegie Endowment for International Peace, May 2008. As of October 19, 2009:
http://www.carnegieendowment.org/files/brown_kuwait2.pdf

Brumberg, Daniel, "Islam Is Not the Solution (or the Problem)," *Washington Quarterly*, Vol. 29, No. 1, Winter 2006, pp. 97–116.

Bruno, Greg, "Iraq's Forgotten Refugees," daily analysis, New York: Council on Foreign Relations, October 16, 2007. As of August 6, 2009:
http://www.cfr.org/publication/14529/iraqs_forgotten_refugees.html

Bunker, Robert J., and John P. Sullivan, "Suicide Bombing in Operation Iraqi Freedom," Arlington, Va.: The Institute of Land Warfare, Paper No. 46W, September 2004.

Byman, Daniel L., and Kenneth Pollack, "Explosive Affinities: Cross-Border Consequences of Civil Strife in Iraq," *Berlin Journal*, Fall 2006. As of May 4, 2008:
http://www.brookings.edu/articles/2006/fall_iraq_pollack.aspx

———, *Things Fall Apart: Containing the Spillover From an Iraqi Civil War*, Washington, D.C.: The Brookings Institution, The Saban Center for Middle East Policy, January 2007.

Cagapty, Soner, "A Middle East Study Tour: Perspectives from Turkey," *PolicyWatch*, No. 1322, December 19, 2007. As of November 6, 2009: http://thewashingtoninstitute.com/templateC05.php?CID=2699

Carapico, Sheila, *Civil Society in Yemen: The Political Economy of Activism in Modern Arabia*, New York: Cambridge University Press, 2007.

Center for Strategic Research, *Foreign Policy* Research Division, "Arab Countries' Concerns About Iran in the Light of the New Environment in the Region," Tehran, 2006. As of December 19, 2006: http://www.csr.ir/departments.aspx?abtid=04&&semid=68

Chamberlin, Wendy, ed., *Viewpoints Special Edition: Iraq's Refugee and IDP Crisis: Human Toll and Implications*, Washington, D.C.: Middle East Institute, 2008. As of October 2009: http://www.mei.edu/Default.aspx?TabID=541

Charbel, Ghassan, "Iran al-Kha'ifa wa al-Mukhifa [Iran: Scared and Scary]," *Dar al-Hayat* (in Arabic), January 17, 2008. Available in English as of October 21, 2009: http://www.daralhayat.com/archivearticle/247694

"Clashes Spread in Northeast Syria, at Least 30 Dead," *New York Times*, March 14, 2004.

"CNOOC Confirms Preliminary Gas Deal with Iran—Xinhua," Reuters, December 22, 2007. As of October 22, 2008: http://www.iht.com/articles/ap/2007/12/10/business/AS-FIN-China-Iran-Oil.php

Cockburn, Patrick, and Jerome Taylor, "Conflict in Iraq: The Sniper Who Shoots on Video," *Independent* (London), November 9, 2006. As of January 2009: http://www.*Independent*.co.uk/news/world/middle-east/conflict-in-iraq-the-sniper-who-shoots-on-video-423530.html

Cole, David, and Jules Lobel, "Are We Safer? A Report Card on the War on Terror," *Los Angeles Times*, November 18, 2007. As of October 21, 2009: http://www.latimes.com/media/acrobat/2007-11/33860990.pdf

Cordesman, Anthony H., "Iraq's Evolving Insurgency," rev. working draft, Washington, D.C.: Center for Strategic and International Studies, December 9, 2005.

Crystal, Jill, "Public Order and Authority: Policing Kuwait," in Paul Dresch and James Piscatori, *Monarchies and Nations: Globalization and Identity in the Arab States of the Gulf*, New York: I.B. Tauris, 2005.

al-Dakhil, Khalid, "Al-Taakul al-Dawr al-Misri fi al-Mintaqa [The Erosion of the Egyptian Role in the Region]," Al Arabiya (in Arabic), July 5, 2006.

Daragahi, Borzou, "Rift over Shiites Is Seen in Bahrain's Royal Court," *Los Angeles Times*, July 7, 2007.

"al-Dawr al-Russi fi 'Amliyat al-Salam fi al-Sharq al-Awsat [The Russian Role in the Middle East Peace Process]," *Ma Wara' al-Khabr* [*Behind the News*], Al Jazeera (in Arabic), March 22, 2008. As of September 29, 2009: http://www.aljazeera.net/NR/exeres/1B7228C4-52BB-4964-8622-1A96C03F3795.htm

"Deadly Gun Battle in Gaza Mosque," BBC News, August 14, 2009. As of October 10, 2009: http://news.bbc.co.uk/2/hi/8202553.stm

Dehghani, Mahmoud, "The Role of the New Iraq in the Security Orders in the Persian Gulf," Tehran: Center for Strategic Research, *Foreign Policy* Research Division, 2003. As of December 20, 2006: http://www.csr.ir/departments.aspx?abtid=07&&semid=306

"Demands Issued on Johnston Tape," BBC News, May 9, 2007. As of October 10, 2009: http://news.bbc.co.uk/2/hi/middle_east/6637507.stm

Department of the Air Force, "Air Force Posture Statement 2008," Washington, D.C., February 27, 2008. As of September 1, 2008: http://www.posturestatement.af.mil/shared/media/document/AFD-080310-037.pdf

al-Dhaheri, Mohammed Mohsen, "Tribes Should Be Social Entities not Political Participants, Says al-Dhaheri," interview by Zaid al Alaya'a, *Yemen Observer*, September 22, 2007. As of October 21, 2009: http://www.yobserver.com/reports/10012989.html

al-Dhaydi, Mshari, "Warning to Those Who Wear Turbans," *Asharq Al-Awsat* (in Arabic), July 19, 2007. As of October 17, 2007: http://www.asharqalawsat.com/leader.asp?section=3&issue=10430&article=424347

al-Dhiyabi, Jamil, "Fa'es Amrika wa Ghatrasat Iran" [America's Ax and Iran's Arrogance]," *Dar Al Hayat*, June, 25, 2007

al-Din, 'Irfan Nizam, "al-'Arab wa al-Fawda al-'Alamiya al-Jadida [The Arabs and the New International Chaos]," *Dar al-Hayat* (in Arabic), September 1, 2008.

Dodge, Toby Craig, "The Social Ontology of Late Colonialism: Tribes and the Mandated State in Iraq," in Faleh A. Jabar and Hosham Dawod, eds., *Tribes and Power: Nationalism and Ethnicity in the Middle East*, London: Saqi Books, 2007, pp. 257–282.

Dreyfuss, Robert, "Beware the NIE," *Tom Paine Common Sense*, website, September 26, 2006. As of October 21, 2009: http://www.tompaine.com/articles/2006/09/26/beware_the_nie.php

Ehteshami, Anoushiravan, "Iran-Iraq Relations After Saddam," *Washington Quarterly*, Autumn 2003.

————, "Iran's International Posture After the Fall of Baghdad," *Middle East Journal*, Vol. 58, No. 2, Spring 2004.

Eisenstadt, Michael, "Target Iraq's Republican Guard," *Middle East Quarterly*, December 1996. As of September 9, 2008:
http://www.meforum.org/article/415

————, "Living With a Nuclear Iran?" *Survival*, Vol. 41, No. 3, Autumn 1999, pp. 124–148.

————, "The Historical and Sociopolitical Context of IEDs: Lessons from the Middle East," presented to the Washington Institute for the National Academies Committee on Defeating IEDs, February 2006.

al-Ekri, 'Abd al-Nabi, "Mutatallabat wa Tabi'at al-Islah al-Khaliji [Requirements and Developments of Gulf Reform]," unpublished paper, Manama, Bahrain, undated (provided to the authors November 2006).

————, "Bahrain: Al-Wefaq and the Challenges of Participation," *Arab Reform Bulletin*, Vol. 5, No. 4, May 2007.

Energy Information Agency, Office of Integrated Analysis and Forecasting, *International Energy Outlook: 2006*, Washington, D.C.: U.S. Department of Energy, June 2006. As of October 21, 2009:
http://www.eia.doe.gov/oiaf/ieo/index.html

————, "Country Analysis Briefs: China," August 2006.

————, "Country Analysis Briefs: Iran," October 2007.

————, "Country Energy Profiles: China," 2008.

Enginsoy, Ümit, "U.S. Upgrades Ties with Iraqi Kurds, Albeit Invisibly," *Turkish Daily News*, May 27, 2008. As of August 13, 2008:
http://www.turkey-now.org/db/Docs/CAP_turkey.pdf

England, Andrew, "Arab Street Warms to Showman Ahmadi-Nejad," *Financial Times*, April 6, 2007.

Ephraim Kam, "Marching Johnny Home: Evacuating the American Forces from Iraq," *Strategic Assessment*, Vol. 8, No. 4, February 2006.

Evron, Yair, "An Israel-Iran Balance of Nuclear Deterrence: Seeds of Instability," in Efraim Kam, ed., *Israel and a Nuclear Iran: Implications for Arms Control, Deterrence, and Defense*, Tel Aviv: Institute for National Security Studies, July 2008.

Ezzat, Dina, "Gaza or Tehran: Is Egypt Ceding Influence to Iran in Gaza and Is the Latter Fighting for It?" *Al-Ahram*, December 14–18, 2008.

FAFO, "Iraqis in Jordan 2007: Their Number and Characteristics," Oslo, 2007. As of August 6, 2009:
http://www.fafo.no/ais/middeast/jordan/Iraqis_in_Jordan.htm

Fagen, Patricia Weiss, *Iraqi Refugees: Seeking Stability in Syria and Jordan*, Washington D.C.: Georgetown University, Institute for the Study of International Migration, 2007.

al-Fajr Media Center, tract, September 2007.

Fandy, Mamoun, "al-'Iraq: Ja'izat al-'Arab al-Kubra [Iraq: The Great Arab Prize]," *Asharq Al-Awsat* (in Arabic), June 9, 2008. As of October 19, 2009:
http://www.asharqalawsat.com/leader.asp?section=3&issueno=10786&article=474218

al-Faqir, 'Abd al-Rahman, "The Real War and the Symbolic War: The 'Scorpio Sting,' Part 1," October 22, 2007. (in English). As of December 8, 2009:
http://www.jihadica.com/wp-content/uploads/2008/09/9-3-08-ekhlaas-real-war-vs-symbolic-ware28094violence-to-eliminate-enemy-vs-terrorist-violence.pdf

Fattah, Hassan M., "An Island Kingdom Feels the Ripples from Iran and Iraq," *New York Times*, April 16, 2006a.

———, "Bickering Saudis Struggle or an Answer to Iran's Rising Influence in the Middle East," *New York Times*, December 22, 2006b.

"Fatwas in Saudi Arabia Calling for Demolishing the Shrine of Imam Al-Husayn and Al-Sayyidah Zaynab, Peace Be Upon Them, and Volunteer Committees of Students of Muhammad Bin-Sa'ud University to Instigate the Demolition of the Shrines," *al-Najaf News* (in Arabic), July 19, 2007. As of July 2007:
http://www.alnajafnews.net

Felter, Joseph, and Brian Fishman, "al-Qa'ida's Foreign Fighters in Iraq: A First Look at the Sinjar Records," West Point, N.Y.: Combating Terrorism Center, Harmony Project, December 2007. As of September 9, 2008:
http://www.ctc.usma.edu

"Fighting in Nahr al-Bared Splits Tripoli into Two Camps," *Daily Star*, July 3, 2007.

Fishman, Brian, "After Zarqawi: The Dilemmas of the Future of Al Qaeda in Iraq," *Washington Quarterly*, Autumn 2006, pp. 19–32.

———, "Dysfunction and Decline: Lessons Learned from Inside al-Qa'ida in Iraq," West Point, N.Y.: Combating Terrorism Center, March 16, 2009. As of 19 April 2009:
http://www.ctc.usma.edu/harmony/pdf/DD_FINAL_FINAL.pdf

Fishman, Brian, Peter Bergen, Joseph Felter, Vahid Brown, and Jacob Shapiro, *Bombers, Bank Accounts, and Bleedout*, West Point, N.Y.: Combating Terrorism Center, Harmony Project, July 2008. As of September 9, 2008: http://www.ctc.usma.edu/harmony/pdf/Sinjar_2_July_23.pdf

Fisk, Robert, "Lebanese Salute Their 'Martyr' in Iraq War," *Independent* (London), July 7, 2006.

Fitzpatrick, Mark, *The Iranian Nuclear Crisis: Avoiding Worst-Case Outcomes*, Washington, D.C.: International Institute for Strategic Studies, Adelphi Paper 398, November 2008. As of September 30, 2009: http://www.iiss.org/publications/adelphi-papers/adelphi-papers-2008/the-iranian-nuclear-crisis/

Fleishman, Jeffrey, "Report on Iran Fuels Arab Fears," *Los Angeles Times*, December 6, 2007.

Freedberg, Sydney J., Jr., "Iraqi Rebels: the New Iraqi Way of War," *National Journal*, June 8, 2007. As of July 28, 2008: http://www.nationaljournal.com/njcover2.htm

Freedman, Robert O., "The Putin Visit to Saudi Arabia, Qatar and Jordan: Business Promotion or Great Power Maneuvering?" *Independent* (London), February 15, 2007a. As of October 14, 2009: http://www.cdi.org/russia/johnson/2007-39-39.cfm

———, "The Russian Resurgence in the Middle East," *China and Eurasia Forum Quarterly*, Vol. 5, No. 3, 2007b, pp. 19–27.

Freeman, Chas W., "The Arabs Take a Chinese Wife: Sino-Arab Relations in the Decade to Come," Remarks to the World Affairs Council of Northern California at Asilomar, Pacific Grove, Calif., May 7, 2006. As of October 23, 2009: http://www.mepc.org/whats/SinoArabRelations.asp

al-Furqan Foundation, "Regarding the Recent Crusader Attack on the Jihadi Media," Islamic State of Iraq, September 13, 2003. As of October 22, 2008: http://www.globalterroralert.com

Furtig, Henner, "Conflict and Cooperation in the Persian Gulf: The Interregional Order and US Policy," *Middle East Journal*, Vol. 61, No. 4, Fall 2007.

Gaballah, Khalifa, "Experts: Iran Mapping The Future of the Region Together with Saudi Arabia in the Absence of an Egyptian Role," *Al-Misri Al-Yawm* (in Arabic), March 9, 2007.

Gambill, Gary C., "Salafi-Jihadism in Lebanon," *Middle East Monitor*, Vol. 3, No. 1, January–March 2008. As of May 2, 2008: http://www.mideastmonitor.org/issues/0801/0801_1.htm

Gause, F. Gregory, III, "Revolutionary Fevers and Regional Contagion: Domestic Structures and the 'Export' of Revolution in the Middle East," *Journal of South Asian and Middle Eastern Studies*, Vol. 14, No. 3, Spring 1991.

———, "Saudi Arabia: Iraq, Iran and the Regional Power Balance and the Sectarian Question," *Strategic Insights*, February 2007.

Georgi, Lydia, "Saudi Oil Reserve for China a Win-Win Proposition," *Middle East Online*, April 25, 2006.

Ghali, Ibrahim, "Russia wa al-Mihwar al-Mumana'in al-'Arab . . . Hudud al-'Alaqa [Russia and the Axis of Arab Rejectionists . . . Limits of the Relationship]," *IslamOnline*, October 28, 2007 (in Arabic). As of October 2009:
http://www.islamonline.net/servlet/Satellite?c=ArticleA_C&cid=1193049192650&pagename=Zone-Arabic-News%2FNWALayout

al-Gheit, Abu, interview, *Nile News*, August 5, 2008. Also available (in Arabic) as of August 6, 2008:
http://www.ndp.org.eg/ar/News/ViewNewsDetails.aspx?NewsID=39123

Gibbons, Robert, "Saudi Says U.S. Policy Handing Iraq to Iran," *San Diego Union-Tribune*, September 21, 2005.

di Giovannangeli, Umberto, "Afghani, Sauditi, Iracheni, Ceceni A Gaza una Legione Straniera Jihadista [Afghans, Saudis, Iraqis, Chechens: Jihadist Foreign Legion in Gaza]," *l'Unita* (in Italian), February 10, 2008. As of January 2009:
http://www.mauronovelli.it/B%20Isr%20Pal%2010%20e%2011%20febb%202008.htm#1959-15534552

Global Islamic Media Front, "Tawqit Dakhul Tanzim al-Qa'ida ila al-Filistin [The Timing of the Entry of al-Qa'ida into Palestine]," al Boraq website (in Arabic), January 28, 2008. As of October 2009:
http://www.alboraq.info/showthread.php?t=39579t

Global Security, "Military: PJAK/PEJAK," Web article, December 11, 2007. As of August 17, 2009:
http://www.globalsecurity.org/military/world/para/pjak.htm

Goldberg, Jacob, "After Iraq: What Will the Middle East Look Like?" *Atlantic Monthly*, January/February 2008.

Gordon, Michael R., and Dexter Filkins, "Hezbollah Said to Help Shiite Army in Iraq," *New York Times*, November 28, 2006. As of October 14, 2009:
http://www.nytimes.com/2006/11/28/world/middleeast/28military.html

Guldimann, Tim, "The Iranian Nuclear Impasse," *Survival*, Vol. 49, No. 3, Autumn 2007, pp. 169–178.

Gundzik, Jephraim P., "The Ties That Bind China, Russia and Iran," *Asia Times*, June 4, 2005. As of October 23, 2009:
http://www.atimes.com/atimes/China/GF04Ad07.html

Gwertzman, Bernard, "Sick: Alliance Against Iran," interview with Gary Sick, Council on Foreign Relations, January 23, 2007. As of September 30, 2009: http://www.cfr.org/publication/12477/

Haahr, Kathryn, "New Reports Allege Foreign Fighters in Iraq Returning to Europe," *Terrorism Focus*, Vol. 3, No. 20, 23 May 2006.

Hafez, Mohammed M., *Suicide Bombers in Iraq: The Strategy and Ideology of Martyrdom*, Washington, D.C.: United States Institute of Peace Press, 2007.

al-Handal, Shaykh Mahruth, *Qabila 'Aniza: Tarikhiha, Rajalatiha, Insabiha fi al-'Iraq wa al-Jazira* [*The Tribe of 'Aniza: Its History, Journeys, and Movement in Iraq and the Arabian Peninsula*], Beirut: Dar al-Rafidayn, 2005.

Harb, Osama al-Ghazali, "al-Hiqba al-Iraniya [The Iranian Epoch]," *al-Siyasa al-Dawliya* (in Arabic), No. 173, July 2008. As of October 22, 2008: http://www.siyassa.org.eg/asiyassa/Index.asp?CurFN=efti0.htm&DID=9630

Harik, Judith, *The Public and Social Services of the Lebanese Militias*, Oxford: Center for Lebanese Studies, 1994.

Hasan Abu Talib, "al-Sin wa al-Sharq al-Awsat: bayn Ramziyat al-Siyasa wa Takamul al-Iqtisad [China and the Middle East: Between Political Symbolism and Economic Integration]," *al-Siyasa al-Dawliya* (in Arabic), No. 173, July 2008.

Haykel, Bernard, "Saudis United," blog posting, Middle East Strategy at Harvard, John M. Olin Institute for Strategic Studies, December 16, 2007. As of August 6, 2009: http://blogs.law.harvard.edu/mesh/2007/12/saudis_united/

Hegghammer, Thomas, "Global Jihadism After The Iraq War," *Middle East Journal*, Vol. 60, No. 1, Winter 2006.

———, "Islamist Violence and Regime Stability," *International Affairs*, July 22, 2008. As of January 2009: http://hegghammer.com/

Henderson, Simon, "The Elephant in the Gulf: The Arab States and Iran's Nuclear Program," Washington Institute for Near East Policy, Policy Watch 1065, December 21, 2005. As of October 2009: http://www.washingtoninstitute.org

Hersh, Seymour M., "Plan B: Annals of National Security," *New Yorker*, Vol. 80, No. 17, June 28, 2004.

Hess, Pamela, "US Intel: al-Qaida May Move Outside Iraq," Associated Press, February 5, 2008.

Heydemann, Steven, "Upgrading Authoritarianism in the Arab World," Washington, D.C.: The Brookings Institution, Analysis Paper No. 13, October 2007. As of October 2009: http://www.brookings.edu/papers/2007/10arabworld.aspx

Hiltermann, Joost, "Iraq and the New Sectarianism in the Middle East," Synopsis of a Presentation at the Massachusetts Institute of Technology, November 12, 2006. As of April 10, 2008:
http://www.crisisgroup.org/home/index.cfm?id=4558

Hindi, Linda, "Iraqi Expatriates Costing Jordan $1 Billion Annually—Interior Ministry," *Jordan Times*, May 7, 2007.

Hitchens, Christopher, "Did the Toppling of Saddam Hussein Lead to Recent Events in Iran?" *Slate*, July 6, 2009. As of July 23, 2009:
http://www.slate.com/id/2222254

Hoffman, Bruce, "The Myth of Grass Roots Terrorism: Why Osama bin Laden Still Matters," *Foreign Affairs Journal*, May/June 2008.

el-Hokayem, Emile, and Matteo Legrenzi, "The Arab Gulf States in the Shadow of the Iranian Nuclear Challenge," working paper, Washington D.C.: The Stimson Center, May 2006. As of June 2007:
http://www.stimson.org/

al-Humayd, Tariq, "'Ala Matha Tufawad Washington Tehran? [What Will Washington Negotiate With Tehran?]," *Asharq Al-Awsat* (in Arabic), October 15, 2007a.

———, "Wartat al-Taqrir al-Istikhbarati 'An al-'Iran [The Implication of the Intelligence Report on Iran," *Asharq Al-Awsat*, December 6, 2007b. As of December 5, 2009:
http://www.aawsat.com/leader.asp?section=3&article=448614&issueno=10600

———, "Betraying the Awakening Council," *Asharq Al-Awsat* (in English), August 24, 2008.

Imam, Sayyid, "The Rationalization of Jihad in Egypt and the World," *al-Masri al-Yawm*, serialized November–December 2007.

"Intelligence Brief: Russia's Moves in Syria," *Power and Interest News Report*, June 30, 2006. As of December 7, 2009:
http://intellibriefs.blogspot.com/2006/07/intelligence-brief-russias-moves-in.html

International Crisis Group, *Iran in Iraq: How Much Influence?* Amman/Brussels, Middle East Report No. 38, March 21, 2005.

International Monetary Fund, "IMF Executive Board Concludes 2007 Article IV Consultation with the Syrian Arab Republic," Public Information Notice No. 07/104, August 15, 2007. As of May 5, 2008:
http://www.imf.org/external/np/sec/pn/2007/pn07104.htm

"Iran and Saudi Arabia Confrontation in the Middle East," *Aftab News* (in Farsi), December 5, 2006. As of December 21, 2006:
http://www.aftabnews.ir/vdchkqn23znkm.html

"Iran Tujadid Qasfuha lil-Qura al-Hadudiya fi Kurdistan al-Iraq [Iran Renews Its Strikes on the Border Villages of Iraqi Kurdistan]," *Asharq Al-Awsat* (in Arabic), September 28, 2007. As of September 9, 2008:
http://www.asharqalawsat.com/

"Iranian Forces Shell Sulmaniya Border Areas," *Aswat al-Iraq* (in English), June 6, 2008.

"Iraq Index: Tracking Reconstruction and Security in Post-Saddam Iraq," website, Washington, D.C.: Brookings Institution, Saban Center for Middle East Policy, October 22, 2008. As of October 22, 2008:
http://www.brookings.edu/saban/iraq-index.aspx

"Iraq Offers Training Opportunities for Gulf Jihadists, but It May Not Be Afghanistan Mark Two," *Gulf States Newsletter*, Vol. 30, No. 783, June 9, 2006.

"Iraqi Security: Female Suicide Bombers Were Mentally Disabled; Bombs Detonated Remotely," *Jihad Watch*, website, February 1, 2008. As of January 2009:
http://www.jihadwatch.org/archives/019781.php

"Israel's Deputy DefMin Interviewed on Iran, Palestinians, Regional Issues," *Jerusalem Post*, November 10, 2006.

Izzak, B., "Interior Minister Rebuffs Tribal Rift," *Kuwait Times*, April 18, 2008.

Ja'far, Qasim Muhammad, "'Awda Russia ila al-Saha al-Dawliya wa Atharha 'ala al-'Arab [Russia's Return to the International Arena and Its Impact on the Arabs]," Al Jazeera (in Arabic), September 2, 2008.

Janardhan, N., "Kuwait Wakes up to the Face of Militant Islam," Terrorism Monitor, Vol. 3, No. 9, May 6, 2005. As of August 13, 2009:
http://www.jamestown.org/single/?no_cache=1&tx_ttnews[tt_news]=159

Jones, Seth, "The Rise of Afghanistan's Insurgency: State Failure and Jihad," *International Security Journal*, Vol. 32, No. 4, Spring 2008.

Jones, Toby Craig, "The Iraq Effect in Saudi Arabia," *Middle East Report*, No. 237, Winter 2005. As of September 18, 2006:
http://www.merip.org/mer/mer237/jones.html

Judson, David, "Israel Denies Helping Iraqi Kurds, Sees One Iraq," *Turkish Daily News*, April 20, 2007.

Kabbara, Rouba, "Al Qaeda Bombers Target Oil Pipelines," *The Age*, December 20, 2004. As of July 20, 2008:
http://www.theage.com.au/news/War-on-Terror/Al-Qaeda-bombers-target-oil-pipelines/2004/12/19/1103391636195.html

Kagan, Frederick W., Kimberly Kagan, and Danielle Pletka, "Iranian Influence in the Levant, Iraq and Afghanistan," paper, Washington, D.C.: American Enterprise Institute for Public Policy, February 19, 2008. As of August 13, 2009:
http://www.aei.org/paper/27526

Kagan, Kimberly, "Iran's Proxy War Against the United States and the Iraqi Government," Institute for the Study of War and the *Weekly Standard*, May 2006–August 2007.

Kassianova, Alla, "Russian Weapons Sales to Iran: Why They Are Unlikely to Stop," Washington, D.C., Center for Strategic and International Studies, Program on New Approaches to Russian Security, Policy Memo 427, December 2006.

Katz, Mark, "Russian-Iranian Relations in the Ahmadinejad Era," *Middle East Journal*, Vol. 62, No. 2, Spring 2008.

Katzman, Kenneth, "Iran's Activities and Influence in Iraq," Washington, D.C.: Congressional Research Service, December 27, 2007.

Kaye, Dalia Dassa, and Frederic M. Wehrey, "A Nuclear Iran: The Reactions of Neighbours," *Survival*, Vol. 49 No. 2, Summer 2007, pp. 111–128.

Kazemi, Nibras, "A Virulent Ideology in Mutation: Zarqawi Upstages Maqdisi," in Hillel Fradkin, Husain Haqqani, and Eric Brown, eds., *Current Trends in Islamist Ideology*, Vol. 2, Washington D.C.: Hudson Institute, Center on Islam, Democracy, and the Future of the Muslim World, 2005. As of December 5, 2009:
http://www.currenttrends.org/docLib/20060130_Current_Trends_v2.pdf

Kemp, Geoffrey, "The U.S. and Iran: The Nuclear Dilemma: Next Steps," paper, Washington D.C.: The Nixon Center, April 2004.

Kemp, Geoffrey, Michael Eisenstadt, Farideh Farhi, and Nasser Hadian, "Iran's Bomb: American and Iranian Perspectives," paper, Washington D.C.: The Nixon Center, March 2004.

Khadduri, Walid, "Oil in a Week (China's Oil Consumption Increased despite Price Hikes)," *Dar Al Hayat*, July 29, 2008.

al-Khalidi, Ashraf, Sophia Hoffmann, and Victor Tanner, *Iraqi Refugees in the Syrian Arab Republic: A Field-Based Snapshot*, Washington D.C.: The Brookings Institution–University of Bern Project on Internal Displacement, June 2007.

Kiernan, Peter, "Middle East Opinion: Iran Fears Aren't Hitting the Arab Street," based on University of Maryland/Zogby International 2006 Annual Arab Public Opinion Survey, New York: Zogby International, March 2, 2007. As of August 16, 2009:
http://www.zogby.com/Soundbites/readclips.cfm?ID=14570

Kostiner, Joseph, "Coping with Regional Challenges: A Case Study of Crown Prince Abdullah's Peace Initiative," in Paul Aarts and Gerd Nonneman, eds., *Saudi Arabia in the Balance: Political Economy, Society, Foreign Affairs*, London: Hurst & Company, 2005, pp. 352–371.

"Kurdish Landmine Kills Three," *The Australian*, July 28, 2008. As of August 13, 2008:
http://www.theaustralian.news.com.au/story/0,25197,24087668-12377,00.html

Kurdish Regional Government, Statement on First High-Level Talks with Turkey, May 2008. As of August 13, 2008:
http://www.krg.org/articles/detail.asp?lngnr=12&smap=02010100&rnr=223&anr=24025

"Kurdish Officials," Agence France Presse, March 17, 2004.

"Kuwait MPs Expelled for Mourning Mughniyah," Al Arabiya (in English), February 20, 2008. As of May 13, 2008:
http://www.alarabiya.net/articles/2008/02/20/45901.html

"Kuwait: Thousands Demonstrate to Protest Crackdown on Illegal Tribal Primaries," Associated Press, May 4, 2008.

Kupchan, Charles, and Ray Takeyh, "Iran Just Won't Stay Isolated," *Los Angeles Times*, March 4, 2008.

"Kuwait Tribes Storm Police Station in Pre-Election Unrest," *Gulf News*, May 4, 2008.

La Franchi, Howard, "As Mideast Realigns, US Leans Sunni," *Christian Science Monitor*, October 9, 2007.

bin Laden, Osama, "Reasons of the Struggle on the Occasion of the 60th Anniversary of the Founding of the Occupying State of Israel," statement "To the Western Peoples," English trans. of audiorecording, May 16, 2008. As of December 5, 2009:
http://www.jihadica.com/wp-content/uploads/2008/05/5-16-08-bin-laden-statement-reasons-for-the-conflict-english.pdf

"Asbab al-Sara'a fi al-Dhikra al-Sittin li-Qiyam Dawla al-Ihtilal al-Isra'ili [The Reasons for the Conflict on the 60th Anniversary of the Creation of the Occupation State of Israel]," produced by Nakhbat al-'Alam al-Jihadi, May 16, 2008. Transcript (in Arabic) as of December 2008:
http://hanein.info/vb/showthread.php?t=67289.

———, "Rissala Muwajaha ila al-*Umma* al-Islamiya" [Letter to the Muslim People]," audio recording (in Arabic), May 18, 2008. As of January 2009:
http://www.aljazeera.net/news/archive/archive?ArchiveId=1090963

Laipson, Ellen, "The Iraqi Refugee Crisis in Regional Context," testimony before the Senate Foreign Relations Committee Subcommittee on the Middle East and South Asia, March 31, 2009. As of October 2009:
http://www.stimson.org/swa/pdf/IraqRefugeesLaipson.pdf

"Lamhat 'an Inba'ath al-Salafiyya fi Suriya" [An Overview of the Salafi Resurgence in Syria]," posted by Abu al-Hussain to the Ana al-Muslim forum (in Arabic), January 21, 2009. As of January 2009:
http://www.muslm.net/vb/showthread.php?t=328790

Larrabee, F. Stephen, "A War of Nerves in Turkey," *Japan Times*, May 12, 2007a.

————, "Turkey Rediscovers the Middle East," *Foreign Affairs*, Vol. 86, No. 4, July/August 2007b.

————, *Turkey as a U.S. Security Partner*, Santa Monica, Calif.: RAND Corporation, MG-694-AF, 2008. As of October 2009:
http://www.rand.org/pubs/monographs/MG694/

Lawson, Fred H., "Syria's Relations with Iran: Managing the Dilemmas of Alliance," *Middle East Journal*, Vol. 61, No. 1, Winter 2007, pp. 29–47.

Lei, W., "China-Arab Energy Cooperation: The Strategic Importance of Institutionalization," *Middle East Economic Survey*, Vol. 49, No. 3, January 16, 2006.

Leverett, Flynt, and Jeffrey Bader, "Managing China-U.S. Energy Competition in the Middle East," *Washington Quarterly*, Winter 2005–2006.

Lischer, Sarah Kenyon, "Security and Displacement in Iraq," *International Security*, Vol. 33, No. 2, Fall 2008.

Lowe, Robert, "The Syrian Kurds: A People Discovered," London: Chatham House, Middle East Programme, January 2006. As of May 4, 2008:
http://www.chathamhouse.org.uk/files/3297_bpsyriankurds.pdf

Lowe, Robert, and Claire Spencer, eds., *Iran, Its Neighbors and the Regional Crises*, London: Chatham House, Royal Institute of International Affairs, 2006.

Lynch, Marc, "Ahmadinejad and the Gulf," posting to author's blog, "Abu Aardvark," December 4, 2007. As of December 5, 2009:
http://abuaardvark.typepad.com/abuaardvark/2007/12/ahmednejad-and.html

————, "Dueling Arab Summits," *Foreign Policy*, January 16, 2009. As of August 14, 2009:
http://lynch.foreignpolicy.com/posts/2009/01/16/dueling_arab_summits

Mack, Andrew, ed., *Human Security Brief 2007*, Vancouver, B.C.: Simon Fraser University, Human Security Report Project, May 21, 2008. As of October 2009:
http://www.humansecuritybrief.info/access.html

bin Mahmud, Hussayn, "Rai al-Shaikh bin Mahmud fi al-Tarshid al-Ma'azum [The Opinion of Shaikh bin Mahmud on the so-called Rationalization]," *al-Hesbah*, website on November 21, 2007.

Malbrunot, George, "Les Milices Libanaises Commencent à Réarmer [The Lebanese Militia Begin to Rearm]," *Le Figaro* (in French), October 15, 2007. As of October 2009:
http://www.lefigaro.fr/international/20070419.WWW000000394_les_milices_libanaises_commencent_a_rearmer.html

Malik, 'Adel, "min al-Bahr al-Abiad ila al-Bahr al-Aswad: Mashari'a Haroob Sakhina wa Barida . . . Bidayat Suqut al-Ahadiya al-Amirkiya wa Inba'ath al-Thunaiya al-Taqlidiya [From the Mediterranean to the Black Sea: Plans for Hot and Cold Wars . . . The Beginning of the Fall of American Unipolarity and the Resurrection of Traditional Bipolarity]," *Dar al-Hayat* (in Arabic), August 31, 2008.

Mansharof, Y., H. Varulkar, D. Lav, and Y. Carmon, "The Middle East on a Collision Course (4): Saudi/Sunni-Iranian/Shiite Conflict—Diplomacy and Proxy Wars," Washington, D.C.: Middle East Media Research Institute, Inquiry and Analysis Series, No. 324, February 9, 2007.

Maqdimi, 'Abd al-Rauf, "Amniyat bi Nasr Amriki fi al-'Iraq [Wishes for an American Victory in Iraq]," *Dar al-Hayat* (in Arabic), May 10, 2007.

al-Marhun, 'Abd al-Jalil Zaid, "Amn al-Khalij wa Ishkaliyat al-Dawr al 'Arabi [Gulf Security and the Problematic of the Arab Role]," Al Jazeera (in Arabic), November 11, 2007. As of October, 8, 2009:
http://www.aljazeera.net/NR/exeres/C10E2163-AE2C-4825-81D8-D8E827544B2B.htm

Marques, Joseph, "World View," column, *Gulf News*, August 2, 2007. As of August 13, 2009:
http://archive.gulfnews.com/articles/07/08/03/10143771.html

The Media Commission for the Victory of the Iraqi People, the Mujahidin Services Center, "Iraq al-Jihad Aamal wa Akhtar: Tahlil Li-Waq'a wa Istishraf Li-l-Mustaqbal wa Khatwat 'Amliya 'ala Tariq al-Jihad al-Mubarak [Iraqi Jihad, Hopes and Risks: Analysis of the Reality and Visions for the Future, and Actual Steps in the Path of the Blessed Jihad]," (in Arabic), undated. As of October 9, 2009:
http://www.e-prism.org/images/book_-_Iraq_al-Jihad.doc

Meyers, Steven Lee, "Iraq Provinces Try to Overcome Political Disarray," *New York Times*, April 16, 2009.

Miller, Greg, "Osama bin Laden's Son May Be in Pakistan too," *Los Angeles Times*, January 17, 2009. Available as of January 2009 at:
http://www.latimes.com/news/nationworld/world/la-fg-intel17-2009jan17,0,7167684.story

Moussa, 'Amr, "Speech to the Arab League Summit in Damascus," Damascus: League of Arab States website (in Arabic), March 29, 2008. As of October 2009:
http://www.arableagueonline.org/las/arabic/details_ar.jsp?art_id=5486&level_id=943#

Movement for Justice and Democracy in Syria, *Shiism in Syria* (in Arabic), 2007. As of May 8, 2008:
http://forsyria.org/newsletterpdf/ShiiasmInSyria.pdf

"al-Mukhabarat al-Misriya Tuhaqaq m'a al-'Aa'idin men Gaza bi-Tahmat Dakhuliha li-l-Qiyam bi-'Amiliyyat Dadd Israel [Egyptian Intelligence Investigates Returnees from Gaza on Suspicion that they Entered to launch offensives against Israel]," *Asharq Al-Awsat* (in Arabic), February 9, 2008. As of January 2009:
http://www.asharqalawsat.com/details.asp?section=4&issueno=10665&article=45 7701&feature=

Nafi'a, Bashir Moussa, "Taraju'a al-Dawr al-Amiriki fi al-Mintaqa La Tuqalil min Makhatir al-Harb [A Retreat in the American Role in the Region Does Not Diminish the Threat of War]," *Al-'Asr* (in Arabic), June 19, 2008. As of October 22, 2008:
http://www.alasr.ws/index.cfm?method=home.con&contentid=10144

Nasr, Vali, *The Shia Revival: How Conflicts Within Islam Will Shape the Future*, New York: W.W. Norton & Co., 2006.

National Counterterrorism Center, Worldwide Incident Tracking System, Web page, undated. As of October 8, 2009:
http://wits.nctc.gov/Incidents.do

———, *2007 Report on Terrorism*, April 30, 2008. As of August 14, 2009:
http://wits.nctc.gov/Reports.do

National Intelligence Council, "Declassified Key Judgments of the National Intelligence Estimate 'Trends in Global Terrorism: Implications for the United States' dated April 2006," press release, McLean, Va.: Office of the Director of National Intelligence, September 26, 2006. As of October 20, 2009:
http://www.dni.gov/press_releases/Declassified_NIE_Key_Judgments.pdf

———, "National Intelligence Estimate: The Terrorist Threat to the US Homeland, press release, McLean, Va.: Office of the Director of National Intelligence, July 17, 2007a. As of October 20, 2009:
http://www.dni.gov/press_releases/20071203_release.pdf

———, "National Intelligence Estimate—Iran: Nuclear Intentions and Capabilities," press release, McLean, Va.: Office of the Director of National Intelligence, November 2007b. As of October 20, 2009:
http://www.dni.gov/press_releases/20071203_release.pdf

New York University Center for Global Affairs, "Iraq Post-2010," *CGA Scenarios*, No. 1, Spring 2007. As of April 2, 2007:
http://www.scps.nyu.edu/globalaffairs

Norton, Augustus Richard, "The Shiite 'Threat' Revisited," *Current History*, December 2007.

"Officials: Teens Trained for Suicide Bombings in Iraq," Cable News Network, May 26, 2008. As of July 20, 2008:
http://www.cnn.com/2008/WORLD/meast/05/26/iraq.main/index.html

Oliker, Olga, Keith Crane, Lowell H. Schwartz, and Catherine Yusupov, Russian *Foreign Policy*: Sources and Implications, Santa Monica, Calif.: RAND Corporation, MG-768-MF, 2009. As of August 16, 2009:
http://www.rand.org/pubs/monographs/MG768/

Olmert, Ehud, Speech to the American-Israeli Public Affairs Conference, March 12, 2007. As of October 2009:
http://www.aipac.org/Publications/SpeechesByPolicymakers/Olmert-PC-2007.pdf

Oppel, Richard A., Jr., "In Iraq, Conflict Simmers on a Second Kurdish Front," *New York Times*, October 23, 2007.

'Othman, Osama, "'Alaama Okhra 'ala al-Taraju'a al-Amiriki [Another Sign of American Retreat]," *al-Quds al-'Arabi* (in Arabic), August 21, 2008.

Ottaway, Marina, "Who Wins in Iraq? Arab Dictators," *Foreign Policy*, March/April 2007. As of April 7, 2008:
http://www.foreignpolicy.com/story/cms.php?story_id=3710

Ottaway, Marina, Nathan J. Brown, Amr Hamzawy, Karim Sadjadpour, and Paul Salem, *The New Middle East*, Washington, D.C.: The Carnegie Endowment for International Peace, 2008.

Partrick, Neil, "Dire Straits for US Mid-East Policy: The Gulf Arab States and US-Iran Relations," commentary, London: Royal United Services Institute, website, January 9, 2008. As of April 2008:
http://www.rusi.org/research/studies/menap/commentary/ref:C4784DF6A9E6B2/

Paz, Reuven, "The Impact of the War in Iraq on Islamist Groups and the Culture of Global Jihad," presented at the International Conference on the Impact of Global Terrorism at the International Policy Institute for Counter-Terrorism, September 11–14, 2004a. As of August 13, 2009:
http://www.e-prism.org/images/Impact_of_the_war_in_Iraq_-_paper.pdf

———, "Qa'idat al-Jihad, Iraq, and Madrid: The First Tile in the Domino Effect?" December 3, 2004b. As of October 2009:
http://www.ict.org.il/Articles/tabid/66/Articlsid/557/currentpage/14/Default.aspx

Peimani, Hooman, "Russia Turns to Iran for Oil Exports," *Asia Times*, February 11, 2003. As of October 2009:
http://www.atimes.com/atimes/Central_Asia/EB11Ag03.html

Peters, Ralph, "Blood Borders: How a Better Middle East Would Look," *Armed Forces Journal*, June 2006. As of April 10, 2008:
http://www.armedforcesjournal.com/2006/06/1833899

Pew—*See* Pew Global Attitudes Project.

Pew Global Attitudes Project, "Islamic Extremism: Common Concern for Muslim and Western Publics," survey findings, Washington, D.C.: Pew Research Center, July 14, 2005. As of August 14, 2009:
http://pewglobal.org/reports/

————, "Global Unease with Major World Powers," survey findings, Washington, D.C.: Pew Research Center, June 27, 2007. As of August 14, 2009:
http://pewglobal.org/reports/

————, "Global Economic Gloom—China and India Notable Exceptions," survey findings, Washington, D.C.: Pew Research Center, June 12, 2008. As of August 14, 2009:
http://pewglobal.org/reports/

————, "Confidence in Obama Lifts U.S. Image Around the World," survey findings, Washington, D.C.: Pew Research Center, July 23, 2009. As of August 14, 2009:
http://pewglobal.org/reports/

Phillips, Sarah, "Cracks in the Yemeni System," *Middle East Report*, July 2005. As of May 1, 2008:
http://www.merip.org/mero/mero072805.html

Pollack, Kenneth, Daniel Byman, David Fromkin, and Dennis Ross, "Lines in the Sand," *Vanity Fair*, January 2008.

Pollock, David, "Kuwait: Between Iraq and Iran," in David Pollock, ed. *With Neighbors Like These: Iraq and the Arab States on Its Borders*, Washington, D.C.: The Washington Institute for Near East Policy, June 2007.

"Press Fears Over Saddam Execution," BBC News, December 31, 2006. As of December 5, 2009:
http://news.bbc.co.uk/2/hi/middle_east/6220833.stm

Qadura, Kamal, "'Opek li-l-Ghaz . . . Hulm am Haqiqa? [An OPEC for Gas . . . Dream or Reality?]," *Asharq Al-Awsat* (in Arabic), May 2 2008.

"The al-Qaeda Organization in the Islamic Maghreb Claims Responsibility for the Attempted Assassination of President Bouteflika and the Attack on the Dellys Barracks," The MEMRI Blog, September 9, 2007. As of July 20, 2008:
http://www.thememriblog.org/blog_personal/en/2818.htm

al-Qaʻida in Iraq, "Situation Report," trans. Harmony Project, West Point, N.Y.: Combating Terrorism Center, IZ-060316-01, undated. As of October 20, 2009:
http://ctc.usma.edu/harmony/harmony_index.asp

"Al-Qaʻida Video Shows Boys Training to Kill" Al Arabiya, February 6, 2008. Also, as of February 2008:
http://www.usatoday.com/news/world/iraq/2008-02-05-camps-usat_N.htm?loc=interstitialskip

"Al-Qanasa wa Assas T 'alim al-Ramiya [Sniping and the Basics of Learning to Shoot]," January 26, 2009. Circa January 2009: http://al-shouraa.com/vb/showthread.php?t=21170

Qandil, 'Abd al-Halim, "Sahwat al-Saif al-Russi [Awakening of the Russian Sword]," *al-Quds al-'Arabi* (in Arabic), September 2, 2008.

Rageh, Rawya, "Al Qaeda Group Said to Post Online Magazine," Associated Press, March 4, 2005. As of October 22, 2008 : http://www.boston.com/news/world/middleeast/articles/2005/03/04/al_qaeda_group_said_to_post_online_magazine/

al-Rashid, 'Abd al-Rahman, "Li Hadhahi al-Asbab, Nakhsha Iran [For These Reasons, We Fear Iran]," *Asharq Al-Awsat* (in Arabic), April 18, 2006. As of September 29, 2009: http://www.aawsat.com/leader.asp?section=3&article=358858&issueno=10003

———, "Iran Taghayarat Ya 'Arab Iran [Arabs of Iran: Iran Has Changed]," *Asharq Al-Awsat* (in Arabic), June 20, 2009. As of September 29, 2009: http://www.aawsat.com/leader.asp?section=3&article=524184&issueno=11162

al-Rashid, Madawi, *Contesting the Saudi State: Islamic Voices from A New Generation*, New York: Cambridge University Press, 2007.

Rosner, Shmuel, "FM Livni: U.S. Must Stand Firm on Iraq," *Ha'aretz*, March 13, 2007. As of October 20, 2009: http://www.haaretz.com/hasen/spages/836463.html

Rosner, Shmuel, Aluf Benn, and Amiram Barkat, "Israel Sees Rapid Exit from Iraq Endangering Jordanian Regime," *Ha'aretz*, March 16, 2007. As of October 20, 2009: http://www.haaretz.com/hasen/spages/838667.html

"Rot Here or Die There: Bleak Choices for Iraqi Refugees in Lebanon," *Human Rights Watch*, Vol. 19, No. 8E, November 2007.

Rougier, Bernard, "Islamistes Sunnites et Hezbollah," *Le Monde Diplomatique*, January 2007. As of May 1, 2008: http://www.monde-diplomatique.fr/2007/01/ROUGIER/14327

Rubin, Alissa, "Arrests Deepen Sunni Bitterness," *New York Times*, April 11, 2009.

Rubin, Alissa, and Sabrina Tavernise, "Turkish Troops Enter Iraq in Pursuit of Kurdish Militants," *New York Times*, February 23, 2008.

Rubin, Barry, "Syria and Iraq: The Inconvenient Truth," in David Pollock, ed., *With Neighbors Like These: Iraq and the Arab States on Its Borders*, Washington, D.C.: Washington Institute for Near East Policy, June 2007.

al-Rukabi, Zain al-'Abidin, "al-Natija: Kharab al-'Iraq wa Khidmat al-Iran wa Tadahur al-Iqtisad al-Amiriki [The Result: The Destruction of Iraq, Service to Iran, and the Decline of the American Economy]," *Asharq Al-Awsat* (in Arabic), March 22, 2008. As of October 22, 2008:
http://www.asharqalawsat.com/leader.asp?section=3&article=463732&issu eno=10707

Ruman, Muhammad Abu, "Al-Tashay 'u fi al-Urdun [Conversion to Shi'ism in Jordan]," *Al-Ghad* (Jordan), October 4–5, 2006. As of September 29, 2009:
http://www.albainah.net/index.aspx?function=Item&id=13311&lang=

"Rusiya Tadraj al-Ikhwan al-Muslimin Dhamn Qa'imat al-Irhab [Russia Includes the Muslim Brotherhood on the List of Terrorism]," *Ma Wara' al-Khabr [Behind the News]*, Al Jazeera (in Arabic), August 22, 2006. As of September 29, 2009:
http://www.aljazeera.net/NR/exeres/BEE20720-CA72-47A6-A781-541761436B12.htm

Russell, James A., *Regional Threats and Security Strategy: The Troubling Case of Today's Middle East*, Carlisle, Pa.: U.S. Army War College, Strategic Studies Institute, November 20, 2007.

Russell, Richard L., "Peering Over the Horizon: Arab Threat Perception and Security Responses to a Nuclear-Ready Iran," Washington, D.C.: Nonproliferation Policy Education Center, February 5, 2005.

"Russia Delivers S-300 Favorit to Iran," *Aviation Week*, December 18, 2008.

"Russian-Saudi JV Finds Hydrocarbon Reserves at Saudi Gas Deposit," *Ria Novosti*, February 12, 2007. As of October 2009:
http://en.rian.ru/business/20070212/60575338.html

Saab, Bilal Y., "The Future of the Syrian-Iranian Alliance," *Dar Al Hayat*, December 21, 2007.

Saab, Bilal Y., and Bruce O. Riedel, "Expanding the 'Jihad': Hizb'allah's Sunni Islamist Network," Washington, D.C.: The Brookings Institution, February 1, 2007. As of October 2009:
http://www.brookings.edu/articles/2007/02islamicworld_saab.aspx

al-Sabeel5 (pseudonym), "How to Deal with Iran," posting to al-Hesbah forum, April 12, 2008, tr. SITE Intelligence Group, April 15, 2008.

Sadjapour, Karim, "The Nuclear Players," *Journal of International Affairs*, Vol. 60, No. 2, Spring/Summer 2007, pp. 125–134.

Sageman, Marc, *Leaderless Jihad: Terror Networks in the 21st Century*, Philadelphia: University of Pennsylvania Press, 2008.

Saif, Ibrahim, and David M. DeBartolo, "The Iraq War's Impact on Growth and Inflation in Jordan," Jordan: University of Jordan, Center for Strategic Studies. July 2007.

Samii, Bill, "Iran: Country Faces Agitated Kurdish Population," *Iran Report*, Radio Free Europe/Radio Liberty, July 22, 2005.

al-Sayyid, Yasin, "Nihayat 'Asr al-Haymana al-Amirikiya al-Mutlaqa [The End of the Age of Unrestrained American Hegemony]," *Dar al-Hayat* (in Arabic), August 31, 2008.

Schemm, Paul, "al-Qa'ida Online Supporters Lash Out at Taliban for Not Remaining True to Global Jihad," *International Herald Tribune* (Associated Press), March 10, 2008.

Scheuer, Michael, "Al-Qaeda Completes Its Organizational Mission in Iraq," *Terrorism Focus*, Vol. 5, No. 3, January 23, 2008.

Schwirtz, Michael, and Nazila Fathi, "Russia Denies Selling Missile System to Iran," *New York Times*, December 23, 2008.

Sfakianakis, John, "Saudi-Russian Trade Relations Deepen," *Arab News*, November 21, 2007. As of November 3, 2009:
http://www.arabnews.com/?page=6&section=0&article=103811&d=21&m=11&y=2007

Shabib, Nabil, "ila Ba 'adh Tayyarna al-Mahalliya . . . Rusiya Imbiriyalia Aidan [To Some of our Local Movements . . . Russia is also Imperialist]," *IslamOnline* (in Arabic), August 27, 2008. As of November 3, 2009:
http://www.islamonline.net/servlet/Satellite?c=ArticleA_C&cid=1219723037670&pagename=Zone-Arabic-News/NWALayout

Shadid, Anthony, "Smoke of Iraq War 'Drifting Over Lebanon,'" *Washington Post*, June 12, 2006.

———, "With Iran Ascendant, U.S. Is Seen at Fault," *Washington Post*, January 30, 2007.

———, "Schism Among Shiites Over Clerical Rule," *Washington Post*, July 29, 2009.

Shaffer, Brenda, *Partners in Need: The Strategic Relationship of Russia and Iran*, Washington, D.C.: The Washington Institute for Near East Policy, 2001.

"Al-Shaif Forms Tribal Coalition Against al-Ahmar's Solidarity Council," *News Yemen*, August 14, 2007. As of August 13, 2009:
http://www.newsyemen.net/en/view_news.asp?sub_no=3_2007_08_14_6810

al-Shaiji, 'Abdullah Khalifa, "al-'Iraq wa Amn Mintaqat al-Khalij al-'Arabi: Tada'iyat al-Wadh'a al-Amni fi al-'Iraq 'ala Majlis al-Ta'awin al-Khaliji [Iraq and the Security of the Arab Gulf Region: Consequences of the Security Situation in Iraq on the Gulf Cooperation Council States]," *Arab Journal of Political Science* (in Arabic), No. 18, Spring 2008.

Shelby, David, "Rice Seeks to Rally Moderate Forces in Middle East," *America.gov*, October 2, 2006. As of November 6, 2009: http://www.america.gov/st/washfile-english/2006/October/20061002121532ndybl ehs0.2561151.html

al-Siba'i, Hani, "Hel Taghad al-Qa'ida al-Tarf 'an Dawla al-Imarat l'Itifaq Musbaq Baynhuma? [Would al-Qa'ida Ignore the Emirates Due to a Prior Agreement Between Them?]," *Hanein Forum*, June 16, 2008. As of August 12, 2008: http://www.hanein.info/vb/showthread.php?t=71556&highlight=%E5%C7%E4% ED+%C7%E1%DE%C7%DA%CF%C9

Simon, Steven, "The Price of the Surge," *International Herald Tribune*, April 16, 2008.

SITE Intelligence Group, "Former ISI Shariah Court Judge Killed in Afghanistan," communique, Bethesda, Md., May 11, 2008.

"Six Al Qaeda Men Awarded Death Penalty in Kuwait," *Dawn*, December 28, 2005. As of August 14, 2009: http://www.dawn.com/2005/12/28/top14.htm

Slackman, Michael, "Iraq Hangings Fuel Sunni-Shiite Sectarianism in the Middle East," *New York Times*, January 17, 2007.

Slackman, Michael, and Hassan M. Fattah, "In Public View, Saudis Counter Iran in Region," *New York Times*, February 6, 2007.

Slavin, Barbara, *Mullahs, Money, and Militias: How Iran Exerts Its Influence in the Middle East*, Washington, D.C.: United States Institute of Peace, Special Report 206, June 2008.

Sluglett, Marion Farouk, and Peter Sluglett, "Sunnis and Shi'is Revisited: Sectarianism and Ethnicity in Authoritarian Iraq," in D. Hopwood, Habib Ishow, and Thomas Kozcinowski, eds., *Iraq: Power and Society*, Reading, UK: Ithaca Press, 1993.

Smith, Mark A., "Russia and the Persian Gulf: The Deepening of Moscow's Middle East Policy," Swindon, UK: Research and Assessment Branch, August 5, 2007.

Socor, Vladimir, "Russian Energy: Toward a Russia-Led 'OPEC for Gas'?" overview and summary, Jamestown Foundation, April 25, 2007. As of October 23, 2009: http://www.jamestown.org/media/events/single/?tx_ttnews[tt_news]=124&tx_ttne ws[backPid]=19&cHash=5210bbf1b3

Sokolski, Henry, and Patrick Clawson, eds., *Getting Ready for a Nuclear-Ready Iran*, Carlisle, Pa.: U.S. Army War College, Strategic Studies Institute, 2005.

Solomon, Jay, "U.S.-Arab Alliance Aims to Deter Terrorism, Iran," *Wall Street Journal*, August 9, 2007.

Spencer, Robert, "Kuwait: Fundamentalists Recruiting Teens for Jihad," *Jihad Watch*, September 7, 2004. As of July 10, 2008:
http://www.jihadwatch.org/archives/003103.php

Steinberg, James, "Real Leaders Do Soft Power: Learning the Lessons of Iraq," *Washington Quarterly*, Vol. 31, No 2, Spring 2008. As of April 4, 2008:
http://www.twq.com/08spring/index.cfm?id=297

Stepanova, Ekaterina, *Russia's Middle East Policy: Old Divisions or New?* Washington, D.C., Center for Strategic and International Studies, Program on New Approaches to Russian Security, Policy Memo 429, December 2006.

"Sunni Iranian Jihadist Groups Claim Shiraz Attack," SITE Report (video), 2008061703, undated.

Susser, Asher, "The Second Lebanon War: The Regional Setting," in Shlomo Brom and Meir Elran, eds., *The Second Lebanon War: Strategic Perspectives*, Tel Aviv: Institute for National Security Studies, 2007a.

———, "Iraq Lebanon and Gaza: Middle Eastern Trends," *Tel Aviv Notes*, The Moshe Dayan Center, July 22, 2007b.

Taheri, Amir, "Iraq and Its Neighbors: A New Approach Takes Shape," *Asharq Al-Awsat* (in Arabic), October 26, 2007. As of July 31, 2008:
http://www.asharqalawsat.com/english/news.asp?section=2&id=10676

Takeyh, Ray, "Iran's Nuclear Calculations," *World Policy Journal*, Vol. 20, No. 2, Summer 2003. As of August 4, 2005:
http://www.worldpolicy.org/journal/

———, "Iran Builds the Bomb," *Survival*, Vol. 46, No. 4, Winter 2004, pp. 51–64.

———, "Iran's New Iraq," *Middle East Journal*, Vol. 62, No. 1, Winter 2008, pp. 13–30.

Talib, Hasan Abu, "al-Sin wa al-Sharq al-Awsat: bayn Ramziyat al-Siyasa wa Takamul al-Iqtisad [China and the Middle East: Between Political Symbolism and Economic Integration]," *al-Siyasa al-Dawliya* (in Arabic), No. 173, July 2008. As of October 22, 2008:
http://www.siyassa.org.eg/asiyassa/Index.asp?CurFN=malf17.htm&DID=9630

Tank, Pinar, "The Effects of the Iraq War on the Kurdish Number in Turkey," *Conflict, Security and Development*, Vol. 5, Number 1, April, 2005.

al-Taqwa, Zadi, "Al-Qa'ida wa Mu 'araka al-Naft [al-Qa'ida and the Battle for Oil," posting, Al Jazeera talk forum, June 2008. As of October 22, 2008:
http://www.aljazeeratalk.net/forum/showthread.php?p=1361502

al-Tariqi, Salih, "al-Sin Namudhjan li-l-'Arab . . . Walakin [China Is a Model for Arabs . . . But]," Al Arabiya (in Arabic), January 15, 2008.

al-Tartusi, Abu Basir, "Rafidi Shi'a and the Issue of Palestine," July 19, 2006. As of October 2009:
http://www.altartosi.com/articles/Artcl097.html

———, "Hizballah and the Spread of Rejectionist, Shi'a Religious Doctrine," February 2, 2004. As of September 29, 2009:
http://abubaseer.bizland.com/articles/read/a65.doc

Tavernise, Sabrina, and Campbell Robertson, "Turkish Premier, in Iraq, Highlights a Warming Trend," *New York Times*, July 11, 2008.

Telhami, Shibley, "2008 Arab Public Opinion Poll: Survey of the Anwar Sadat Chair for Peace and Development at the University of Maryland (with Zogby International)," March 2008, p. 65. As of October 2009:
http://www.brookings.edu/topics/~/media/Files/events/2008/0414_middle_east/0414_middle_east_telhami.pdf

Terrill, Andrew W., *Strategic Implications of Intercommunal Warfare in Iraq*, Carlisle, Pa.: U.S. Army War College, Strategic Studies Institute, January 2005.

Theyab, Jameel, "Who Appointed Them?" *Dar al-Hayat* (in Arabic), circa February 2008. As of February 2008:
http://www.alhayat.com

"Tribe Versus National Interest Battle Looms for Kuwaiti Constituencies," *Gulf States Newsletter*, Vol. 30, No. 779, April 14, 2006.

Ulph, Stephen, *Jihadi After Action Report: Syria*, West Point, N.Y.: Combating Terrorism Center at West Point, 2006a.

———, "Al-Zawahiri Takes Hamas to Task," *Terrorism Focus*, Vol. 3, Issue 9, March 7, 2006b. As of October 22, 2008:
http://jamestown.org/terrorism/news/article.php?articleid=2369916

United Nations Conference on Trade and Development, *Information Economy Report 2007–2008—Science and Technology for Development: The New Paradigm of ICT*, New York and Geneva: United Nations, 2007. As of October 2009:
http://www.pogar.org/publications/other/unctad/info-eco-rep-08e.pdf

"U.S.-Allied Sunnis Alarmed at Baghdad Crackdown," Associated Press, March 30, 2009.

U.S. Department of Defense, *National Defense Strategy*, June 2008. As of September 1, 2008:
http://www.defenselink.mil/pubs/2008NationalDefenseStrategy.pdf

U.S. Department of State, "Country Reports on Terrorism," website, undated. As of January 5, 2010:
http://www.state.gov/s/ct/rls/crt/

———, "Country Reports on Terrorism 2007: Middle East and North Africa Overview II," Washington, D.C., 2007. As of August 30, 2008: http://www.state.gov/documents/organization/105904.pdf

———, "Egypt: Bureau of Democracy, Human Rights and Labor, International Religious Freedom Report 2009," October 26, 2009. As of December 11, 2009: http://www.state.gov/g/drl/rls/irf/2009/127346.htm

———, Bureau of Population, Refugees, and Migration, Office of Admissions, Refugee Processing Center, "Summary of Refugee Admissions as of January 31, 2009," As of February 11, 2009: http://www.wrapsnet.org/WRAPS/Reports/AdmissionsArrivals/tabid/211/Default. aspx

al-'Utaybi, 'Abdallah bin Bijad, "al-Mutafarrasun al-'Arab wa Ahdath Iran [The 'Persianized Arabs' and the Events of Iran]," Al Arabiya, July 6, 2009.

Valbjørn, Morten, and André Bank, "Signs of a New Arab Cold War: The 2006 Lebanon War and the Sunni-Shi'i Divide," *Middle East Report*, Spring 2007.

Vanden Brook, Tom, "Iraq Sniper Attacks Overestimated," November 1, 2007. As of November 6 2009: http://www.marinecorpstimes.com/news/2007/10/gns_snipers_071030/

Verlin, Yevgeny, "A Most Dangerous Game: Russian Gambles, American Distractions," *The National Interest*, March 26, 2003.

Vissar, Reidar, "Other People's Maps," *Wilson Quarterly*, Winter 2007. As of April 10, 2008: http://www.wilsoncenter.org/index.cfm?fuseaction=wq.essay&essay_id=215618

al-Wa'ili, 'Abd al-Hakim, ed., *Musu'at Qaba'il al-'Arab* [*Encyclopedia of Arab Tribes*], Amman: Dar Usama lil-Nushr wa al-Tawzi'a, 2002.

Walt, Stephen, *The Origins of Alliances*, Ithaca, N.Y.: Cornell University Press, 1990.

Watts, Clinton, "Foreign Fighters: How Are They Being Recruited? Two Imperfect Recruitment Models," *Small Wars Journal*, June 22, 2008. As of September 09, 2008: http://smallwarsjournal.com/blog/2008/06/foreign-fighters-how-are-they/

Wehrey, Frederic M., "A Clash of Wills: Hizballah's Psychological Campaign Against Israel," *Small Wars and Insurgencies*, Vol. 13, No. 3, Autumn 2002, pp. 53–74.

———, "Saudi Arabia: Shiites Pessimistic on Reform But Seek Reconciliation," *Arab Reform Bulletin*, Vol. 5, No. 5, June 2007.

Wehrey, Frederic, David E. Thaler, Nora Bensahel, Kim Cragin, Jerrold D. Green, Dalia Dassa Kaye, Nadia Oweidat, and Jennifer Li, *Dangerous But Not Omnipotent: Exploring the Reach and Limitations of Iranian Power in the Middle East*, Santa Monica, RAND Corporation, MG-781-AF, 2009. As of October 2009: http://www.rand.org/pubs/monographs/MG781/

Weymouth, Lally, "A Conversation with King Abdullah of Jordan," interview, *Washington Post*, June 22, 2008. As of September 30, 2009: http://www.washingtonpost.com/wp-dyn/content/article/2008/06/19/AR2008061903151.html

"The Widening Perception Gap: U.S. Policies and the Arab World," event transcript, Washington, D.C.: The Brookings Institution, March 27, 2007. As of December 4, 2007: http://www.brookings.edu/events/2007/0327islamic-world.aspx

Wilson, Scott, "Iraqi Refugees Overwhelm Syria: Migrants Who Fled Violence Put Stress on Housing Market, Schools, *Washington Post*, February 3, 2005.

Wood, Graeme, "The Militant Kurds of Iran," *Jane's Intelligence Review*, August 1, 2006.

Worth, Robert F., "Arab Leaders, Angry at Syrian President, Threaten Boycott of Summit Meeting," *New York Times*, March 8, 2008a, p. 8.

———, "In Democracy Kuwait Trusts, But Not Much," *New York Times*, May 6, 2008b.

Wright, Robin, "U.S. vs. Iran: Cold War, Too," *Washington Post*, July 29, 2007, B01.

Yacoub, Sameer N., "Al-Qaida in Iraq Sought War Between United States and Iran," Associated Press, June 16, 2006. As of August 12, 2008: http://www.nctimes.com/articles/2006/06/16/news/nation/15_01_226_15_06.txt

Yaphe, Judith S., and Charles D. Lutes, *Reassessing the Implications of a Nuclear-Armed Iran*, McNair Paper 69, Washington DC: National Defense University, 2005.

Yousafzai, Sami, and Ron Moreau, "Unholy Allies," *Newsweek*, September 26, 2005. As of July 19, 2008: http://www.newsweek.com/id/104670/page/1

Zakaria, Fareed, "World View: The Only Thing We Have to Fear," *Newsweek*, Vol. 151, No. 22, June 2, 2008, p. 37.

Zaks, Dmitry, "Putin: Iraq War Worst Crisis Since Cold War," *Middle East Online*, March 28, 2003. As of November 13, 2009: http://www.middle-east-online.com/english/?id=4927

al-Zawahiri, Ayman, letter to bin Laden, intercepted by Coalition Provisional Authority, February 12, 2004. As of August 12, 2008:
http://www.libertypost.org/cgi-bin/readart.cgi?ArtNum=96132&Disp=230

al-Zawahiri, Ayman, letter to Abu Mus'ab al-Zarqawi, intercepted by American Forces, July 9, 2005. Available (in Arabic) as of January 2009:
http://www.nabdh-alm3ani.net/nabdhat/nabdh79/nabdh15291.html
    Available (in English) as of December 11, 2009
http://www.washingtonpost.com/wp-srv/world/iraq/zawahiri.10.11.05.pdf

al-Zawahiri, Ayman, "Qara'a al-Ahdath: Liqa' al-Sahab al-Rab'a ma al-Shaikh Ayman al-Zawahiri [Review of Events: al-Sahab's Fourth Interview with Ayman al-Zawahiri]," video prod. by al-Sahab media, December 2007. Available in two English translations as of October 2009:
    Mansfield Report: Global Strategic Translations & Analysis, December 2007:
http://www.lauramansfield.com/subscribers/20071216_zawahiri.asp
    EFA Foundation, December 2007:
http://nefafoundation.org/miscellaneous/nefazawahiri1207-2.pdf

———, "The Open Meeting with Shaykh Ayman al-Zawahiri Part One," video prod. by al-Sahab media, March 2008. English transc. by Mansfield Report: Global Strategic Translations & Analysis, undated. As of October 21, 2009:
http://www.lauramansfield.com/OpenMeetingZawahiri_Part%201.pdf

———, "Selected Questions and Answers from Dr. Ayman al-Zawahiri, Part Two," English trans. and transc., video prod. by al-Sahab media, April 17, 2008. English transc. by NEFA Foundation. As of January 2009:
http://www.nefafoundation.org/miscellaneous/FeaturedDocs/nefazawahiri0508-2.pdf

Zoellick, Robert B., "Whither China: From Membership to Responsibility?" remarks to the National Committee on U.S.–China Relations, September 21, 2005. As of November 6, 2009:
http://www.ncuscr.org/files/2005Gala_RobertZoellick_Whither_China1.pdf

Zogby International/Arab American Institute, "Four Years Later: Arab Opinion Troubled By Consequences of Iraq War," results of poll conducted February 26–March 10, 2007, Washington, D.C.: Arab American Institute, 2007. As of August 16, 2009:
http://www.aaiusa.org/page/-/Polls/2007_poll_four_years_later_arab_opinion.pdf

al-Zubaydi, Sayf al-Din, "Akhwatna fi-l-Urdun, Ihdheru [Beware, Brothers in Jordan]," circa 2008. As of August 12, 2008:
http://www.albainah.com/index.aspx?function=Item&id=10455&lang=

al-Zubaydi, Shaykh Majid, *al-'Ash'ir al'Iraqiya* [*The Iraqi Tribes*], Vols. 1 and 2, Beirut: Dar al-Mahaja al-Bayda', 2005.